Lecture Notes in Computer Science   13564

More information about this series at http://www.springer.com/bookseries/558

Islem Rekik · Ehsan Adeli · Sang Hyun Park ·
Celia Cintas (Eds.)

Predictive Intelligence in Medicine

5th International Workshop, PRIME 2022
Held in Conjunction with MICCAI 2022
Singapore, September 22, 2022
Proceedings

Springer

Editors
Islem Rekik ⓘ
Istanbul Technical University
Istanbul, Turkey

Ehsan Adeli ⓘ
Stanford University
Stanford, CA, USA

Sang Hyun Park ⓘ
Daegu Gyeongbuk Institute of Science
and Technology
Daegu, Korea (Republic of)

Celia Cintas ⓘ
IBM Research - Africa
Nairobi, Kenya

ISSN 0302-9743   ISSN 1611-3349 (electronic)
Lecture Notes in Computer Science
ISBN 978-3-031-16918-2   ISBN 978-3-031-16919-9 (eBook)
https://doi.org/10.1007/978-3-031-16919-9

This Springer imprint is published by the registered company Springer Nature Switzerland AG
The registered company address is: Gewerbestrasse 11, 6330 Cham, Switzerland

Preface

It would constitute a stunning progress in medicine if, in a few years, we contribute to engineering a predictive intelligence able to predict missing clinical data with high precision. Given the outburst of big and complex medical data with multiple modalities (e.g., structural magnetic resonance imaging (MRI) and resting function MRI (rsfMRI)) and multiple acquisition timepoints (e.g., longitudinal data), more intelligent predictive models are needed to improve diagnosis of a wide spectrum of diseases and disorders while leveraging minimal medical data. Basically, predictive intelligence in medicine (PRIME) primarily aims to facilitate diagnosis at the earliest stage using minimal clinically non-invasive data. For instance, PRIME would constitute a breakthrough in early neurological disorder diagnosis as it would allow accurate early diagnosis using multimodal MRI data (e.g., diffusion and functional MRIs) and follow-up observations all predicted from only T1-weighted MRI acquired at baseline timepoint.

Existing computer-aided diagnosis methods can be divided into two main categories: (1) analytical methods and (2) predictive methods. While analytical methods aim to efficiently analyze, represent, and interpret data (static or longitudinal), predictive methods leverage the data currently available to predict observations at later time-points (i.e., forecasting the future) or predict observations at earlier time-points (i.e., predicting the past for missing data completion). For instance, a method which only focuses on classifying patients with mild cognitive impairment (MCI) and patients with Alzheimer's disease (AD) is an analytical method, while a method which predicts if a subject diagnosed with MCI will remain stable or convert to AD over time is a predictive method. Similar examples can be established for various neurodegenerative or neuropsychiatric disorders, degenerative arthritis, or in cancer studies, in which the disease/disorder develops over time.

Following the success of the past editions of PRIME MICCAI, the fifth edition of the workshop (PRIME MICCAI 2022) aimed to drive the field of 'high-precision predictive medicine', where late medical observations are predicted with high precision, while providing explanation via machine and deep learning, and statistically, mathematically- or physically-based models of healthy, disordered development and aging. Despite the terrific progress that analytical methods have made in the last twenty years in medical image segmentation, registration, or other related applications, efficient predictive intelligent models and methods are somewhat lagging behind. As such predictive intelligence develops and improves – and this is likely to happen exponentially in the coming years – it will have far-reaching consequences for the development of new treatment procedures and novel technologies. These predictive models will begin to shed light on one of the most complex healthcare and medical challenges we have ever encountered, and, in doing so, change our basic understanding of who we are.

What are the Key Challenges We Aim to Address?

The main aim of PRIME MICCAI is to propel the advent of predictive models in a broad sense, with application to medical data. To this end, the workshop accepts paper of 8–12 pages in length describing new cutting-edge predictive models and methods that solve challenging problems in the medical field. We envision that the PRIME MICCAI workshop will become a nest for high-precision predictive medicine, one that is set to transform multiple fields of healthcare technologies in unprecedented ways. Topics of interests for the workshop include but are not limited to predictive methods dedicated to the following:

- Modeling and predicting disease development or evolution from a limited number of observations;
- Computer-aided prognostic methods (e.g., for brain diseases, prostate cancer, cervical cancer, dementia, acute disease, neurodevelopmental disorders);
- Forecasting disease or cancer progression over time;
- Predicting low-dimensional data (e.g., behavioral scores, clinical outcome, age, gender);
- Predicting the evolution or development of high-dimensional data (e.g., shapes, graphs, images, patches, abstract features, learned features);
- Predicting high-resolution data from low-resolution data;
- Prediction methods using 2D, 2D+t, 3D, 3D+t, ND, and ND+t data;
- Predicting data of one image modality from a different modality (e.g., data synthesis);
- Predicting lesion evolution;
- Predicting missing data (e.g., data imputation or data completion problems);
- Predicting clinical outcomes from medical data (genomic, imaging data, etc).

Key Highlights

This year's workshop mediated ideas from both machine learning and mathematical/statistical/physical modeling research directions in the hope of providing a deeper understanding of the foundations of predictive intelligence developed for medicine, as well as to where we currently stand and what we aspire to achieve through this field. PRIME MICCAI 2022 featured a single-track workshop with keynote speakers with deep expertise in high-precision predictive medicine using machine learning and other modeling approaches – PRIME MICCAI which are believed to stand in opposing directions. The workshop was organized as a hybrid event (in-person and virtual), and keynote talks were streamed live due to the COVID-19 pandemic. Pre-recorded videos of accepted papers and keynote presentations were posted on the PRIME web page[1]. Eventually, this will increase the outreach of PRIME publications to a broader audience while steering a wide spectrum of MICCAI publications from being 'only analytical' to being 'jointly analytical and predictive.'

We received a total of 20 submissions and accepted 19 papers. All papers underwent a rigorous double-blind review process, with at least two (and mostly four) members of

---

[1] http://basira-lab.com/prime-miccai-2022/.

the Program Committee reviewing each paper. The Program Committee was composed of 21 well-known research experts in the field. The selection of the papers was based on technical merit, significance of results, and relevance and clarity of presentation. Based on the reviewing scores and critiques, all but one PRIME submission was scored highly by reviewers, i.e., had an average score above the acceptance threshold.

Diversity and inclusion have been one of main focuses of PRIME MICCAI, and the workshop continues to strongly support gender balance and geographic diversity in the Program Committee. The authors of this year's accepted papers were affiliated with institutions in four continents: Africa, Europe, America, and Asia. We also provided a BASIRA Scholarship[2] to register the paper of a talented minority student in a low-middle income country. The eligibility criteria of the BASIRA Scholarship were included in the CMT submission system, and the scholarship was ultimately awarded to a student from Africa. We will strive to continue this initiative in the upcoming years and hope to see a similar trend in other conferences and workshops.

August 2022

Islem Rekik
Ehsan Adeli
Sang Hyun Park
Celia Cintas

---

[2] https://basira-lab.com/.

Organization

Workshop Chairs

Islem Rekik   Istanbul Technical University, Turkey
Ehsan Adeli   Stanford University, USA
Sang Hyun Park   DGIST, South Korea
Celia Cintas   IBM Research Africa, Kenya

Program Committee

Ahmed Nebli   University of Sousse, Tunisia
Alaa Bessadok   University of Sousse, Tunisia
Chinasa Okolo   Cornell University, USA
Daniel Moyer   Massachusetts Institute of Technology, USA
Dong Hye Ye   Marquette University, USA
Febrian Rachmadi   RIKEN, Japan
Gang Li   University of North Carolina at Chapel Hill, USA
Ilwoo Lyu   Ulsan National Institute of Science and
     Technology, South Korea
Jaeil Kim   Kyungpook National University, South Korea
Jiahong Ouyang   Stanford University, USA
Li Wang   University of North Carolina at Chapel Hill, USA
Lichi Zhang   Shanghai Jiao Tong University, China
Manhua Liu   Shanghai Jiao Tong University, China
Maria A. Zuluaga   EURECOM, France
Melissa Woghiren   University of Alberta, Canada
Pew-Thian Yap   University of North Carolina at Chapel Hill, USA
Qian Wang   Shanghai Jiao Tong University, China
Qingyu Zhao   Stanford University, USA
Reza Azad   RWTH University, Germany
Seong Tae Kim   Kyung Hee University, South Korea
Seungyeon Shin   National Institutes of Health, USA
Soochahn Lee   Kookmin University, South Korea
Ulas Bagci   Northwestern University, USA
Won Hwa Kim   POSTECH, South Korea
Ziga Spiclin   University of Ljubljana, Slovenia

Contents

Federated Time-Dependent GNN Learning from Brain Connectivity Data with Missing Timepoints

Zeynep Gürler and Islem Rekik[(✉)]

BASIRA Lab, Faculty of Computer and Informatics, Istanbul Technical University,
Istanbul, Turkey
irekik@itu.edu.tr
http://basira-lab.com

Abstract. Predicting changes in brain connectivity between anatomical regions is essential for brain mapping and neural disorder diagnosis across different age spans from a limited data (e.g., single timepoint). Such learning tasks become more difficult when handling a single dataset with missing timepoints, let alone multiple decentralized datasets collected from different hospitals and with varying incomplete acquisitions. With the new paradigm of federated learning (FL) one can learn from decentralized datasets without data sharing. However, to the best of our knowledge, no FL method was designed to predict time-dependent graph data evolution trajectory using non-iid training longitudinal datasets with varying acquisition timepoints. In this paper, we aim to significantly boost the predictive power of data owners (e.g., local hospitals) trained with several missing timepoints while benefiting from other hospitals with available timepoints in a fully data-preserving way. Specifically, we propose a novel 4D GNN federated architecture, namely 4D-FED-GNN+, which acts as a graph self-encoder when the next timepoint is locally missing or as a graph generator when the next timepoint is locally available in the training set. We further design a mixed federation strategy that alternates (i) GNN layer-wise weight aggregation at each timepoint and (ii) pairwise GNN weight exchange between hospitals in a random order. Our comprehensive experiments on both real and simulated longitudinal datasets show that overall 4D-FED-GNN+ significantly outperform locally trained models. Our 4D-FED-GNN+ code available at https://github.com/basiralab/4D-FED-GNN.

Keywords: Longitudinal graphs · Federated learning · Brain graph evolution trajectory prediction · Missing brain connectivity data

1 Introduction

The non-invasive magnetic resonance imaging (MRI) revealed the brain mapping as a highly interconnected system, commonly modeled as a graph (network) where nodes denote anatomical regions of interest (ROIs) and edge weights

I. Rekik et al. (Eds.): PRIME 2022, LNCS 13564, pp. 1–12, 2022.
https://doi.org/10.1007/978-3-031-16919-9_1

encode the level of interaction between ROIs (e.g., synchrony in neural activity) [1,2]. Charting the connectivity landscape of the brain graph in different states (e.g., health and disease) and across different MRI modalities (e.g., functional, structural) advanced our understanding of the brain as a system as well as the genesis and development of neurodegenerative disorders such as Alzheimer's Disease (AD) and Mild Cognitive Impairment (MCI) [3,4]. For instance, [5] showed that AD causes progressive neuronal and synaptic loss alongside diminishing neuronal connectivities, thereby damaging functional and structural brain networks. Still, the *temporal* nature of the brain development, aging as well as abnormality unfolding, remains the least explored in the literature due to the scarcity of longitudinal (4D) MRI datasets. This presents even a bigger hurdle to deep learning models which are data hungry, limiting their generalizability potential. Such data scarcity can be remedied by the design of predictive models that aim to predict the evolution trajectory of brain graphs from limited data (e.g., a single baseline timepoint). In particular, generative models can probe the field of temporal brain disorder mapping and early diagnosis, while relying on a single MRI acquisition [6,7].

In this context, several research papers proposed methods for time-dependent brain evolution trajectory prediction from a single observation [7]. Landmark works [8,9] proposed supervised sample selection techniques for brain connectome evolution trajectory prediction in infant and aging populations, respectively. However, such methods resorted to vectorizing the brain graph into a feature vector, failing to preserve its topology [7]. To address this issue, [10,11] leveraged graph neural networks (GNNs), which generalized spatial convolutions to non-Euclidean spaces such as graphs. [10] used a graph convolutional adversarial network to learn the non-linear mapping between timepoints. [11] proposed Recurrent Brain Graph Mapper (RBGM) composed of a set of recurrent neural network-inspired mappers at each timepoint, where each mapper evolves the current brain graph onto its next timepoint.

However, all these methods share a prime challenge. They are not inherently designed to handle training datasets with *missing timepoints* –let alone multiple decentralized datasets collected from different hospitals and *with varying* incomplete acquisitions. We note that [9] exceptionally used tensor completion to linearly impute the missing brain connectomes in the training trajectories, however one needs first to have access to the data for the target imputation task. Second, such approach fails to preserve the brain topology by (i) linearly approximating the temporal dependency between brain connectomes and (ii) vectorizing the connectivity matrices. To remedy the lack of training data while securing data privacy, federated learning (FL) [12] offers a training paradigm that is compelling to researchers in medicine. Using FL, multiple clients (i.e., hospitals) train their local models on their local datasets, independently, while benefiting from the learning of other hospitals via a central server, in a fully privacy-preserving manner [13]. Conventionally, FL uses a central server that receives the local model weights then aggregates them into a global model weights, which are then broadcasted to the local clients [14]. Since the amount of data each client has is insufficient, the global model provides better performance to the clients [15]. However, FL is challenged by heterogeneous and non-iid datasets across clients [16]. Such challenge needs to be solved when learning from local datasets with varying sequences of missing timepoints (e.g., one missing timepoint or two consecutive ones) in FL.

To the best of our knowledge, there is no FL GNN framework that predicts the brain graph evolution trajectory from a single timepoint [14] –let alone learning from local clients with varying temporal patterns in missing observations. Here we set out to boost the predictive performance of local hospitals with missing timepoints using local hospitals that have available data at the corresponding timepoints in a federated way and propose 4D-FED-GNN+. Specifically, for each hospital, 4D-FED-GNN+ has a GNN per timepoint that (i) acts as a brain graph generator for the next timepoint if the hospital has available training data at the next timepoint or (ii) as a brain graph self-encoder for the follow-up timepoint if the hospital lacks the training data at the next timepoint. Besides, 4D-FED-GNN+ adopts a mixed federation strategy that alternates two different federation methods. In the first strategy, the central server first performs a GNN layer-wise weight aggregation then broadcasts the averaged weights to all local hospitals. For the second strategy, the central server exchanges GNN layer weights of hospitals in a random order. The contributions of our work are multifold:

1. We design the first FL framework to predict time-dependent graph evolution trajectory using non-iid training longitudinal datasets with varying acquisition training timepoints.
2. Our 4D-FED-GNN+ is the first federated graph neural network that predicts time-dependent brain graph evolution trajectory from a single timepoint while mixing different federation rules.
3. A novel time-dependent ordered model exchange is also proposed.
4. Our FL strategy is generic –i.e., not restricted in application to graphs.

2   Proposed Method

In the following sections, we will detail each of the key steps and the rationale of our proposed 4D-FED-GNN+. Figure 1 displays the two key blocks of our 4D-FED-GNN+: **A)** GNN-based time-dependent prediction, and **B)** Mixed federation strategy. We denote the matrices as boldface capital letters, e.g., $\mathbf{X}$, and scalars as lowercase letters, e.g., n.

A) GNN-Based Time-Dependent Prediction. Our 4D-FED-GNN+ uses a GNN per timepoint where each GNN learns a mapping between consecutive timepoints. Given the local hospitals tend to scan their patients in an ordered timepoint sequence of varying lengths resulting missing acquisitions in some timepoints, there are four possible conditions a hospital might encounter when a GNN learns how to map a brain graph at t onto its next timepoint $t + 1$:

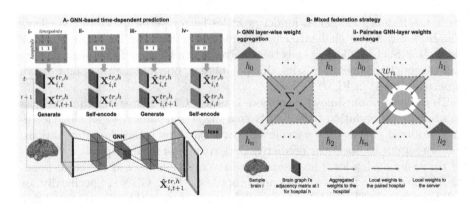

Fig. 1. *Proposed 4D-FED-GNN+.* **(A)** *GNN-based time-dependent prediction.* We design a GNN that takes the adjacency matrix $\mathbf{X}_{i,t}^{tr,h}$ of the training brain graph of subject i or its prediction $\hat{\mathbf{X}}_{i,t}^{tr,h}$ based on the temporal order of hospital h at timepoint t, which defines its state as a generator or a self-encoder at the next timepoint $t+1$. **(B)** *Mixed federation strategy.* We alternate two federation strategies where: (i) the central server receives the GNN layer-wise weights from the hospitals, averages them, then broadcasts the averaged weights to the hospitals, and (ii) the GNN layer-wise weights of local hospitals are exchanged with each other randomly.

(1, 1) the data for both current and next timepoints are available (i.e., consecutive timepoints being available), **(0, 1)** the data for the current timepoint is missing, **(1, 0)** the data for the next timepoint is missing, or **(0, 0)** the data for both current and next timepoints are missing (i.e., consecutive timepoints are missing). As seen in Fig. 1-A, we display the timepoint-wise data-availability of the hospitals in a matrix $\mathbf{M} \in \mathbb{R}^{n \times m}$, where n denotes the number of hospitals and m the total number of timepoints. Each element $\mathbf{M}_{k,t}$ expresses the availability information between a row-wise hospital h_k and a column-wise timepoint t where $\mathbf{M}_{k,t}$ is 1 if the connectivity data is available and 0 otherwise. Further, we assign two different tasks to our GNN based on the temporal availability of the next timepoint. A GNN acts as a (i) *brain graph generator* if the brain connectivity data of the corresponding hospital is present at the next-timepoint (e.g., (1, 1), (0, 1)) or it acts as a (ii) *brain graph self-encoder* if the hospital-of-interest lacks the brain connectivity data at the next timepoint (e.g., (1, 0), (0, 0)). In order to train a GNN on sample i for timepoint $t+1$, where its hospital h lacks the data at timepoint t, the hospital meeting such condition continues to predict using cascaded self-encoding GNNs until reaching an available timepoint where the GNN switches to a generator and obtains $\hat{\mathbf{X}}_{i,t}^{tr,h}$ to use it as an input to the GNN. Further, the GNN at timepoint t uses its ground-truth brain graph $\mathbf{X}_{i,t}^{tr,h}$ or predicted $\hat{\mathbf{X}}_{i,t}^{tr,h}$ as input based on the availability information of timepoint t and computes the loss using the ground-truth brain graph $\mathbf{X}_{i,t+1}^{tr,h}$ at timepoint $t+1$ when the next timepoint is present. If the connectivity data is missing at the next timepoint $t+1$, the GNN self-encodes the data and uses

$\mathbf{X}_{i,t}^{tr,h}$ or predicted $\hat{\mathbf{X}}_{i,t}^{tr,h}$ as an input and also as the ground-truth for $t+1$. Basically, the GNN acts as a generator or a self-encoder based on the condition of the next timepoint.

The GNN Network Architecture
Our 4D-FED-GNN+ uses the RBGM architecture introduced in [11]. RBGM generates a brain graph at timepoint $t+1$ given its observation at timepoint t as an input. The proposed recurrent graph convolution captures the dynamic alterations in the brain connectivity patterns between consecutive timepoints. Our prediction loss consists of an l_1 loss and a topological loss term. The l_1 loss preserves the general characteristics of the connectivity data and is robust to outliers [17]. Therefore, we add the l_1 loss to improve the predicted brain graph quality. For the topological loss, we draw inspiration from [11] and define a node strength vector for each ROI in the brain graph to preserve topological soundness of the generated graphs. For each brain graph, we create a node strength vector $\mathbf{N}$ by summing up all edge weights of each node as: $\mathbf{N} = [N_1, N_2, \ldots, N_{n_r}]$, where N_j is the node strength of node j and n_r is the number of ROIs. The topological loss minimizes the topological dissimilarity between the predicted and ground-truth brain graphs at each timepoint $t+1$ for the training set tr, and is defined as:

$$\mathcal{L}_{tp}(\hat{\mathbf{N}}^{tr} - \mathbf{N}^{tr}) = \frac{1}{n_r} \sum_{j=1}^{n_r} (\hat{\mathbf{N}}_j^{tr} - \mathbf{N}_j^{tr})^2 \tag{1}$$

Let $\hat{\mathbf{X}}_{i,t+1}^{tr,h}$ denote the predicted brain graph for training sample i of hospital h at timepoint $t+1$. Our full loss function is then expressed as follows:

$$\mathcal{L}_{full} = \lambda \mathcal{L}_{tp}(\hat{\mathbf{N}}_{i,t+1}^{tr,h} - \mathbf{N}_{i,t+1}^{tr,h}) + \mathcal{L}_{L1}(\hat{\mathbf{X}}_{i,t+1}^{tr,h}) \tag{2}$$

Dynamic Edge Filtered Convolution. Each GNN in our 4D-FED-GNN+ uses graph convolutional layers inspired by the dynamic graph convolution with edge-conditioned filter proposed by [18]. Let $G = (V, E)$ be a directed or undirected graph where V is a set of n_r ROIs and $E \subseteq V \times V$ is a set of m_r edges. We represent the layer index as l in the neural network. For each layer $l \in \{1, 2, \ldots, L\}$, we define the transformation matrix (i.e., function) that generates edge weights for the message passing between ROIs i and j given features of e_{ij} as $T^l : \mathbb{R}^{d_s} \to \mathbb{R}^{d_l \times d_{l-1}}$ where d_s and d_l are the dimensionality indices. We define $\mathcal{N}(i) = \{j; (j, i) \in E\} \cup \{i\}$ as the neighborhood containing all adjacent ROIs to a node i. We update using the following rule:

$$\mathbf{n}_i^l = \boldsymbol{\Theta}^l \mathbf{n}_i^{l-1} + \frac{1}{\mathcal{N}(i)} \sum_{j \in \mathcal{N}(i)} T^l(e_{ij}; \mathbf{W}^l) \mathbf{n}_j^{l-1} + \mathbf{b}^l \tag{3}$$

where $\mathbf{n}_i^l$ is the node embedding for the ROI i at layer l. $\boldsymbol{\Theta}^l$ is the dynamically generated edge weights by T^l. We denote $\mathbf{W}^l$ as the weights of T^l, $\mathbf{b}^l \in \mathbb{R}^{d_l}$ as the bias term and note that T can be *any type* of neural network.

Graph Recurrent Filter. Each GNN in 4D-FED-GNN+ uses an edge-based recurrent graph neural network firstly introduced in [11]. It redesigns the edge-conditioned filter [18] in the graph convolution layer as a graph recurrent-filter. Graph recurrent-filter remembers the earlier information thanks to its hidden state, which works as a memory by capturing the learned information in the previous layer, and processes the current data accordingly. Each RNN cell takes two specific inputs: the input brain graphs at the current timepoint, and the hidden state values learned from the brain graphs at the previous timepoint. While training, it updates the hidden state with the knowledge representation of the current timepoint. Specifically, let $\mathbf{e}^{t+1} \in \mathbb{R}^{m_r \times 1}$ be the set of edges for a given timepoint $t + 1$ and $\mathbf{H}^t \in \mathbb{R}^{m_r \times m_r}$ be the hidden state matrix from the previous timepoint t, the recurrent edge-filtering function $T^l(\mathbf{e}^{t+1}, \mathbf{H}^t)$ is expressed as follows:

$$\mathbf{H}^{t+1} = tanh([\mathbf{e}^{t+1}, \mathbf{H}^t] \odot [\mathbf{W}_{ph}, \mathbf{W}_{hh}] + \mathbf{B}_h) \tag{4}$$

where $\mathbf{H}^{t+1} \in \mathbb{R}^{m_r \times m_r}$ is the hidden state at the current timepoint $t+1$ and $\mathbf{W}_{ph}$ and $\mathbf{W}_{hh}$ are learnable parameters for input-to-hidden weights and hidden-to-hidden weights. $\mathbf{B}_h \in \mathbb{R}^{m_r \times m_r}$ is the bias term. We use tanh [19] to force the state values to fall in the range of $[-1, 1]$ for avoiding the vanishing gradient problem that tends to happen when we use an activation function such as sigmoid, causing the training to diverge.

B) Mixed Federation Strategy. 4D-FED-GNN+ is trained using a mixed strategy alternating two federation methods. The first method is GNN layer-wise weight aggregation (Fig. 1-B-i). After training the GNN for several rounds, the hospitals send their GNN layer weights to the central server which first aggregates them then broadcasts the averaged weights to all hospitals. As aggregation function, we use the basic FedAvg proposed by [20]. FedAvg is expressed as $w^t = \frac{1}{n} \sum_{k=0}^{n} w_k^t$ while w_k^t denotes the GNN layer weights of hospital k at time-point t with n being the number of hospitals and w^t representing the GNN layer weights of the global model at timepoint t. The second federation method is a model exchange between pairs of hospitals (Fig. 1-B-ii). One of the challenges that FL algorithms encounter is local clients with non-iid data. In our case, the local hospitals (i.e., clients) acquire their time-dependent brain connectivity data in a ordered temporal sequence of varying lengths and scan a different number of patients (i.e., samples) causing the data to be non-iid. Hence, simply averaging the GNN layer weights might degrade the performance of the federation when dealing with non-iid data. Therefore, since model exchange emerged as a promising method to handle non-iid data [21–23], we design a dual federation strategy. Specifically, after training the GNN for a couple of rounds, the hospitals send

---

Algorithm 1: 4D-FED-GNN+

Server Input: the GNN layer weights $\mathbf{W}_k^t$ of hospital h_k at timepoint t, federation mode f

Hospital k's Input: initial global model $\mathbf{W}^t$, local data D_k; brain graphs are missing at timepoint t for hospital h_k if $\mathbf{X}_{i,t}^{tr,h_k} \notin D_k$; $\forall$ $1 \leq i \leq n_k$, n_k is the number of samples for h_k, number of rounds per averaging n_a, number of rounds per model exchange n_e, number of rounds R, number of timepoints T,

Hospitals:

for $t \leftarrow 1$ *to* T do

    for $r \leftarrow 1$ *to* R do

        Sample hospitals $H \subseteq \{h_1, \ldots, h_n\}$;

        $f = 1$

        for *each hospital* $k \in H$ do

            Initialize local model $\mathbf{W}_k^t \leftarrow \mathbf{W}^t$;

            $\mathbf{W}_k^t \leftarrow$ **Hospital Training**$(\mathbf{D}_k, \mathbf{W}_k^t, n_e)$;

            Communicate $\mathbf{W}_k^t$ to the server;

        $f = 0$

        for *each hospital* $k \in H$ do

            Initialize local model $\mathbf{W}_k^t \leftarrow \mathbf{W}_j^t$;

            $\mathbf{W}_k^t \leftarrow$ **Hospital Training**$(\mathbf{D}_k, \mathbf{W}_k^t, n_a)$;

            Communicate $\mathbf{W}_k^t$ to the server;

Server:

if $f == 1$ then

    for *each hospital* $k \in H$ do

        Communicate $\mathbf{W}_k^t$ to hospital h_{k+1};

else

    Construct $\mathbf{W}^t = \frac{1}{n} \sum_{k \in H} \mathbf{W}_k^t$;

    Communicate $\mathbf{W}^t$ to all hospitals $k \in H$;

Server output: $\mathbf{W}^t$, $\mathbf{W}_k^t$ to hospital h_{k+1}

Hospital k's output: $\mathbf{W}_k^t$

---

their GNN layer weights to the central server and the central server randomly exchanges the GNN layer weights of the hospitals with each other. We detail the steps of 4D-FED-GNN+ in Algorithm 1, where TrainHospital function differs based on the data availability condition of the hospital at both current and next timepoints as explained in **A**). Algorithm 1 first performs the pairwise hospital exchange then the GNN layer-wise weight aggregation in each round.

3 Results and Discussion

Longitudinal Brain Graph Dataset. We evaluated our 4D-FED-GNN+ using 113 subjects from the OASIS-2 longitudinal dataset [24]. This set consists of a longitudinal collection of 150 subjects aged 60 to 96. Each subject was scanned on two or more visits, separated by at least one year. For each subject, we use structural T1-w MRI to construct a cortical morphological network derived from cortical thickness as proposed in [25]. Each cortical hemisphere is parcellated into 35 ROIs using Desikan-Killiany cortical atlas. We built our 4D-FED-GNN+ with PyTorch Geometric library [26]. We also conducted our experiments with simulated data with denser timepoints. To do so, we compute the mean connectivity values and correlation matrices of the OASIS-2 dataset and calculate the multivariate normal distribution to generate simulated brain graph data since the mean connectivity values and correlation matrices capture the patterns of the brain connectivity dataset. We simulate 120 brain graphs at 6 timepoints.

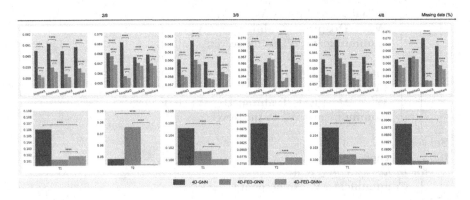

Fig. 2. (1) Prediction accuracy using mean absolute error (MAE) of our 4D-FED-GNN+ and comparison methods at t_1 and t_2 timepoints (top row). (2) The node strength of predicted brain graphs by 4D-FED-GNN+ and its variants (bottom row). ****: $p-value < 0.001$ using two-tailed paired t-test.

Evaluation and Parameter Setting. To evaluate 4D-FED-GNN+, we conducted each experiment using 5-fold cross-validation where in each run, one fold is used for testing while each of the remaining folds serves as the local training data for one hospital resulting in 4 hospitals to federate. To better observe the effect of the missing timepoint ratio on the performance, we selected 3 different ratio values of the missing to the total timepoints. We work under the assumption that the baseline timepoint (i.e., first observation) is always available. The OASIS dataset has 3 timepoints, which implies that, excluding the baseline, there are totally 8 timepoints for 4 hospitals. We randomly mask different timepoints with size 2, 3, and 4 to vary the ratio of the missing data. We perform this randomized masking twice for each ratio and carried out 6 experiments for each method. For the simulated dataset, we set 3 ratio values as 1/20, 8/20, and 5/20 (20 = 6 timepoints × 4 hospitals) to vary the ratio of the missing data and conducted two experiments with different masking variations for each ratio value. For the RBGM training, we used ADAM [27] as our default optimizer and

Table 1. Prediction accuracy using mean absolute error (MAE) of our 4D-FED-GNN+ and comparison methods at t_1, t_2, t_3, t_4, and t_5 timepoints for the simulated dataset.

	Methods	10/20				8/20				5/20			
		h_0	h_1	h_2	h_3	h_0	h_1	h_2	h_3	h_0	h_1	h_2	h_3
	4D-GNN	0.0508	0.0503	0.0534	0.0527	0.0512	0.0502	0.0525	0.0533	0.0516	0.0513	0.0537	0.0527
t_1	4D-FED-GNN	0.0374	0.0376	0.0374	0.0376	0.0374	0.0378	0.0377	0.0374	0.0377	0.0372	0.0378	0.0377
	4D-FED-GNN+	**0.0371**	**0.0371**	**0.0370**	**0.0371**	**0.0369**	**0.0372**	**0.0371**	**0.0369**	**0.0371**	**0.0366**	**0.0371**	**0.0372**
	4D-GNN	0.0964	0.0578	0.0837	0.0612	0.0775	0.0599	0.0627	0.0886	0.0783	0.1020	0.0853	0.0875
t_2	4D-FED-GNN	0.0448	0.0447	0.0439	0.0447	0.0451	0.0452	0.0456	0.0453	0.0449	0.0438	0.0445	0.0448
	4D-FED-GNN+	**0.0439**	**0.0434**	**0.0425**	**0.0438**	**0.0444**	**0.0440**	**0.0447**	**0.0446**	**0.0441**	**0.0430**	**0.0433**	**0.0443**
	4D-GNN	0.1515	0.1517	0.2574	0.1512	0.1494	0.1125	0.1571	0.2745	0.1488	0.3752	0.2615	0.2659
t_3	4D-FED-GNN	0.0531	0.0540	0.0550	0.0544	0.0545	0.0551	0.0559	0.0566	0.0569	0.0580	0.0579	0.0594
	4D-FED-GNN+	**0.0515**	**0.0517**	**0.0524**	**0.0515**	**0.0524**	**0.0526**	**0.0532**	**0.0525**	**0.0538**	**0.0532**	**0.0534**	**0.0535**
	4D-GNN	0.4046	0.3251	0.5668	0.4289	0.5719	0.2749	0.3062	0.6997	0.5684	1.2237	0.5970	1.0096
t_4	4D-FED-GNN	0.0799	0.0881	0.0932	0.0929	0.0833	0.0858	0.0871	0.0958	0.1122	0.1151	0.1142	0.1277
	4D-FED-GNN+	**0.0727**	**0.0775**	**0.0797**	**0.0768**	**0.0732**	**0.0778**	**0.0761**	**0.0775**	**0.0945**	**0.0950**	**0.0953**	**0.0974**
	4D-GNN	1.7104	1.4239	4.0096	1.6694	2.8495	1.1352	1.0630	7.2772	2.8276	14.6458	4.6099	11.2775
t_5	4D-FED-GNN	0.1879	0.2012	0.2241	0.2346	0.2064	0.2017	0.2223	0.2405	0.2614	0.2717	0.2959	0.3090
	4D-FED-GNN+	**0.1536**	**0.1718**	**0.1697**	**0.1722**	**0.1738**	**0.1768**	**0.1873**	**0.1880**	**0.2199**	**0.2252**	**0.2503**	**0.2433**

set the learning rate to 0.001. We empirically set the hyperparameter λ to 10 in our loss function, the number of rounds for averaging as 14, and for model exchange as 7 during FL mixing.

Benchmarks and 4D-FED-GNN+ Variants. Since our 4D-FED-GNN+ is the first FL method aiming to predict the brain graph evolution trajectory from a single timepoint using brain connectivity data with varying missing timepoints, we benchmarked our framework against 2 of its variants: **(1) 4D-GNN:** the vanilla method where hospitals train their local data without federation; **(2) 4D-FED-GNN:** the variant where we use a single federation strategy based on GNN layer-wise weight aggregation (i.e., no mixed strategy).

Real 4D Data. Figure 2 displays the MAE results between the ground-truth and predicted brain graphs as well as their MAE in node strength representations for OASIS dataset at t_1 and t_2 timepoints, respectively. We also report the p-values using a two-tailed paired t-test between 4D-FED-GNN+ and each benchmark method. As seen in Fig. 2, our proposed technique 4D-FED-GNN+ significantly outperformed the comparison methods 4D-GNN and 4D-FED-GNN ($p < 0.001$). Considering the prediction performance of 4D-GNN, we can say that the federation strategy significantly boosts the prediction performance of the local hospitals. Next, our proposed federation technique outperforming 4D-FED-GNN shows that GNN layer-wise weight exchange works well together with GNN layer-wise weight aggregation and increases the federation performance for non-iid data. Given that preserving the graph topology is a harder task comparatively to predicting edge weights, still our 4D-FED-GNN+ achieved the best performance in 4 out of 6 evaluation scenarios.

Simulated 4D Data. Further, we conducted our experiments on the simulated dataset to further demonstrate the generalizability of our proposed 4D-FED-

GNN+. The simulated data allows us to simulate more difficult scenarios where 3 consecutive timepoints can be missing in $\mathbf{M}$. When the number of timepoints increases, the risk of facing a bad condition such as several consecutive missing timepoints for a hospital arises. Therefore, predicting for the latter timepoints becomes even more challenging. Table 1 shows that our proposed 4D-FED-GNN+ significantly outperforms all comparison methods in all experiments using 5-fold cross-validation.

Although our 4D-FED-GNN+ produced the best results in predicting brain graph evolution trajectory by learning from brain connectivity data with missing timepoints, there are a few limitations. First, the proposed framework particularly works on unimodal brain graphs with only one connectivity type (e.g., structural) [28]. Therefore, we aim to extend our proposed frameworks to handling multi-modal brain graphs with varying missing modalities and timepoints. Second, we used FedAvg [20] as aggregation method in our mixed federation strategy. FedAvg is the most popular and easiest to implement strategy in classical FL tasks. However, when it comes to learning from non-iid data, FedAvg might be slow in convergence in most cases [29]. Thus, we aim to design a better federation scenario to learn from our temporally varying non-iid graph data.

4   Conclusion

In this paper, we introduced the *first* federated brain graph evolution trajectory prediction framework that learns from brain connectivity data with missing timepoints coming in varying patterns. Specifically, we proposed 4D-FED-GNN+, which learns a federated GNN-based time-dependent prediction where each hospital has a GNN that acts as a generator or a self-encoder based on the data availability at both current and next timepoints. To federate, it performs a federation strategy mixing GNN layer averaging and exchange. The proposed federation technique outperformed benchmark methods on both real and simulated 4D connectomic datasets. In our future work, we will work on how to better aggregate received model weights learned from non-iid temporal data using techniques such as local batch normalization [30].

Acknowledgments. I. Rekik is supported by the European Union's Horizon 2020 research and innovation programme under the Marie Sklodowska-Curie Individual Fellowship grant agreement No 101003403 (http://basira-lab.com/normnets/) and the Scientific and Technological Research Council of Turkey under the TUBITAK 2232 Fellowship for Outstanding Researchers (no. 118C288, http://basira-lab.com/reprime/). However, all scientific contributions made in this project are owned and approved solely by the authors.

References

1. Fornito, A., Zalesky, A., Breakspear, M.: Graph analysis of the human connectome: promise, progress, and pitfalls. Neuroimage **80**, 426–444 (2013)

2. Mišić, B., et al.: The functional connectivity landscape of the human brain. PLoS ONE **9**, e111007 (2014)
3. Fornito, A., Zalesky, A., Breakspear, M.: The connectomics of brain disorders. Nat. Rev. Neurosci. **16**, 159–172 (2015)
4. van den Heuvel, M.P., Sporns, O.: A cross-disorder connectome landscape of brain dysconnectivity. Nat. Rev. Neurosci. **20**, 435–446 (2019)
5. Yu, M., Sporns, O., Saykin, A.J.: The human connectome in Alzheimer disease-relationship to biomarkers and genetics. Nat. Rev. Neurol. **17**, 545–563 (2021)
6. Shrivastava, A., Li, P.: A new space for comparing graphs (2014)
7. Bessadok, A., Mahjoub, M.A., Rekik, I.: Graph neural networks in network neuroscience. arXiv preprint arXiv:2106.03535 (2021)
8. Ezzine, B.E., Rekik, I.: Learning-guided infinite network atlas selection for predicting longitudinal brain network evolution from a single observation. In: Shen, D., et al. (eds.) MICCAI 2019. LNCS, vol. 11765, pp. 796–805. Springer, Cham (2019). https://doi.org/10.1007/978-3-030-32245-8_88
9. Ghribi, O., Li, G., Lin, W., Shen, D., Rekik, I.: Multi-regression based supervised sample selection for predicting baby connectome evolution trajectory from neonatal timepoint. Med. Image Anal. **68**, 101853 (2021)
10. Hong, Y., Kim, J., Chen, G., Lin, W., Yap, P.T., Shen, D.: Longitudinal prediction of infant diffusion MRI data via graph convolutional adversarial networks. IEEE Trans. Med. Imaging **38**, 2717–2725 (2019)
11. Tekin, A., Nebli, A., Rekik, I.: Recurrent brain graph mapper for predicting time-dependent brain graph evaluation trajectory. In: Albarqouni, S., et al. (eds.) DART/FAIR -2021. LNCS, vol. 12968, pp. 180–190. Springer, Cham (2021). https://doi.org/10.1007/978-3-030-87722-4_17
12. McMahan, B., Moore, E., Ramage, D., Hampson, S., Arcas, B.A.: Communication-efficient learning of deep networks from decentralized data. In: Artificial Intelligence and Statistics, pp. 1273–1282 (2017)
13. Tom, E., et al.: Protecting data privacy in the age of AI-enabled ophthalmology. Transl. Vis. Sci. Technol. **9**, 36 (2020)
14. Liu, R., Yu, H.: Federated graph neural networks: overview, techniques and challenges. arXiv preprint arXiv:2202.07256 (2022)
15. Saha, S., Ahmad, T.: Federated transfer learning: concept and applications. Intelligenza Artificiale **15**, 35–44 (2021)
16. Zhang, C., Xie, Y., Bai, H., Yu, B., Li, W., Gao, Y.: A survey on federated learning. Knowl.-Based Syst. **216**, 106775 (2021)
17. Anagun, Y., Isik, S., Seke, E.: SRLibrary: comparing different loss functions for super-resolution over various convolutional architectures. J. Vis. Commun. Image Represent. **61**, 178–187 (2019)
18. Simonovsky, M., Komodakis, N.: Dynamic edge-conditioned filters in convolutional neural networks on graphs. CoRR abs/1704.02901 (2017)
19. Shewalkar, A.N., Nyavanandi, D., Ludwig, S.A.: Performance evaluation of deep neural networks applied to speech recognition: RNN, LSTM and GRU. J. Artif. Intell. Soft Comput. Res. **9**, 235–245 (2019)
20. McMahan, H.B., Moore, E., Ramage, D., Hampson, S., Arcas, B.A.: Communication-efficient learning of deep networks from decentralized data (2017)
21. Mao, Z., et al.: FedExg: federated learning with model exchange. In: 2020 IEEE International Symposium on Circuits and Systems (ISCAS), pp. 1–5 (2020)
22. Kamp, M., Fischer, J., Vreeken, J.: Federated learning from small datasets. arXiv preprint arXiv:2110.03469 (2021)

23. Matsuda, K., Sasaki, Y., Xiao, C., Onizuka, M.: FedMe: federated learning via model exchange. arXiv preprint arXiv:2110.07868 (2021)
24. LaMontagne, P.J., et al.: Oasis-3: longitudinal neuroimaging, clinical, and cognitive dataset for normal aging and Alzheimer disease. MedRxiv (2019)
25. Mahjoub, I., Mahjoub, M., Rekik, I.: Brain multiplexes reveal morphological connectional biomarkers fingerprinting late brain dementia states. Sci. Rep. **8**, 1–14 (2018)
26. Fey, M., Lenssen, J.E.: Fast graph representation learning with Pytorch geometric. CoRR abs/1903.02428 (2019)
27. Kingma, D.P., Ba, J.: Adam: a method for stochastic optimization. arXiv preprint arXiv:1412.6980 (2014)
28. Bullmore, E., Sporns, O.: The economy of brain network organization. Nat. Rev. Neurosci. **13**, 336–349 (2012)
29. Li, X., Huang, K., Yang, W., Wang, S., Zhang, Z.: On the convergence of FedAvg on non-IID data. arXiv preprint arXiv:1907.02189 (2019)
30. Li, X., Jiang, M., Zhang, X., Kamp, M., Dou, Q.: FedBN: federated learning on non-IID features via local batch normalization. arXiv preprint arXiv:2102.07623 (2021)

Bridging the Gap Between Deep Learning and Hypothesis-Driven Analysis via Permutation Testing

Magdalini Paschali[1], Qingyu Zhao[1], Ehsan Adeli[1], and Kilian M. Pohl[1,2(✉)]

[1] Department of Psychiatry and Behavioral Sciences,
Stanford University School of Medicine, Stanford, CA, USA
kpohl@stanford.edu
[2] Center for Health Sciences, SRI International, Menlo Park, CA, USA

Abstract. A fundamental approach in neuroscience research is to test hypotheses based on neuropsychological and behavioral measures, i.e., whether certain factors (e.g., related to life events) are associated with an outcome (e.g., depression). In recent years, deep learning has become a potential alternative approach for conducting such analyses by predicting an outcome from a collection of factors and identifying the most "informative" ones driving the prediction. However, this approach has had limited impact as its findings are not linked to statistical significance of factors supporting hypotheses. In this article, we proposed a flexible and scalable approach based on the concept of permutation testing that integrates hypothesis testing into the data-driven deep learning analysis. We apply our approach to the yearly self-reported assessments of 621 adolescent participants of the National Consortium of Alcohol and Neurodevelopment in Adolescence (NCANDA) to predict negative valence, a symptom of major depressive disorder according to the NIMH Research Domain Criteria (RDoC). Our method successfully identifies categories of risk factors that further explain the symptom.

Keywords: Permutation testing · Risk factor identification · Classification · Behavioral data · Outcome prediction · Disease prediction

1 Introduction

Neuropsychological studies often collect a wide range of measurements by asking participants to fill out self-reports and undergo cognitive assessments [1] in order to gain insights into the intervention and prevention of mental diseases. To support hypotheses motivating study creation, they then select a few measurements and test the statistical significance of their associations with the disease [2]. Alternatively, deep neural networks (DNNs) can be trained on all collected measurements to predict disease outcomes, and the decision process can be interpreted by identifying critical factors contributing to the prediction [3]. The identification of such factors is generally based on 'importance' scores, i.e., relative measurements (of arbitrary units) [4]. Failing to provide an absolute metric

© The Author(s), under exclusive license to Springer Nature Switzerland AG 2022
I. Rekik et al. (Eds.): PRIME 2022, LNCS 13564, pp. 13–23, 2022.
https://doi.org/10.1007/978-3-031-16919-9_2

of significance, findings from deep models generally fail to support hypotheses and hence have limited impact on advancing neuropsychology. To bridge the gap between hypothesis-driven analysis and data-driven deep learning, we propose a procedure for testing whether a category (domain) of factors significantly drives the prediction of a DNN. We do so by constructing the distribution of prediction accuracy under the null hypothesis that the tested category does not contain useful information for prediction.

This null distribution is derived based on a permutation procedure, which has been used to analyze different characteristics of machine learning models. Golland et al. [5] relied on permutation analysis to test whether the observed accuracy of a classifier could be achieved by chance. Other methods [6] computed permutation-based p-values to quantify whether a classifier exploits the dependency between input features. Permutation testing has also been used for selecting important attributes over a single or a set of prediction models [7] in decision trees [8], random forests [9–11], and DNNs [12]. Specifically, Mi et al. [12] proposed a permutation-based feature importance test that, based on normal distributions, identified predictors for survival of kidney-cancer patients.

Compared to these prior approaches, our proposed method has several advantages: 1) our method seamlessly connects data-driven learning approach with traditional hypothesis-driven analysis by quantifying statistical significance of categories of factors; 2) the approach does not require re-training the model as our null hypothesis is linked to a specific trained model; 3) thanks to the non-parametric nature of the permutation test, our method can be adapted to any machine or deep learning model regardless of the accuracy metric used for training.

We applied the proposed procedure to test the significance of categories of neuropsychological and behavioral measurements for predicting the depressive symptom of negative valence of the NIMH Research Domain Criteria (RDoC) [13]. To illustrate the generality of our test procedure, we apply it to a cross-sectional and a longitudinal variant of the prediction model, which is trained on annual acquired records of 621 participants (ages 12 to 17 years) provided by the National Consortium on Alcohol and Neurodevelopment in Adolescence (NCANDA). In both scenarios, our permutation procedure identified meaningful categories distinguishing non-symptomatic youth from participants with symptoms of negative valence.

2   Methodology

Problem Setup. Let $X \in \mathbb{R}^{n \times m}$ be the data matrix recording m measures (capturing demographic, neurospychological, and behavior factors) from n subjects, where X_i denotes the i-th row of X, associated with subject i. We also assume the m measures can be grouped into C categories so that $X := [X^1, ..., X^C]$. Each category $X^j \in \mathbb{R}^{n \times m_j}$ consists of m_j measures assessing one specific domain of cognition or behavior (e.g., all measures associated with sleep) for the n subjects ($\sum_{j=1}^{C} m_j = m$). Furthermore, each subject is linked to a label y_i, where $y_i = 0$

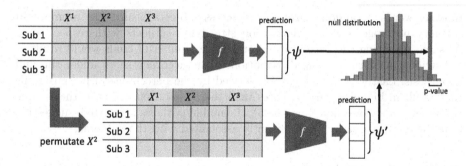

Fig. 1. Overview of the proposed permutation method, which we use to compute the significance of a category X^2 of factors for driving the prediction of model f. We first permute the values of X^2 across subjects (rows) and then measure the prediction accuracy based on the permuted input to derive a null distribution of the accuracy score $\hat{\psi}$. The percentile of the true accuracy ψ then defines the category's statistical significance (or p-value).

refers to non-symptomatic (healthy) subjects and $y_i = 1$ to a subject of the cohort of interest (e.g., certain disease or negative valence).

To find the association between factors X and outcome y, an emerging approach is to build a deep neural network $f(\cdot)$ so that $y_i' = f(X_i)$. After deriving the prediction $y' = [y_1', ..., y_n']^\top$ based on proper cross-validation, an accuracy metric $\psi = \mathcal{M}(y, y')$ is then computed to quantify the predictive power of the model. Examples for $\mathcal{M}(\cdot)$ are the classification accuracy, F1, AUC, mean absolute error, and R2 coefficient. To better understand the complex relationship between brain and behavior relationships associated with the group of interest, the last and yet most important step of the deep learning analysis is to identify which specific categories of factors are significantly associated with the outcome.

Permutation Test. Instead of using typical model interpretation techniques (such as Gradient-weighted Class Activation Maps (Grad-CAM) [4]) to compute "importance" of factors (which is a relative score), we formulate the problem as a hypothesis testing procedure. To test whether a category X^j significantly drives the prediction of the network f, our null hypothesis is that

$\mathcal{H}_0$: *The accuracy of the prediction model f is the same as ψ after permutation of the information in X^j.*

Since both the network f and the accuracy metric function $\mathcal{M}$ are possibly highly non-linear functions, we propose to use the permutation test as the test procedure. A permutation test is a non-parametric statistical test that constructs the null distribution of any test statistic (ψ in our case) by calculating all possible values of the test statistic under all possible rearrangements of the observed data points (see also Fig. 1). Specifically, let $\pi(\cdot)$ denote a random permutation of n objects such that $\pi(X^j)$ denotes the row-permutated matrix for the jth factor category. A new accuracy score is then computed as

$$\hat{\psi} = \mathcal{M}(f([X^1, ..., \pi(X^j), ..., X^C]), y). \tag{1}$$

In other words, a random permutation across subjects ensures the permutated category no longer carries information stratifying subjects with respect to y. As such, repeating the permutation for a large number of trials would result in a distribution of $\hat{\psi}$, i.e., the distribution of the accuracy score under the null hypothesis. Lastly, a p-value can be derived by the percentage of permutations that result in higher accuracy scores than the actual accuracy ψ. If the p-value is smaller than a threshold (e.g., 0.05), the null hypothesis is rejected, suggesting that the tested category is significantly associated with the outcome.

3   Experimental Setup

Depression Symptom Prediction. In this work, we predict the depression symptom of negative valence among adolescents from their demographics, self-reports, and neuropsychological and behavioral measures. Negative valence is a symptom describing feelings of sadness, loss, anxiety, fear, and threat. The literature has shown that youth with negative valence tend to develop major depressing disorder (MDD) [13] resulting in increased risk for chronic and recurrent depression and suicide attempts.

Dataset. The NCANDA [14] study recruited 831 youths across five sites in the U.S. (University of California at San Diego (UCSD), SRI International, Duke University Medical Center, University of Pittsburgh (UPMC), and Oregon Health & Science University (OHSU)) and followed them annually [15]. As our goal was to analyze adolescent depressive symptoms, we used data from 621 participants who completed at least one assessment before turning 18 years old. The data were part of the public release NCANDA_PUBLIC_6Y_REDCAP_V01 [14]. Among the 621 subjects, 81 reported symptoms of negative valence in at least one of their assessments. These subjects had, on average, 3.20 ± 1.66 assessments collected every 1.05 ± 0.15 years. 310 subjects were female and 311 male with an average age of 15.02 ± 1.69 at the baseline assessment.

We used a total of $m = 126$ measurements at each assessment and grouped them into the following categories ($C = 8$) according to their content:

- *Personality*, which includes traits such as extraversion, agreeableness, acceptance, and emotion regulation.
- *Life*, which describes life events, emotional neglect and trauma.
- *Sleep*, which includes information regarding a subject's sleep and wake-up time and sleep duration.
- *Support*, which describes the involvement of a subject in social clubs and their relationship with their family, friends, and teachers.
- *Neuropsych*, which includes emotion recognition, attention, and working memory measures.
- *Substance Use*, which corresponds to alcohol and substance use, marijuana dependence, and history.
- *Demographics*, which includes age, sex, ethnicity, and pubertal development score.

Table 1. p-value of each category in predicting negative valence and the null distribution of BACC resulting from category-specific permutations. Bold marks p-values of significant importance (p < 0.05). Cross-Sectional refers to models trained on the average across each subject's assessments, and Longitudinal to models trained on all yearly subject assessments.

Category	Cross-sectional		Longitudinal	
	Null distribution	p-value	Null distribution	p-value
Personality	65.72 ± 0.085	**<0.002**	58.72 ± 0.065	**<0.002**
Life	69.84 ± 0.092	**0.036**	70.22 ± 0.068	**0.030**
BRIEF	69.35 ± 0.094	**0.044**	72.29 ± 0.079	0.074
Support	69.89 ± 0.071	0.068	71.05 ± 0.096	**0.050**
Sleep	70.48 ± 0.094	0.108	71.95 ± 0.111	0.094
Neuropsych	70.49 ± 0.083	0.116	74.07 ± 0.090	0.430
Substance use	72.39 ± 0.098	0.534	74.13 ± 0.095	0.362
Demographics	71.84 ± 0.093	0.366	78.04 ± 0.112	0.992

- *BRIEF*, or the Behavior Rating Inventory of Executive Function [16], which measures aspects of executive functioning.

Model Training. To showcase our testing approach can be applied to any deep neural network, we trained a cross-sectional and a longitudinal model. Specifically, for the cross-sectional setting, we computed the average value of each feature across all assessments of a subject. Afterward, we classified subjects as having negative valence or being non-symptomatic via a deep learning model consisting of three Fully Connected (FC) layers, ReLU activation, and dropout layers with probability of 0.2. The model was trained for 55 epochs with a learning rate of 0.001.

For the longitudinal setting, a deep learning model consisting of a Gated Recurrent Unit (GRU) [17] layer, and two FC layers identified negative valence in the last assessment of a subject, i.e., in a Sequence-to-One fashion. The model was trained for 30 epochs with learning rate of 0.0001 and Adam Optimizer [18].

The loss function used in both settings was the weighted binary cross entropy [19]. To combat the severe class imbalance, we calculated the ratio of non-symptomatic to symptomatic subjects, $R = \frac{N_{non-symptomatic}}{N_{symptomatic}}$ as our loss weight. Additionally, we employed ℓ_1 regularization to avoid overfitting. We implemented our models and our evaluation in PyTorch 1.10.0 [20]. Our code is publicly available[1].

Identifying Important Feature Categories. We trained all models using stratified 5-fold cross-validation with subject-level splits across folds. The accuracy of each model was determined via the F1-Score and the balanced accuracy

---

[1] https://github.com/MaggiePas/Permutations_MICCAIPRIME2022.

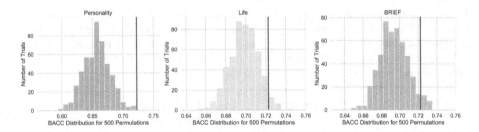

Fig. 2. Null distributions of BACC derived by permutation for the three categories that were significant for predicting negative valence when using the cross-sectional model. The red line denotes the observed BACC with the original (un-permutated) data, from which we infer the p-values of the categories as listed in Table 1 (Color figure online).

(BACC) [21], which account for the severe class imbalance. We used the proposed approach to test whether each of the 8 categories significantly contributed to the observed BACC. To do so, we performed 500 permutations within each test fold (a total of 2500 permutations) to generate the null distribution of BACC.

4   Results and Discussion

We now present and discuss the results of our models for the cross-sectional and longitudinal training setting. First, we review the significant categories identified by the permutation analysis. Afterward, we test for the specificity of our approach by re-training the models once using only significant categories and once only non-significant categories. Subsequently, we calculate the Shapley values [22] for each category feature and show their overlap with the significant categories identified by our permutation analysis. Finally, we perform hierarchical hypothesis testing by dividing the significant feature categories into meaningful subcategories and repeating the permutation experiment on each of them.

Cross-Sectional Model. Based on the 5-fold cross-validation, the cross-sectional model resulted in a BACC of 72.25%. Table 1(left) summarizes the null distribution of BACC for each category resulting from 500 permutations and the corresponding p-value. Figure 2 plots the distributions for the significant categories. In all three cases, the mean BACC of the null distribution is clearly lower than the true BACC of 72.25% (shown in red).

Specifically, *Personality* is the most significant category for predicting negative valence as permuting personality variables caused the highest drop of 6.5% (comparing true model BACC with the mean of null distribution). This result was in line with the depression literature, frequently reporting on the connection between depression and personality traits, which could impact mood through altered reactivity to emotional cues and result in depressive symptoms [23–25].

The second category where random permutations caused a significant decrease in model BACC was *Life*. It has been consistently documented that

Table 2. BACC and F1-scores of models trained with all feature categories, trained only with the categories identified as significant by our approach and only with the non-significant categories. Bold marks the highest BACC and F1-Score.

Categories	Cross-sectional		Longitudinal	
	BACC	F1-Score	BACC	F1-Score
All	**0.7225**	**0.6404**	0.7456	**0.6482**
Only significant	0.7146	0.6322	**0.7668**	0.6221
Non-significant	0.6200	0.5457	0.6683	0.5255

youth experiencing more adverse life events are more susceptible to developing depression [26]. Moreover, strong relationships between childhood abuse and depression have also been previously reported [27]. In the cross-sectional setting, *BRIEF* was also a significant predictor for negative valence. Cognitive and behavioral shifts (that are described by *BRIEF*) have been associated with negative valence, while depression is reciprocally linked with executive dysfunction [28].

Longitudinal Model. Our longitudinal model resulted in a 74.56% BACC. The 2% increase compared to the cross-sectional model could be attributed to the temporal information provided to our RNN and the higher number of individual assessments. In line with the cross-sectional setting, *Personality* and *Life* were significant in predicting the outcome. Slightly deviating from the cross-sectional results, permutating *BRIEF* variables only resulted in trend-level significance ($p = 0.074$; cross-sectional setting: $p = 0.044$) and *Support* (which was at a trend-level $p = 0.068$ with respect to the cross-sectional setting) reached the significance threshold. The literature has shown the crucial role of social support in preventing depression [29]. Moreover, the presence and quality of friendships in adolescence is a significant factor that influences mental health, while limited social interactions could lead to depressive symptoms [30]. The general agreement in the importance of categories (top 4 vs. bottom 4) between cross-sectional and longitudinal analyses suggests the robustness of our proposed test procedure.

Specificity Testing of Significant Categories. To explore the specificity of our test procedure, we retrained our models using only the significant categories as the input (*Personality, Life* and *BRIEF* in the cross-sectional setting and *Personality, Life* and *Support* in the longitudinal setting) and also using only the non-significant categories. Table 2 shows that results from using only significant categories roughly aligned with the ones using all categories. This indicates that the significant categories identified by our method contained the majority of the information for prediction.

Notably, in the longitudinal setting, the model trained only on the significant categories led to a 2.2% improvement in BACC, potentially suggesting that removing irrelevant features reduced the chance of overfitting in the RNN. In both settings, training the model on the non-significant categories led to a drastic

Table 3. Results of permutation testing on fine-grained feature categories within *Personality* and *Life*. Bold marks p-values of significant importance ($p < 0.05$) for each category sub-scales.

Sub-category		Cross-sectional		Longitudinal	
		p-value	Difference	p-value	Difference
Pesonality	TIPI	**0.006**	-0.033 ± 0.089	**<0.002**	-0.124 ± 0.056
	RSQ	0.074	-0.017 ± 0.090	0.084	-0.029 ± 0.082
	UPPS	0.374	-0.005 ± 0.103	0.964	$+0.021 \pm 0.089$
Life	LEQ	0.098	-0.017 ± 0.090	**0.010**	-0.049 ± 0.070
	CTQ	0.452	-0.000 ± 0.101	0.864	$+0.011 \pm 0.105$

decrease in BACC by 10% in the cross-sectional model and 8% in the longitudinal one. These results further highlight that the variables of the non-significant categories did not substantially aid the prediction process.

Comparison with SHAP Values. To relate the significance of categories to the importance of features, we generated the Deep SHapley Additive exPlanations (SHAP) [31], which assign an importance value (Shapley values [32]) to each feature for a particular prediction. Shapley values calculate the average marginal contribution of each feature towards the model prediction. Figure 3 plots the ranked SHAP values for all 126 features of our model in the cross-sectional setting. Notably, the variables of the categories identified as significant by our approach (i.e., *Personality*, *Life* and *BRIEF*) have also been assigned high SHAP scores.

Hierarchical Hypothesis Testing. We further show our test procedure's versatility by embedding it into a nested analysis. As *Personality* and *Life* were the two significant categories in both models, we tested the statistical significance of subcategories within each category. Specifically, we split *Personality* into the subcategories of measurements collected by the *Ten-Item Personality Inventory* (TIPI) [33], the *Responses to Stress Questionnaire* (RSQ) [34], and *Urgency, Premeditation (lack of), Perseverance (lack of), Sensation Seeking* (UPPS) [35]. TIPI assesses Extraversion, Agreeableness, Conscientiousness, Emotional Stability, and Openness to Experience. RSQ measures coping and involuntary stress responses, and UPPS measures multiple aspects of impulsive personality. Furthermore, we split *Life* into the measurements associated with Life Events Questionnaire (LEQ) [36] and Childhood Trauma Questionnaire (CTQ) [37]. LEQ captures life events mostly associated with work and family, and CTQ records physical and emotional abuse and neglect.

Table 3 summarizes the outcome when permutating each subcategory, which revealed that *TIPI* is the most significant predictor of negative valence among factors of *Personality* for both settings. These results highlight our approach's ability to scale from more extensive category variables to fine-grained variable subsets.

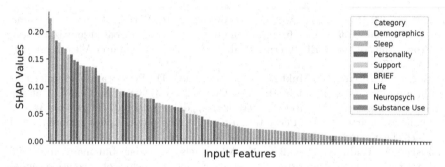

Fig. 3. Feature Importance Scores for all our model features computed by the Deep SHapley Additive exPlanation (SHAP) [31] derived for our cross-sectional model. The significant categories identified by our approach (Table 1) have also been assigned high SHAP values.

5   Conclusion

This paper proposed a flexible and scalable approach that successfully combined hypothesis testing with data-driven deep learning analysis. Based on permutation testing, the approach relates the importance of a category of factors in the data-driven prediction process to p-values used in hypothesis testing. We evaluated our permutation scheme for identifying the major depressive symptom of negative valence from the psycho-social and cognitive factors recorded in 621 NCANCA youths. In line with the literature, personality traits and life events were of significant importance for the predictions performed by the cross-sectional DNN and longitudinal RNN. In summary, our comprehensive analysis can identify potential predictors of negative valence during adolescence that might be important for timely intervention, especially given the increased risk for depression starting with the COVID pandemic [38].

Acknowledgements. This study was in part supported by the National Consortium on Alcohol and Neurodevelopment in Adolescence (NCANDA) by means of research grants from the National Institute on Alcohol Abuse and Alcoholism (NIAAA) AA021697 (PI: KMP) and AA028840 (PI: QZ). The research was also supported by the Stanford Human-Centered Artificial Intelligence (HAI) Google Cloud Credit (PI: KMP).

References

1. Gurd, J., Kischka, U., Marshall, J.C., Halligan, P.W.: Handbook of Clinical Neuropsychology, 2nd edn. Oxford University Press, Oxford (2010)
2. Blakesley, R., et al.: Comparisons of methods for multiple hypothesis testing in neuropsychological research. Neuropsychology **23**, 255–264 (2009)
3. Kang, M., et al.: Prediction of cognitive impairment via deep learning trained with multi-center neuropsychological test data. BMC Med. Inform. Decis. Mak. **19** (2019)

4. Selvaraju, R.R., Cogswell, M., Das, A., Vedantam, R., Parikh, D., Batra, D.: Grad-CAM: visual explanations from deep networks via gradient-based localization. In: Proceedings of the IEEE International Conference on Computer Vision, pp. 618–626 (2017)
5. Golland, P., Liang, F., Mukherjee, S., Panchenko, D.: Permutation tests for classification. In: Auer, P., Meir, R. (eds.) COLT 2005. LNCS (LNAI), vol. 3559, pp. 501–515. Springer, Heidelberg (2005). https://doi.org/10.1007/11503415_34
6. Ojala, M., Garriga, G.C.: Permutation tests for studying classifier performance. J. Mach. Learn. Res. **11**(6) (2010)
7. Fisher, A., Rudin, C., Dominici, F.: All models are wrong, but many are useful: learning a variable's importance by studying an entire class of prediction models simultaneously. J. Mach. Learn. Res. **20**(177), 1–81 (2019)
8. Frank, E., Witten, I.H.: Using a permutation test for attribute selection in decision trees. In: Shavlik, J.W. (ed.) Proceedings of the Fifteenth International Conference on Machine Learning, pp. 152–160. Morgan Kaufmann (1998)
9. Breiman, L.: Random forests. Mach. Learn. **45**(1), 5–32 (2001)
10. Altmann, A., Toloşi, L., Sander, O., Lengauer, T.: Permutation importance: a corrected feature importance measure. Bioinformatics **26**(10), 1340–1347 (2010)
11. Ishwaran, H., Lu, M.: Standard errors and confidence intervals for variable importance in random forest regression, classification, and survival. Stat. Med. **38**(4), 558–582 (2019)
12. Mi, X., Zou, B., Zou, F., Hu, J.: Permutation-based identification of important biomarkers for complex diseases via machine learning models. Nat. Commun. **12**(1), 1–12 (2021)
13. Insel, T., et al.: Research Domain Criteria (RDoC): toward a new classification framework for research on mental disorders (2010)
14. Pohl, K.M., et al.: The NCANDA_PUBLIC_6Y_REDCAP_V01 data release of the national consortium on alcohol and neurodevelopment in adolescence (NCANDA) (2021). https://doi.org/10.7303/syn25606546
15. Brown, S.A., et al.: The national consortium on alcohol and neurodevelopment in adolescence (NCANDA): a multisite study of adolescent development and substance use. J. Stud. Alcohol Drugs **76**(6), 895–908 (2015)
16. Gioia, G.A., Isquith, P.K., Guy, S.C., Kenworthy, L.: Test review behavior rating inventory of executive function. Child Neuropsychol. **6**(3), 235–238 (2000)
17. Cho, K., et al.: Learning phrase representations using RNN encoder-decoder for statistical machine translation. arXiv preprint arXiv:1406.1078 (2014)
18. Kingma, D.P., Ba, J.: Adam: a method for stochastic optimization. arXiv preprint arXiv:1412.6980 (2014)
19. Murphy, K.P.: Machine Learning: A Probabilistic Perspective. MIT Press, Cambridge (2012)
20. Paszke, A., et al.: PyTorch: an imperative style, high-performance deep learning library. In: Advances in Neural Information Processing Systems, vol. 32, pp. 8024–8035. Curran Associates Inc. (2019)
21. Brodersen, K.H., Ong, C.S., Stephan, K.E., Buhmann, J.M.: The balanced accuracy and its posterior distribution. In: 2010 20th International Conference on Pattern Recognition, pp. 3121–3124. IEEE (2010)
22. Suhara, Y., Xu, Y., Pentland, A.: DeepMood: forecasting depressed mood based on self-reported histories via recurrent neural networks, pp. 715–724 (2017)
23. Rottenberg, J., Gotlib, I.H.: Socioemotional functioning in depression. In: Mood Disorders: A Handbook of Science and Practice, pp. 61–77 (2004)

24. Klinger-Koenig, J., Hertel, J., Terock, J., Voelzke, H., Van der Auwera, S., Grabe, H.J.: Predicting physical and mental health symptoms: additive and interactive effects of difficulty identifying feelings, neuroticism and extraversion. J. Psychosom. Res. **115**, 14–23 (2018)
25. Watson, D., Stasik, S.M., Ellickson-Larew, S., Stanton, K.: Extraversion and psychopathology: a facet-level analysis. J. Abnorm. Psychol. **124**(2), 432 (2015)
26. De Venter, M., Demyttenaere, K., Bruffaerts, R.: The relationship between adverse childhood experiences and mental health in adulthood. A systematic literature review. Tijdschr. Psychiatr. **55**(4), 259–268 (2013)
27. Kendler, K.S., Bulik, C.M., Silberg, J., Hettema, J.M., Myers, J., Prescott, C.A.: Childhood sexual abuse and adult psychiatric and substance use disorders in women: an epidemiological and cotwin control analysis. Arch. Gen. Psychiatry **57**(10), 953–959 (2000)
28. Gotlib, I.H., Joormann, J.: Cognition and depression: current status and future directions. Annu. Rev. Clin. Psychol. **6**, 285–312 (2010)
29. Lamblin, M., Murawski, C., Whittle, S., Fornito, A.: Social connectedness, mental health and the adolescent brain. Neurosci. Biobehav. Rev. **80**, 57–68 (2017)
30. Ueno, K.: The effects of friendship networks on adolescent depressive symptoms. Soc. Sci. Res. **34**(3), 484–510 (2005)
31. Lundberg, S.M., Lee, S.-I.: A unified approach to interpreting model predictions. In: Advances in Neural Information Processing Systems, vol. 30 (2017)
32. Shapley, L.S.: A value for n-person games, contributions to the theory of games, vol. 2, pp. 307–317 (1953)
33. Gosling, S.D., Rentfrow, P.J., Swann, W.B., Jr.: A very brief measure of the Big-Five personality domains. J. Res. Pers. **37**(6), 504–528 (2003)
34. Connor-Smith, J.K., Compas, B.E., Wadsworth, M.E., Thomsen, A.H., Saltzman, H.: Responses to stress in adolescence: measurement of coping and involuntary stress responses. J. Consult. Clin. Psychol. **68**(6), 976 (2000)
35. Cyders, M.A., Smith, G.T., Spillane, N.S., Fischer, S., Annus, A.M., Peterson, C.: Integration of impulsivity and positive mood to predict risky behavior: development and validation of a measure of positive urgency. Psychol. Assess. **19**(1), 107 (2007)
36. Masten, A.S., Neemann, J., Andenas, S.: Life events and adjustment in adolescents: the significance of event independence, desirability, and chronicity. J. Res. Adolesc. **4**(1), 71–97 (1994)
37. Bernstein, D.P., et al.: Initial reliability and validity of a new retrospective measure of child abuse and neglect. Am. J. Psychiatry **152**, 1535–1537 (1994)
38. Alzueta, E., et al.: Risk for depression tripled during the COVID-19 pandemic in emerging adults followed for the last 8 years. Psychol. Med. 1–8 (2021)

Multi-tracer PET Imaging Using Deep Learning: Applications in Patients with High-Grade Gliomas

Mirwais Wardak[1,2(✉)], Sarah M. Hooper[1,3], Christiaan Schiepers[4], Wei Chen[4], Carina Mari Aparici[1], Guido A. Davidzon[1], Ophir Vermesh[1], Timothy F. Cloughesy[5], Sung-Cheng Huang[4], and Sanjiv Sam Gambhir[1,2,6]

[1] Department of Radiology, Molecular Imaging Program at Stanford (MIPS), Stanford University School of Medicine, Stanford, CA, USA
mwardak@stanford.edu
[2] Stanford Cardiovascular Institute, Stanford University School of Medicine, Stanford, CA, USA
[3] Department of Electrical Engineering, Stanford University, Stanford, CA, USA
[4] Department of Molecular and Medical Pharmacology, Ahmanson Translational Imaging Division, David Geffen School of Medicine at UCLA, Los Angeles, CA, USA
[5] Department of Neurology, UCLA Neuro-Oncology Program, David Geffen School of Medicine at UCLA, Los Angeles, CA, USA
[6] Department of Bioengineering, Department of Materials Science and Engineering, and Stanford Bio-X, Stanford University, Stanford, CA, USA

Abstract. One of the great strengths of positron emission tomography (PET) is its ability to quantitatively image a wide array of molecular targets for disease evaluation. However, multi-tracer PET imaging is hindered because current technology permits only one PET tracer to be imaged at a time. The aim of this study was to develop a deep learning system that uses a PET image obtained with one tracer to predict a synthetic PET image of a different tracer without having to actually inject the second tracer. Deep neural networks were designed to generate synthetic 3′-deoxy-3′-[^{18}F]-fluorothymidine (^{18}F-FLT) PET images from 3,4-dihydroxy-6-[^{18}F]-fluoro-L-phenylalanine (^{18}F-FDOPA) PET and magnetic resonance imaging scans of nineteen patients with glioblastoma. Here, we show that the proposed image synthesis method closely predicts the ground truth ^{18}F-FLT PET images (MAE = 0.024 ± 0.004, SSIM = 0.832 ± 0.035, PSNR = 27.521 ± 1.606). Moreover, a blinded image evaluation by three nuclear medicine physicians determined that the synthetic images were rated significantly better on spatial resolution ($p < 0.015$), image noise ($p < 0.001$) and overall image quality ($p < 0.0001$) than the true PET images. This study offers a new strategy for multi-tracer PET imaging using machine learning and reduces radiation dose to the patient by at least 50%.

S. S. Gambhir—Deceased.

Supplementary Information The online version contains supplementary material available at https://doi.org/10.1007/978-3-031-16919-9_3.

© The Author(s), under exclusive license to Springer Nature Switzerland AG 2022
I. Rekik et al. (Eds.): PRIME 2022, LNCS 13564, pp. 24–35, 2022.
https://doi.org/10.1007/978-3-031-16919-9_3

Keywords: Deep learning · Multi-tracer PET · Synthetic images

1   Introduction

Positron emission tomography (PET) is a quantitative medical imaging technique that uses radiotracers to examine tissue and organ biochemistry in vivo [17]. Each radiotracer reveals unique information about different biological processes [12,17] (e.g., glucose metabolism, receptor densities, protein synthesis) which can lead to improved diagnosis and clinical management. Multi-tracer PET imaging thus offers great potential for image-guided personalized medicine.

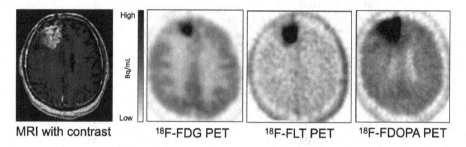

| MRI with contrast | ^{18}F-FDG PET | ^{18}F-FLT PET | ^{18}F-FDOPA PET |

Fig. 1. Multi-tracer PET images of a patient with a glioblastoma. Imaging a patient with multiple radiotracers can characterize and monitor different aspects of tumor physiology, providing complementary information. Contrast-enhanced MRI is shown for anatomical reference on the far left. ^{18}F-FDOPA and ^{18}F-FLT overcome some of the current limitations of [^{18}F]-fluorodeoxyglucose (18F-FDG), such as high physiologic background uptake of ^{18}F-FDG in normal grey matter, nonspecific uptake of ^{18}F-FDG by immune cells, and the fact that ^{18}F-FDG uptake in low-grade brain tumors is usually similar to that in normal white matter.

Two tracers useful for studying glioblastoma (GBM) include the nucleoside tracer 3′-deoxy-3′-[^{18}F]-fluorothymidine (^{18}F-FLT), which provides information about a tumor's DNA replication activity [6,7], and the amino acid analog 3,4-dihydroxy-6-[^{18}F]-fluoro-L-phenylalanine (^{18}F-FDOPA), which can help measure the level of amino acid transport into a tumor [6,19]. Clinically, ^{18}F-FDOPA is useful for detecting low- and high-grade brain tumors and evaluating tumor extent for surgical resection [6], while ^{18}F-FLT has been shown to correlate with patient outcome in high-grade brain tumors [22]. Imaging with both radiotracers can therefore help inform patient care [6,12] (Fig. 1).

PET tracers are typically administered and studied one at a time because each tracer gives rise to indistinguishable 511 keV annihilation photon pairs [1]. As a result, multi-tracer PET imaging has posed a formidable technical and logistical challenge. To obtain PET scans with multiple tracers, several imaging sessions need to be scheduled, resulting in high costs, image alignment issues, potential changes in pathophysiology, and an arduous experience for the patient. Further, administering multiple radiotracers increases radiation dose to

Table 1. Clinical characteristics of patients with ^{18}F-FLT and ^{18}F-FDOPA PET and contrast-enhanced MRI scans. *GBM = glioblastoma; †AA = anaplastic astrocytoma.

Patient no.	Sex	Age (y)	Pathology at initial diagnosis	Initial WHO grade	Pathology at recurrence	WHO grade at recurrence
1	M	69	GBM*	4	GBM	4
2	F	65	GBM	4	GBM	4
3	F	59	GBM	4	GBM	4
4	M	64	GBM	4	GBM	4
5	M	37	AA†	3	GBM	4
6	M	68	GBM	4	GBM	4
7	F	35	AA	3	GBM	4
8	F	54	GBM	4	GBM	4
9	M	45	GBM	4	GBM	4
10	M	26	AA	3	GBM	4
11	F	40	GBM	4	GBM	4
12	F	47	GBM	4	GBM	4
13	F	70	GBM	4	GBM	4
14	F	61	GBM	4	GBM	4
15	F	37	GBM	4	GBM	4
16	M	57	GBM	4	GBM	4
17	F	62	GBM	4	GBM	4
18	M	76	GBM	4	GBM	4
19	M	46	GBM	4	GBM	4

the patient. For these reasons, the vast potential of multi-tracer PET imaging has not yet been fully realized.

In this study, we investigate the utility of machine learning (ML) for multi-tracer PET imaging. Recent ML advances show tremendous promise for image analysis, classification, and synthesis tasks [23]. We hypothesized that convolutional neural networks (CNNs) could leverage the information in a PET image acquired with one tracer to predict the distribution of a second tracer. Here, we report a general ML framework that transforms an existing PET scan taken with a specific tracer into a synthetic PET scan of a second tracer without having to inject the second tracer. We trained these networks to generate synthetic ^{18}F-FLT PET images from ^{18}F-FDOPA PET and contrast-enhanced MRI (ceMRI) images and present proof-of-principal results. This system sets forth a new method for multi-tracer PET imaging that delivers additional information about disease states without increasing patient radiation dose or requiring additional imaging sessions.

2   Methods

2.1   PET and MR Dataset

We utilized a retrospective dataset of 19 patients with high-grade recurrent brain tumors, which was collected under an approved IRB and deidentified (Table 1)

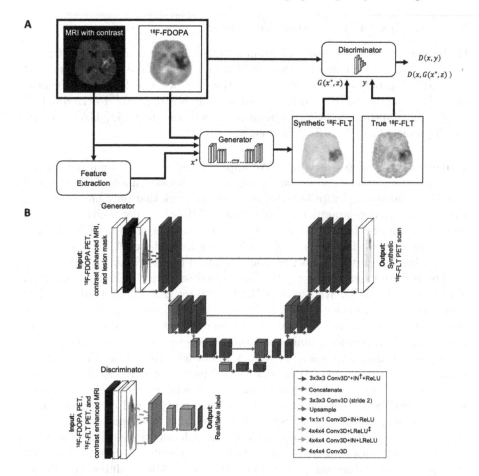

Fig. 2. A. Diagram of image generation method. An MRI is processed by a 3D CNN to extract a lesion mask. Next, the ^{18}F-FDOPA PET, MRI, and lesion mask are input into a generator, which produces the synthetic ^{18}F-FLT PET scan. During training, the scans are analyzed by a discriminator. **B. cGAN network architectures.** *3D convolutional layer; † Instance normalization; ‡ Leaky ReLU.

[22]. Each patient received an ^{18}F-FLT PET, ^{18}F-FDOPA PET, and a T1-weighted ceMRI scan; details on image acquisition and preprocessing are in the Supplementary. The data was randomly split into 14 training, 2 validation, and 3 test patients. In addition to evaluating model performance on the test split, we used leave-one-out cross-validation (LOO-CV) on the combined training and validation sets (n = 16) to perform ablations. Over the 16 training and validation patients, there were 7,348,382 voxels within the brain region for each of the MRI and PET scans. Over the three test patients, there were 1,430,060 voxels within the brain region.

2.2   Description of Proposed Framework

Overview. Figure 2A shows a diagram summarizing our framework, which predicts an ^{18}F-FLT PET image given a ceMRI and ^{18}F-FDOPA PET image. First, the ceMRI is processed by a feature extraction network, which predicts the mask of the lesion in the ceMRI. Then, the lesion mask, ceMRI, and ^{18}F-FDOPA PET image are fed into a conditional generative adversarial network (cGAN) [11,16], which predicts the ^{18}F-FLT PET image.

Feature Extraction Network. We implemented an application-specific feature extraction network to extract features (e.g., a lesion mask) from the ceMRIs. By training a separate feature extraction network that only processes ceMRIs, larger training datasets containing only ceMRIs (i.e., not multi-tracer PET images, which are difficult to collect) could be used for training. The separate feature extractor offloads some of the learning from the cGAN, which is constrained by the limited number of available multi-tracer training images.

The feature extraction network was trained to output a lesion mask given a T1-weighted ceMRI. We used the BraTS dataset [2,3,15] for training, which contained 274 patients with GBM and lower grade gliomas from multiple institutions that were segmented by one to four human raters. We used an 80/20% split of the BraTS dataset for training and validation respectively; no BraTS images were reserved as test images since they were not used to test the PET synthesis network. Our feature extraction network architecture was modeled after previous work [10]. To train the feature extraction network, we used full scan volumes from the BraTS dataset augmented by random flips as well as random transposes. Training was done with batch size of two due to memory constraints of the GPU. We trained for 300 epochs with the Adam optimizer [13], which was initialized with a learning rate of 5e−6 that was scheduled to drop by a factor of 0.5 when the validation loss plateaued for 10 epochs. After training with BraTS, the feature extraction network's weights were frozen and the cGAN was trained.

cGAN. The cGAN generator takes as input the ceMRI, ^{18}F-FDOPA PET image, and lesion mask, and outputs a synthetic ^{18}F-FLT PET image. The cGAN discriminator is employed only during training to encourage the generator to output realistic images, as is standard in cGANs (cGAN background provided in Supplementary). The cGAN generator was inspired by U-Net [18] and the discriminator was modeled after PatchGAN [11] (Fig. 2B). Detailed architecture descriptions of the networks depicted in Fig. 2B as well as detailed loss functions used for training are provided in the Supplementary.

The 19-patient dataset containing the PET scans was used to train the cGAN. We first initialized the weights of the cGAN generator by again utilizing the BraTS dataset; specifically, we trained the generator to predict the lesion masks of contrast-enhanced MRIs in the BraTS dataset. After this pretraining to initialize the generator's weights, we trained the cGAN with the PET and MR dataset for 150 epochs. Data augmentation was performed on every iteration of training. Specifically, from each $128 \times 128 \times 63$ image volume, a random

Table 2. Performance metrics on the test set for our network and two common image synthesis networks. The mean value over all synthetic test images is listed with the standard error of the mean shown in parentheses.

	MAE	SSIM	PSNR
Proposed method	0.024 (0.004)	0.832 (0.035)	27.521 (1.606)
Image-to-Image	0.026 (0.001)	0.810 (0.023)	24.516 (1.098)
U-Net	0.033 (0.002)	0.785 (0.002)	22.108 (1.030)

$64 \times 64 \times 32$ image patch was chosen as a training sample. We used a combination of random affine transformations, horizontal flips, and elastic transforms to further augment the dataset. For validation and test images, no data augmentation was performed and full image volumes were processed instead of image patches. Random hyperparameter search was used to choose the learning rates, weight decay, and dropout probability. The dropout rate in the generator was set to 0.2. The generator learning rate was initialized to $5e{-}4$ and scheduled to drop by a factor of 0.1 after 100 epochs with a weight decay set to 0.08. The discriminator learning rate was initialized to $1e{-}5$ and scheduled to drop by a factor of 0.1 after 100 epochs with a weight decay of zero.

2.3   Evaluation Procedure

Quantitative Evaluation. We evaluated the synthetic images using the mean absolute error (MAE), the structural similarity index (SSIM), and the peak signal-to-noise ratio (PSNR) (equations in Supplementary). SSIM (range $[0, 1]$) measures visually perceived image quality while MAE and PSNR measure voxelwise differences between two images. Lower MAE and higher PSNR and SSIM values indicate synthetic images closer to the ground truth. We report the mean performance metrics with the standard error of the mean.

Nuclear Medicine Physician Analysis. Synthetic and true ^{18}F-FLT PET images were presented to three nuclear medicine physicians who were blinded to whether the images were real or synthetic. They evaluated the PET images in 3D while having the ceMRI for anatomical reference. The physicians rated each ^{18}F-FLT PET image's spatial resolution, image noise, and overall image quality on a 5-point scale (1: poor/non-diagnostic; 2: below average; 3: average/acceptable; 4: good; 5: excellent). The average ratings for the real and synthetic images were compared with a t-test.

3   Results

3.1   Quantitative Evaluation

We compared our proposed system against two common image synthesis networks: Image-to-Image [11] and U-Net [18]. The MAE, SSIM, and PSNR of our

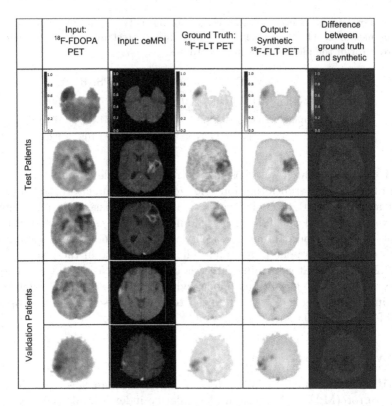

Fig. 3. Axial slices from three test patients and two validation patients. All images are normalized to [0, 1]. The last column shows the absolute value of the difference between the normalized ground truth and synthetic ^{18}F-FLT PET images.

proposed approach on the test set were 0.024 ± 0.004, 0.832 ± 0.035, and 27.521 ± 1.606, respectively, representing a 7.69%, 2.72%, and 12.26% improvement over the next-best baseline (Table 2). In Fig. 3, axial slices of the ^{18}F-FDOPA PET, ceMRI, ground truth ^{18}F-FLT PET, and synthetic ^{18}F-FLT PET images are shown. Zoomed-in images of the tumors are shown in Supplementary Figure S1 and additional patients are shown in Figure S2.

3.2 Nuclear Medicine Physician Analysis

When pooling the ratings from the three nuclear medicine physicians for the 19 patients (Fig. 4; predictions on the training and validation images generated via LOO-CV), the synthetic ^{18}F-FLT PET images were rated significantly better than the true ^{18}F-FLT PET images on spatial resolution (4.40 ± 0.10 vs. 4.05 ± 0.08, $p < 0.015$), image noise (4.63 ± 0.08 vs. 4.21 ± 0.10, $p < 0.001$) and overall image quality (4.56 ± 0.08 vs. 4.07 ± 0.09, $p < 0.0001$). On average, the raters were unable to distinguish whether the ^{18}F-FLT PET images were real or synthetic.

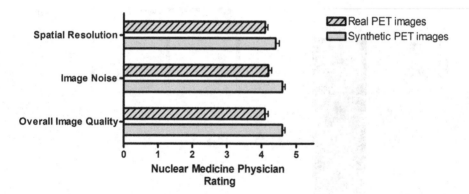

Fig. 4. Nuclear medicine physician ratings of the real and synthetic ^{18}F-FLT PET images. Overall mean ratings by three nuclear medicine physicians of the real and synthetic ^{18}F-FLT PET images; error bars show the standard deviation of the mean ($n = 57$). The synthetic PET images were rated significantly better than the true PET images on spatial resolution ($p < 0.015$), image noise ($p < 0.001$) and overall image quality ($p < 0.0001$).

3.3 Ablations

We evaluated the impact of various changes to our system input on the quality of the synthetic images.

Effect of Multi-modal Input. We assessed the effect of the tumor mask and multi-modal input on the synthetic ^{18}F-FLT PET images by retraining the cGAN with fewer input imaging modalities. Using combined training and validation sets, we ran LOO-CV six times, each time providing the network with a different set of inputs. We found that multi-modal inputs in the image synthesis network improved the quality of the synthetic images: the mean PSNR of the synthetic images generated using the contrast-enhanced MRI, ^{18}F-FDOPA PET, and lesion mask was 5.39% and 2.02% higher than that of the synthetic images generated with only the contrast-enhanced MRI and ^{18}F-FDOPA images, respectively (Supplementary Table S1). The contrast-enhanced MR and PET scans collectively contain anatomical and molecular information that illuminate the underlying system, so training with both modalities was expected to produce better synthetic images than training with a single modality alone. Example images generated with varying inputs during LOO-CV are shown in Fig. 5.

Effect of Volumetric Processing. Processing volumetric data instead of 2D axial slices has both pros and cons. Training with volumetric patches allows for dependencies between axial slices to be analyzed. Conversely, training on axial slices often requires fewer network parameters and is a simple means of data augmentation. To evaluate the effect of training on 2D vs. 3D inputs, we retrained the network using single axial slices, many axial slices, and all axial slices per training sample. To train with one axial slice, all 3D operations in the

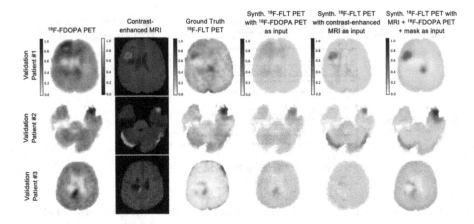

Fig. 5. ^{18}**F-FDOPA PET, contrast-enhanced MRI, ground truth** ^{18}**F-FLT PET, and three synthetic** ^{18}**F-FLT PET images generated with varying inputs during LOO-CV for three validation patients.** Multimodal inputs to the cGAN improved the quality of the synthetic images. The differences in the three synthetic images show the effect of varying the input to the cGAN. All images are normalized to [0, 1].

Table 3. Performance metrics from LOO-CV on the combined training and validation sets showing the effect of training the network with different numbers of axial slices. The mean value over all synthetic training and validation images is listed with the standard error of the mean shown in parentheses.

	MAE	SSIM	PSNR
1 slice	0.041 (0.006)	0.727 (0.029)	21.359 (1.079)
16 slices	0.027 (0.002)	0.814 (0.012)	25.957 (0.634)
32 slices	0.026 (0.002)	0.832 (0.011)	26.620 (0.599)
48 slices	0.026 (0.003)	0.818 (0.013)	26.432 (0.650)
63 slices	0.027 (0.003)	0.818 (0.012)	26.137 (0.695)

network were changed to 2D operations. Image quality metrics from LOO-CV on the combined training and validation sets are summarized in Table 3.

Training with volumetric data produced synthetic ^{18}F-FLT PET images that most closely matched the ground truth images. Comparing the network trained on one axial slice to 32 axial slices (as used in the final network), the MAE dropped 36.59%, the SSIM rose 14.44%, and the PSNR increased 24.63%. We observed that processing volumetric data discouraged small erroneous hot spots in the image from appearing, which occurred when training with only one axial slice. Even though processing 2D slices increased the effective number of samples in our training set, the errors resulted in lower overall performance.

4 Discussion and Conclusion

Image-guided personalized medicine requires a detailed exploration of disease status. However, acquiring multiple PET scans can increase cost, time, radiation dose and patient discomfort. To overcome these challenges, we developed a deep learning system that takes a PET image of one tracer to predict a second PET image of a different tracer. This work opens up a new way forward in molecular imaging, allowing multiple targets to be interrogated without having to inject imaging agents for each and every target.

Previous works have proposed multi-tracer PET imaging strategies, such as using the difference in half-lives of various radioisotopes [8], detecting a third prompt gamma ray [1], or co-injecting a tracer cocktail [9]. These techniques, nevertheless, still increase the patient's radiation exposure. Staggered tracer injections have also been proposed for multi-tracer imaging using tracer kinetic constraints [8,12], though require dynamic imaging (of potentially long duration) and are sensitive to the tracer combination/imaging protocol used [12]. Past ML research has explored cross-modal image synthesis to generate a PET image from an anatomical image such as a CT [4] or MRI scan [20]. Other works have used ML to synthesize a standard-dose PET from an ultra-low-dose PET image of the same tracer [5].

Limitations of this work include the small number of patients and that images were acquired at a single center. Since large numbers of patients are rarely imaged with multiple tracers due to logistical and technical challenges, this work is intended as a proof-of-principle. A larger dataset would likely improve results and strengthen the analyses. Additionally, the values in the synthetic PET images are not in units of percent injected dose per gram of tissue; however, the ratio of uptake values (e.g., tumor-to-background) can still be used.

To extend this study, we are interested in studying the conditions under which the mapping between different tracers can be learned, possibly using the tracer kinetic models. This line of inquiry may also lead to improved results by incorporating domain knowledge into training. Finally, extensions of this work to different pathologies, tracers, organs, and imaging modalities are being explored, with the potential to generalize the system into an N-input→M-output molecular imaging agent mapping.

In conclusion, we implemented a deep learning framework that can take ^{18}F-FDOPA PET images and ceMRIs and generate synthetic ^{18}F-FLT PET images that closely match the true ^{18}F-FLT PET images of GBM patients. We showed superior MAE, SSIM and PSNR with our method. Furthermore, nuclear medicine physicians found the synthetic images to have excellent image quality. This study advances a new strategy for multi-tracer PET imaging using ML and reduces radiation dose to the patient and the number of required imaging scans.

Acknowledgements. We want to thank all the patients and their families as well as the healthcare professionals involved in this work. We dedicate this manuscript to the loving memory of our visionary colleague and friend, Dr. Sanjiv Sam Gambhir. Funding: This study was supported in part by funding from the Ben and Catherine

Ivy Foundation and the Canary Foundation. Sarah Hooper is supported by the Fannie and John Hertz Foundation, the National Science Foundation Graduate Research Fellowship under Grant No. DGE-1656518, and as a Texas Instruments Fellow under the Stanford Graduate Fellowship in Science and Engineering. Google LLC generously provided Google Cloud Platform research credits to train and test the neural networks. S.M.H., M.W., and S.S.G. are co-inventors on a United States patent entitled "Systems and Methods for Synthetic Medical Image Generation" (U.S. Patent 62/825,714; filing date, March 28, 2019) that is related to this work.

References

1. Andreyev, A., Celler, A.: Dual-isotope PET using positron-gamma emitters. Phys. Med. Biol. **56**(14), 4539 (2011)
2. Bakas, S., et al.: Advancing the cancer genome atlas glioma MRI collections with expert segmentation labels and radiomic features. Sci. Data **4**, 170117 (2017)
3. Bakas, S., et al.: Identifying the best machine learning algorithms for brain tumor segmentation, progression assessment, and overall survival prediction in the brats challenge. arXiv preprint arXiv:1811.02629 (2018)
4. Bi, L., Kim, J., Kumar, A., Feng, D., Fulham, M.: Synthesis of positron emission tomography (PET) images via multi-channel generative adversarial networks (GANs). In: Cardoso, M.J., et al. (eds.) CMMI/SWITCH/RAMBO -2017. LNCS, vol. 10555, pp. 43–51. Springer, Cham (2017). https://doi.org/10.1007/978-3-319-67564-0_5
5. Chen, K.T., et al.: Ultra-low-dose ^{18}F-florbetaben amyloid PET imaging using deep learning with multi-contrast MRI inputs. Radiology **290**(3), 649 (2019)
6. Chen, W.: Clinical applications of PET in brain tumors. J. Nucl. Med. **48**(9), 1468–1481 (2007)
7. Chen, W., et al.: Predicting treatment response of malignant gliomas to bevacizumab and irinotecan by imaging proliferation with [^{18}F] fluorothymidine positron emission tomography: a pilot study. J. Clin. Oncol. **25**(30), 4714–4721 (2007)
8. Huang, S., Carson, R., Hoffman, E., Kuhl, D., Phelps, M.: An investigation of a double-tracer technique for positron computerized tomography. J. Nucl. Med. **23**(9), 816–822 (1982)
9. Iagaru, A., et al.: Novel strategy for a cocktail ^{18}F-fluoride and ^{18}F-FDG PET/CT scan for evaluation of malignancy: results of the pilot-phase study. J. Nucl. Med. **50**(4), 501–505 (2009)
10. Isensee, F., Kickingereder, P., Wick, W., Bendszus, M., Maier-Hein, K.H.: Brain tumor segmentation and radiomics survival prediction: contribution to the BRATS 2017 challenge. In: Crimi, A., Bakas, S., Kuijf, H., Menze, B., Reyes, M. (eds.) BrainLes 2017. LNCS, vol. 10670, pp. 287–297. Springer, Cham (2018). https://doi.org/10.1007/978-3-319-75238-9_25
11. Isola, P., Zhu, J.Y., Zhou, T., Efros, A.A.: Image-to-image translation with conditional adversarial networks. In: Proceedings of the IEEE Conference on Computer Vision and Pattern Recognition, pp. 1125–1134 (2017)
12. Kadrmas, D.J., Hoffman, J.M.: Methodology for quantitative rapid multi-tracer PET tumor characterizations. Theranostics **3**(10), 757 (2013)
13. Kingma, D.P., Ba, J.: Adam: a method for stochastic optimization. arXiv preprint arXiv:1412.6980 (2014)

14. Mao, X., Li, Q., Xie, H., Lau, R.Y., Wang, Z., Paul Smolley, S.: Least squares generative adversarial networks. In: Proceedings of the IEEE International Conference on Computer Vision, pp. 2794–2802 (2017)
15. Menze, B.H., et al.: The multimodal brain tumor image segmentation benchmark (BRATS). IEEE Trans. Med. Imaging **34**(10), 1993–2024 (2014)
16. Mirza, M., Osindero, S.: Conditional generative adversarial nets. arXiv preprint arXiv:1411.1784 (2014)
17. Phelps, M.E.: PET: Molecular Imaging and its Biological Applications. Springer, Cham (2004)
18. Ronneberger, O., Fischer, P., Brox, T.: U-Net: convolutional networks for biomedical image segmentation. In: Navab, N., Hornegger, J., Wells, W.M., Frangi, A.F. (eds.) MICCAI 2015. LNCS, vol. 9351, pp. 234–241. Springer, Cham (2015). https://doi.org/10.1007/978-3-319-24574-4_28
19. Schwarzenberg, J., et al.: Treatment response evaluation using ^{18}F-FDOPA PET in patients with recurrent malignant glioma on bevacizumab therapy. Clin. Cancer Res. **20**(13), 3550–3559 (2014)
20. Sikka, A., Peri, S.V., Bathula, D.R.: MRI to FDG-PET: cross-modal synthesis using 3D U-Net for multi-modal Alzheimer's classification. In: Gooya, A., Goksel, O., Oguz, I., Burgos, N. (eds.) SASHIMI 2018. LNCS, vol. 11037, pp. 80–89. Springer, Cham (2018). https://doi.org/10.1007/978-3-030-00536-8_9
21. Vollmar, S., Cizek, J., Sué, M., Klein, J., Jacobs, A., Herholz, K.: Vinci-volume imaging in neurological research, co-registration and ROIs included. Forschung und wissenschaftliches Rechnen **2004**(114), 115–131 (2003)
22. Wardak, M., Schiepers, C., Cloughesy, T.F., Dahlbom, M., Phelps, M.E., Huang, S.C.: ^{18}F-FLT and ^{18}F-FDOPA PET kinetics in recurrent brain tumors. Eur. J. Nucl. Med. Mol. Imaging **41**(6), 1199–1209 (2014)
23. Zaharchuk, G., Gong, E., Wintermark, M., Rubin, D., Langlotz, C.: Deep learning in neuroradiology. Am. J. Neuroradiol. **39**(10), 1776–1784 (2018)

Multiple Instance Neuroimage Transformer

Ayush Singla[1]($\boxtimes$), Qingyu Zhao[1], Daniel K. Do[1], Yuyin Zhou[1,2],
Kilian M. Pohl[1], and Ehsan Adeli[1]

[1] Stanford University, Stanford, CA 94305, USA
{ayushsingla,eadeli}@stanford.edu
[2] University of California Santa Cruz, Santa Cruz, CA 95064, USA

Abstract. For the first time, we propose using a multiple instance learning based convolution-free transformer model, called Multiple Instance Neuroimage Transformer (MINiT), for the classification of T1-weighted (T1w) MRIs. We first present several variants of transformer models adopted for neuroimages. These models extract non-overlapping 3D blocks from the input volume and perform multi-headed self-attention on a sequence of their linear projections. MINiT, on the other hand, treats each of the non-overlapping 3D blocks of the input MRI as its own instance, splitting it further into non-overlapping 3D patches, on which multi-headed self-attention is computed. As a proof-of-concept, we evaluate the efficacy of our model by training it to identify sex from T1w-MRIs of two public datasets: Adolescent Brain Cognitive Development (ABCD) and the National Consortium on Alcohol and Neurodevelopment in Adolescence (NCANDA). The learned attention maps highlight voxels contributing to identifying sex differences in brain morphometry. The code is available at https://github.com/singlaayush/MINIT.

1 Introduction

Transformers, self-attention based architectures widely used in natural language processing (NLP) [37], have recently been successfully adapted for numerous computer vision (CV) tasks, including classification [13], detection [8], and segmentation [38] in both images and videos [4]. However, the analysis of MRIs still relies heavily on convolutional architectures [2,28]. Noting the success of transformer models in NLP and CV, some contemporary works combine Convolutional Neural Network (CNN) encoders and decoders with transformer blocks for medical images [10,20,27].

The transformer-based prior work on MRIs relies on CNN-encoded MRI representations as the input to the transformer blocks and involves sophisticated pre-training and fine-tuning paradigms. For instance, they train different blocks of the model [20] with differing loss objectives [27]. Compared to CNNs, the key advantage of convolution-free self-attention based architectures, like transformers, is that the attention kernels are dynamically computed for an input region at inference [37], whereas they are fixed after training for CNNs. This dynamic

I. Rekik et al. (Eds.): PRIME 2022, LNCS 13564, pp. 36–48, 2022.
https://doi.org/10.1007/978-3-031-16919-9_4

kernel computation allows for contextual information in the input regions to be taken into account, thus greatly improving the generalizability of the model. Recent developments in NLP and CV have suggested significant improvements that enable training convolution-free transformers from scratch [11,34] with the help of data augmentation and regularization. Although some of these techniques were developed for 3D data, such as point clouds [43] or videos [4], their usage for neuroimages is yet to be explored.

In this paper, we propose a novel Multiple Instance Neuroimage Transformer (MINiT) architecture for classification of 3D T1-weighted (T1w) MRIs. We first adopt the standard vision transformer models [4,13] to use cases involving 3D neuroimages. We refer to these new architectures as Neuroimage Transformers (NiT) and create different variants of them by incorporating various attention factorizations, similar to [4], and positional embedding [35]. We then extend our models by encapsulating them with multiple instance learning (MIL) frameworks that have previously been explored for brain disease diagnosis using convolutional models [7,24]. Specifically, MINiT extracts non-overlapping 3D blocks from the input volume and then treats each block as its own instance (3D neuroimage). It splits each block further into non-overlapping 3D patches, computes multi-headed self-attention for each patch, and ultimately combines the results across all patches. As a result, MINiT aggregates feature embeddings in a hierarchical fashion, similar to [30].

We compare MINiT with other variants of Neuroimage Transformers, recent 3D CNN models [2], and an MIL implementation of CNNs. Each model is evaluated on identifying sex from T1w MRIs of two large-scale adolescent brain image datasets: Adolescent Brain Cognitive Development (ABCD) [9] and the National Consortium on Alcohol and Neurodevelopment in Adolescence (NCANDA) [6]. We follow the set up from prior work (e.g., in vivo neuroimaging [17,31] and computational learning-based methods [36,39]) to identify morphological sex differences in brain development during childhood and adolescence. To ensure fair analysis in our study, we first preprocess the MRIs to correct for head size differences by affinely registering all MRIs to a template. All models are then trained in a supervised fashion (with no excessive pretraining/finetuning of any components). We finally visualize the attention maps learned by MINiT, highlighting voxels contributing to identifying sex differences.

2 Method

In this section, we describe our base transformer model, called Neuroimage Transformer (NiT). Next, we present Multiple Instance NiT (MINiT).

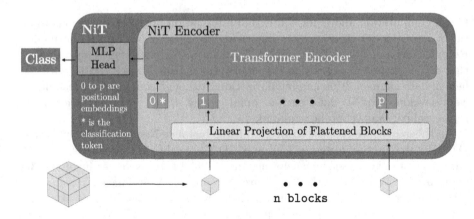

Fig. 1. Base NiT model: We split 3D neuroimages into n fixed-size blocks, linearly embed each of them, add position embeddings and a class token, and feed the sequence to a standard NiT Transformer encoder.

2.1 Neuroimage Transformer (NiT)

For our base transformer model, we follow the overarching model design of [13]. First, we map the input neuroimage $M \in \mathbb{R}^{L \times W \times H}$ to a sequence of flattened blocks $\tilde{z}^{n \times (B^3)}$, where L, W, and H are the length, width, and height of the input, (B, B, B) is the shape of each block and $n = LWH/B^3$ is the resulting number of blocks. Similar to tubelet embeddings in [4], we extract non-overlapping cubiform patches from the input volume, which are subsequently flattened. Second, we project these patches to D dimensions, i.e., the inner dimension of the transformer layers using a learned linear projection, generating the sequence of input patches $z^{n \times D}$. We add learned positional embeddings to retain positional information [37] in the blocks and prepend a learned classification token [12] to their sequence serving as the input neuroimage representation.

The input sequence is then forwarded to a the transformer encoder consisting of L transformer layers. Each layer contains a multi-headed self-attention (MSA) block [37] and a Multi-Layer Perceptron (MLP) block. The MLP block includes two linear projections with a Gaussian Error Gated Linear Units (GEGLU) non-linearity [32] applied between them. Layer norm [5] is applied before and residual connections are added after every block in a transformer layer [18]. Finally, a layer norm and an MLP head consisting of a single $D \times C$ linear layer projects the classification token to $\mathbb{R}^C$, where C is the number of classes (Fig. 1).

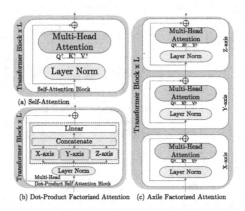

(b) Dot-Product Factorized Attention   (c) Axile Factorized Attention

Fig. 2. Factorized NiT Encoders overview: (a) Vanilla NiT encoder, which uses standard MSA [37]. (b) Dot-Product Factorized NiT encoder, which factorizes MSA itself to split attention computation along all axes. (c) Axile Factorized NiT encoder, which computes factorized self-attention over all axes separately. Note that we chose the word 'axile' to name this factorization to prevent confusion with commonly used 'axial' plane for imaging of the brain.

Factorized and Dot-Product Factorized Encoders. Factorizing attention over input dimensions has shown effectiveness, e.g., in modeling spatio-temporal interactions in videos [4,41], than standard self-attention. We take a similar approach and extend factorized self-attention and factorized dot-product attention by factorizing both attention and MSA over the 3 input dimensions (Fig. 2).

For the factorized dot-product encoder (Fig. 2(b)), we factorize the MSA operation itself. We compute attention weights for each block by splitting the available attention heads into 3. Thus, a third of the attention heads are assigned to each axis dimension to compute attention by modifying the keys and values of each query in MSA to attend only over the assigned axis, as in [4] for the temporal index. The outputs of all heads are concatenated and linearly projected to compute attention across all axes.

In the axile factorized encoder (Fig. 2(c)), we factorize the attention operation into 3 parts by performing MSA axially. First, we only compute MSA among all blocks along the x-axis, followed by MSA computation along the y-axis and the z-axis. We efficiently compute factorized self-attention along a single axis in the same manner that [4] computes temporal self-attention, namely, by reshaping the flattened patches to extract the axis in question to the leading dimension.

Multi-View Factorized NiT (MVNiT). The factorized self-attention methods described in [4] differentiate the axes of the input video into spatial axes and a temporal axis. In neuroimage analysis, an analogous operation is to split a 3D neuroimage into a 2D plane combining two axes, and the orthogonal axis to the plane. We can form the 2D plane to be one of 3 views commonly used in neuroimage analysis, namely, transverse, coronal, and sagittal. Using 2D slices of a 3D neuroimage has been found to be beneficial [20], and thus we consider

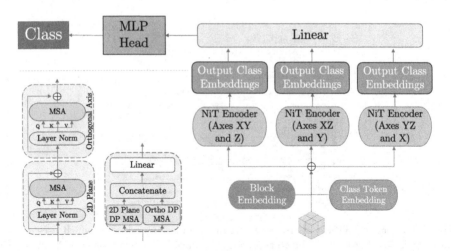

Fig. 3. Multi-View Factorized NiT Model. The encoders on the left show the Axile Factorized and Dot Product Factorized NiT encoders for this Multi-View approach.

a multi-view factorized NiT that uses factorized or dot-product factorized NiT encoders on all 3 views (Fig. 3).

We build factorized and dot-product factorized MSA blocks, which perform their respective attention operations on a combined 2D plane and the orthogonal axis. Thus, given one of the transverse, coronal, or sagittal planes with the respective orthogonal axis, the block would perform MSA treating the 2D plane as the spatial dimension and the orthogonal axis as the third dimension. We create three distinct encoders with these MSA blocks that consider the combined plane to be the transverse, coronal, and sagittal planes, respectively. The input sequence of patches is fed to all three encoders with distinct classification tokens, which then produce their respective class embeddings. These embeddings are concatenated and linearly projected to generate the class prediction.

Rotary Embeddings. As an alternative, we modify our positional embedding to use rotary embeddings (RE) [35]. RE has been shown to enhance prediction accuracies by incorporating explicit relative position dependency in self-attention. We adapt this method by calculating rotary embeddings along each axis, concatenating them, and then calculating self-attention as normal.

2.2   Multiple Instance NiT (MINiT)

Inspired by some prior MIL deep learning models applied to medical images [7, 24], we next develop a convolution-free transformer-based architecture inspired by the MIL paradigm, called MINiT. Given the input neuroimage, we first map it to a sequence of n_B cubiform blocks. Each of these n_B blocks is fed to an NiT model, in which each block is considered the input neuroimage of the model.

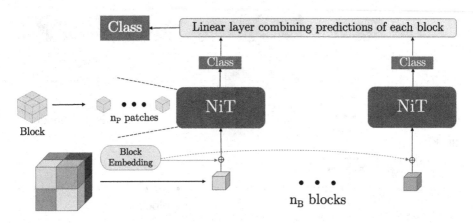

Fig. 4. MINiT: We split the 3D image into n_B fixed-size blocks, add block embeddings, and feed each to a standard NiT encoder. For MINiT, the resulting sequence of predictions is concatenated and linearly projected to arrive at the final class predictions.

The NiT model further maps each block to a sequence of n_P smaller flattened patches. Here, each of the n_B blocks is considered to be the bag of instances, while the n_P flattened patches are analogous to the instances in MIL [24] (Fig. 4).

The sequence of patches for each block is processed similar to NiT, albeit with one modification. In addition to adding learned positional embeddings to the patches (patch embeddings), and prepending a learned classification token to their sequence, we add learned block embeddings, which retain the positional information of the block within the neuroimage to each patch. This is crucial to loosely emulating the benefits of non-overlapping hierarchical attention, as in [30], because block embeddings ensure that each patch learns its position within the input neuroimage. After this step, the patches are processed by the NiT block to produce class predictions for each block, which are concatenated and linearly projected to generate class predictions for the original input neuroimage.

MiGNiT: Multiple Instance Global NiT. In this architecture, we compute global attention [16] by additionally computing self-attention on the output class embeddings produced by each block using an NiT model block. Modifying the MINiT model architecture, we change the NiT blocks to NiT encoders by stripping the final class prediction MLP head. Thus, given an individual 3D block from the input neuroimage, the NiT encoder block produces output class embeddings in $\mathbb{R}^D$. This sequence of output class embeddings produced from each block is fed into a complete NiT block producing class predictions (Fig. 5).

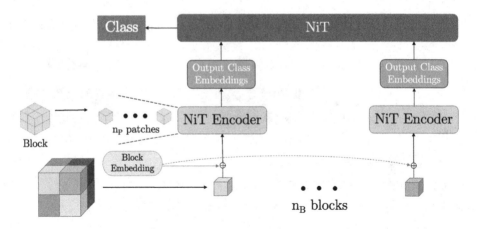

Fig. 5. MiGNiT overview: We split the 3D image into n_B fixed-size blocks, add block embeddings, and feed each to a standard NiT encoder. The output class embeddings are input into a transformer to generate the final class predictions.

3   Experiments

As a proof-of-concept, we apply and compare MINiT with other models on identifying sex from the t1-w MRIs of two large-scale adolescent brain image datasets: ABCD [9] and NCANDA [6]. We compare MINiT with both variants of NiTs and two CNN models, namely a 3D-CNN from [2] and an MIL-based version of a CNN, called MICNN. To identify brain regions contributing to sex classification, we visualize the attention maps learned by NiT and MINiT. All methods were implemented using Python 3.7.10 and its libraries (NumPy 1.15.1, Scikit-Learn 0.19.2, PyTorch 1.9.1 and TorchIO 0.18.41) on Debian GNU/Linux 10.

Data. We use 8653 baseline T1w MRI of participants from the ABCD Study Release 2.0 (ages 10.2 ± 0.78 years; 52.2% boys and 47.8% girls). From the NCANDA Study (release `NCANDA_PUBLIC_6Y_STRUCTURAL_V01` [29]), we consider the T1-w MRIs from all available visits of 808 participants at-risk recruited between ages 12–21 years (49.16% boys and 50.84% girls). Participants made 4.77 average visits to collect 3856 scans (age among all scans 18.77 ± 3.14 years). Observed sex for all the participants across both datasets is defined as sex at birth.

In line with prior studies [28,44], all T1-w MRIs in the following experiments are first pre-processed by a pipeline composed of denoising, bias field correction, skull stripping, correcting for differences in head size via affine registration to a template, and re-scaling to a $64 \times 64 \times 64$ volume. This downsampling allows for models with smaller number of network parameters, boosting training speed.

Post data pre-processing, our dataset combining both ABCD and NCANDA studies totals 12,506 T1-w MRIs, which we split into training, validation, and test sets. We use 80% of the training split for training, 10% for validation, and another 10% for computing test metrics.

We further augment the training data by applying random flip and random affine transformations, adding gaussian noise, and swapping $16 \times 16 \times 16$ patches within the MRIs at random. This process increases the size of the training set by a factor of 10. Based on the augmented training set, we perform the training of both MINiT and all NiT and CNN based comparison models from scratch. Due to the higher proportion of MRIs provided by the ABCD study, our augmented training set has class imbalance skewed towards males. We use weighted random sampling to train all models to account for class imbalance [14].

Training Strategy and Hyperparameters. For all NiT based models, the $64 \times 64 \times 64$ input neuroimage volume is split into $n = 8$ blocks of size $8 \times 8 \times 8$. All MIL-based models, however, use $n_B = 4$ blocks of size $16 \times 16 \times 16$, which are further split into $n_P = 4$ volumetric patches of size $4 \times 4 \times 4$. We apply dropout [33] and weight decay [26] to both MINiT and all NiT and CNN based comparison models, as in [13,34]. In addition, we perform run-time data augmentations, relying on the combination of Mixup [42] and Cutmix [40]. We train both MINiT and all NiT and CNN based comparison models using two optimizers - AdamW [26] using $\beta_1 = 0.9$ and $\beta_2 = 0.99$ and with SAM minimization [11] with Adam [22] using $\beta_1 = 0.9$ and $\beta_2 = 0.99$, and present results from the best of the two. We use a cosine decay learning rate schedule [25] with gradual warmup [15], and train for 200 epochs. With the exception of all MIL NiTs, which took 48 hours, all NiT models train to convergence within 24 hours on a machine with 8 NVIDIA Tesla V100 GPUs with 16GBs of memory.

We perform a search of training hyperparameters, including learning rate, dropout rates, number of warm up epochs, number of scaling epochs and their multiplier, weight decay, and probabilities to apply cutmix and mixup for both MINiT and all NiT and CNN based comparison models. For all NiT based models, we additionally perform a search for the best combination of (L, N_H, D, D_{MLP}), where L is the number of transformer encoder layers, each with an MSA block of N_H heads, D dimension, and D_{MLP} hidden MLP dimension.

Hyperparameter Settings. We share the NiT model-specific hyperparameters used for training in Table 1. We also present the total number of trainable parameters for each model. The memory footprint of these models is smaller to that of most vision transformer models. Compared to small versions of contemporary vision transformer models (ViT-Small has 22.2M parameters) [13,34], MiNiT, has 3.6M trainable parameters. Small memory footprints make our models more appropriate for training on small datasets on smaller GPUs, thus making our work accessible to a large audience. Note that all models are trained and evaluated exactly once using these hyperparameters.

Evaluation Metrics. The classification accuracy and the Area Under the Receiver Operating Characteristic (ROC) curve (AUC) of each method are computed by first binarizing the final prediction score of each participant to 0 (girl) or 1 (boy) followed by comparison to the observed sex. We additionally calculate the F-1 score (F1), sensitivity (SEN), specificity (SPE), and precision (PRC).

Table 1. NiT model-specific hyperparameters for all NiT variants. These hyperparameters are Transformer Layers (L), N_H attention heads, D dimension, D_{MLP} MLP dimension, Learning Rate (LR) and Weight Decay (WD).

Model	Factorization	Trainable parameters	L	N_H	D	$D_M LP$	LR	WD
NiT	✗	1.8M	4	8	256	234	$1e{-}4$	0.16
NiT	Axile	5.1M	6	8	256	64	$1.3e{-}5$	0.05
NiT	DP	4M	3	12	512	175	$6.5e{-}5$	0.25
MVNiT	MV & Axile	15M	6	8	512	209	$9e{-}4$	0.21
MVNiT	MV & DP	8.9M	6	4	512	215	$5e{-}4$	0.13
MiGNiT	✗	8.5M	6	8	256	309	$2e{-}4$	0.3
MiNiT	Axile	3.1M	6	8	128	128	$1e{-}4$	0.01
MiNiT	DP	3.9M	6	12	258	128	$5e{-}5$	0.24
MiNiT	✗	3.6M	6	8	256	309	$1e{-}4$	0.125

Apart from our NiT based comparison methods, we further compare MINiT with two contemporary CNN based models. First, we include the aforementioned 3D-CNN architecture from [2], modified to accommodate $64 \times 64 \times 64$ inputs, in contrast to the original input of $64 \times 64 \times 32$. This CNN architecture contains 4 convolutional blocks connected by $2 \times 2 \times 2$ 3D Max-Pooling, where each convolutional block consists of $3 \times 3 \times 3$ 3D convolution (16/32/64/128 as number of channels for the 4 blocks), Batch Normalization [19] and Re-LU [3]. The resulting 4,096 dimensional features were fed into a three final linear projections of dimensions 64, 32, and 1 with *tanh*, *tanh* and *sigmoid* activations respectively, to generate the final class predictions. Secondly, in line with our own MIL based approach, we create a Multiple Instance CNN (MICNN) model, which applies multiple instance learning to the inputs using the CNN framework described above. The overarching approach from Sect. 2.2 remains the same, with the only difference in architecture being the replacement of the NiT Transformer with the CNN model. We equally conduct hyperparameter search for both MINiT and all NiT and CNN based comparison models.

Results. According to the accuracy scores in Table 2, all but one of the transformer models have better or comparable accuracy to the 3D-CNN model, with the MINiT model reporting the highest classification accuracy of 92.1% as well as the highest F-1 and AUC scores of 92.1% and 97.2%. The MVNiT using Dot-Product Factorization also reports a comparable classification accuracy of 91.9% to the MINiT model, with both models surpassing the 3D-CNN with over 1.5%.

MINiT's performance indicates that the use of a hierarchical attention scheme helps add positional inductive biases similar to convolutional inductive biases, while retaining the advantages of integrating information from the entire volume, even in the earlier transformer layers from self-attention [13]. These results show that our MINiT model is capable of capturing identifying characteristics between sexes, while not being insensitive to class imbalances in comparison to the 3D-

Table 2. ACCuracy, area under the curve (AUC), F-1 score, SENsitivity, SPEcificity, and precision (PRC) for predicting sex from MRIs. Second column shows the factorization method: Axile, Dot-Product (DP), or Multi-View (MV).

Model	Factorization	Rotary embedding	ACC (%)	AUC (%)	F1 (%)	SEN (%)	SPE (%)	PRC (%)
3D-CNN [2]	—	—	90.4	96.8	91.5	**94.7**	84.9	88.6
MI-CNN	—	✗	90.1	96.0	88.6	84.9	94.3	92.5
NiT	✗	✗	86.4	93.5	86.7	87.4	85.4	86.1
NiT	✗	✓	89.1	95.0	88.9	87.6	**90.7**	**90.2**
NiT	Axile	✗	90.0	96.6	91.7	94.2	86.3	89.3
NiT	DP	✗	89.5	96.1	91.0	95.0	82.7	87.3
MVNiT	MV & Axile	✗	88.0	94.0	87.4	88.2	87.7	86.5
MVNiT	MV & DP	✗	91.9	96.2	91.6	93.8	88.8	89.5
MIGNiT	✗	✓	90.1	96.1	89.9	90.8	89.4	88.9
MINiT	Axile	✗	87.9	94.1	88.0	87.6	88.1	88.3
MINiT	DP	✗	90.7	96.2	89.9	88.3	92.9	91.6
MINiT	✗	✗	**92.1**	**97.2**	**92.1**	94.2	90.0	90.1

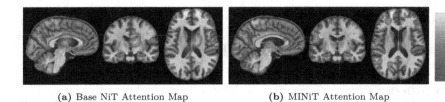

(a) Base NiT Attention Map   (b) MINiT Attention Map

Fig. 6. Attention maps learned by (a) NiT and (b) MINiT models. The bar shows the color-map (from red = 0.4 to yellow = 0.8; thresholded on the lower bound for clarity).

CNN. The 3D-CNN is extremely sensitive to class imbalances, as evidenced by the ≈ 10% gap between sensitivity and specificity. All but one of the NiT models are significantly less sensitive to class imbalances, a common problem in medical image analysis [23]. Factorized encoders by themselves have high sensitivity to class imbalances, but using them in Multi-View or MIL settings reduces this sensitivity. MVNiT and MINiT with Axile Factorization have the lowest gaps between sensitivity and specificity, which allows them to generalize well against class imbalances, at some cost to accuracy.

We compute the attention maps for the base NiT from the output token to the input space using Attention Rollout [1]. For MINiT, we use Attention Rollout to calculate attention weights for each patch in a block, which we concatenate and then average to build attention weights for a block. We proceed to use Attention Rollout using the block attention weights to compute the final attention maps. From Fig. 6, we observe that MINiT attends between numerous different voxels in the neuroimage (due to MIL nature), in contrast to the focused attention between fewer, but larger, voxels by the base NiT. Considering existing documented evidences [21] that sex differences in youth are widespread in the brain and the significant difference in accuracy between the two models, it is evident that MINiT is able to better generalize by capturing features spread all around the brain.

4   Conclusion

In this paper, we propose Multiple Instance Neuroimage Transformer (MINiT), a multiple instance learning based convolution-free transformer model for classification of 3D T1w MRIs. They consider the entire 3D volume and train end-to-end in a supervised fashion, with no excessive pre-training or fine-tuning required. As a proof-of-concept, we train MINiT on identifying sex from T1w MRIs and obtain state-of-the-art results. The visualization of the attention map learned by our MiNiT model demonstrates its ability to sensitively capture identifying differing morphological characteristics between sexes, while not being insensitive to class imbalances. Further extensions could investigate the transfer learning capabilities of MINiT by fine-tuning on small-sized datasets for different tasks.

Acknowledgements. This work was partially supported by the NIH grants AA021697 and AA028840, and the Stanford Institute for Human-centered Artificial Intelligence (HAI) Google Cloud Credits (GCP) credits.

References

1. Abnar, S., Zuidema, W.: Quantifying attention flow in transformers. arXiv:2005.00928 (2020)
2. Adeli, E., et al.: Deep learning identifies morphological determinants of sex differences in the pre-adolescent brain. Neuroimage **223**, 117293 (2020)
3. Agarap, A.F.: Deep learning using rectified linear units (ReLU). arXiv:1803.08375 (2018)
4. Arnab, A., Dehghani, M., Heigold, G., Sun, C., Lučić, M., Schmid, C.: ViViT: a video vision transformer. In: ICCV, pp. 6836–6846 (2021)
5. Ba, J.L., Kiros, J.R., Hinton, G.E.: Layer normalization. arXiv:1607.06450 (2016)
6. Brown, S.A., et al.: The national consortium on alcohol and neurodevelopment in adolescence (NCANDA): a multisite study of adolescent development and substance use. JSAD **76**(6), 895–908 (2015)
7. Carbonneau, M.A., Cheplygina, V., Granger, E., Gagnon, G.: Multiple instance learning: a survey of problem characteristics and applications. Pattern Recogn. **77**, 329–353 (2018)
8. Carion, N., Massa, F., Synnaeve, G., Usunier, N., Kirillov, A., Zagoruyko, S.: End-to-end object detection with transformers. In: Vedaldi, A., Bischof, H., Brox, T., Frahm, J.-M. (eds.) ECCV 2020. LNCS, vol. 12346, pp. 213–229. Springer, Cham (2020). https://doi.org/10.1007/978-3-030-58452-8_13
9. Casey, B., et al.: The adolescent brain cognitive development (ABCD) study: imaging acquisition across 21 sites. Dev. Cogn. Neurosci. **32**, 43–54 (2018)
10. Chen, J., et al.: TransUNet: transformers make strong encoders for medical image segmentation. arXiv:2102.04306 (2021)
11. Chen, X., Hsieh, C.J., Gong, B.: When vision transformers outperform ResNets without pre-training or strong data augmentations. arXiv:2106.01548 (2021)

12. Devlin, J., Chang, M.W., Lee, K., Toutanova, K.: BERT: pre-training of deep bidirectional transformers for language understanding. arXiv:1810.04805 (2018)
13. Dosovitskiy, A., et al.: An image is worth 16 × 16 words: transformers for image recognition at scale. arXiv:2010.11929 (2020)
14. Efraimidis, P.S., Spirakis, P.G.: Weighted random sampling with a reservoir. Inf. Process. Lett. **97**(5), 181–185 (2006)
15. Goyal, P., et al.: Accurate, large minibatch SGD: training ImageNet in 1 hour. arXiv:1706.02677 (2017)
16. Han, K., Xiao, A., Wu, E., Guo, J., Xu, C., Wang, Y.: Transformer in transformer. In: NeurIPS, vol. 34 (2021)
17. Hänggi, J., Buchmann, A., Mondadori, C.R., Henke, K., Jäncke, L., Hock, C.: Sexual dimorphism in the parietal substrate associated with visuospatial cognition independent of general intelligence. JoCN **22**(1), 139–155 (2010)
18. He, K., Zhang, X., Ren, S., Sun, J.: Deep residual learning for image recognition. In: CVPR, pp. 770–778 (2016)
19. Ioffe, S., Szegedy, C.: Batch normalization: accelerating deep network training by reducing internal covariate shift. In: ICML, pp. 448–456. PMLR (2015)
20. Jun, E., Jeong, S., Heo, D.W., Suk, H.I.: Medical transformer: universal brain encoder for 3D MRI analysis. arXiv:2104.13633 (2021)
21. Kaczkurkin, A.N., Raznahan, A., Satterthwaite, T.D.: Sex differences in the developing brain: insights from multimodal neuroimaging. Neuropsychopharmacology **44**(1), 71–85 (2019)
22. Kingma, D.P., Ba, J.: Adam: a method for stochastic optimization. arXiv:1412.6980 (2014)
23. Larrazabal, A.J., Nieto, N., Peterson, V., Milone, D.H., Ferrante, E.: Gender imbalance in medical imaging datasets produces biased classifiers for computer-aided diagnosis. Proc. Natl. Acad. Sci. **117**(23), 12592–12594 (2020)
24. Liu, M., Zhang, J., Adeli, E., Shen, D.: Landmark-based deep multi-instance learning for brain disease diagnosis. Med. Image Anal. **43**, 157–168 (2018)
25. Loshchilov, I., Hutter, F.: SGDR: stochastic gradient descent with warm restarts. arXiv:1608.03983 (2016)
26. Loshchilov, I., Hutter, F.: Decoupled weight decay regularization. arXiv:1711.05101 (2017)
27. Malkiel, I., Rosenman, G., Wolf, L., Hendler, T.: Pre-training and fine-tuning transformers for FMRI prediction tasks. arXiv:2112.05761 (2021)
28. Ouyang, J., et al.: Longitudinal pooling & consistency regularization to model disease progression from MRIs. IEEE J. Biomed. Health Inform. **25**(6), 2082–2092 (2020)
29. Pohl, K.M., et al.: The 'NCANDA_PUBLIC_6Y_STRUCTURAL_V01' data release of the National Consortium on Alcohol and NeuroDevelopment in Adolescence (NCANDA). Sage Bionetworks Synapse (2022). https://doi.org/10.7303/syn32773308
30. Pramono, R.R.A., Chen, Y.T., Fang, W.H.: Hierarchical self-attention network for action localization in videos. In: ICCV, pp. 61–70 (2019)
31. Sacher, J., Neumann, J., Okon-Singer, H., Gotowiec, S., Villringer, A.: Sexual dimorphism in the human brain: evidence from neuroimaging. JMRI **31**(3), 366–375 (2013)
32. Shazeer, N.: GLU variants improve transformer. arXiv:2002.05202 (2020)
33. Srivastava, N., Hinton, G., Krizhevsky, A., Sutskever, I., Salakhutdinov, R.: Dropout: a simple way to prevent neural networks from overfitting. JMLR **15**(1), 1929–1958 (2014)

34. Steiner, A., Kolesnikov, A., Zhai, X., Wightman, R., Uszkoreit, J., Beyer, L.: How to train your ViT? data, augmentation, and regularization in vision transformers. arXiv:2106.10270 (2021)

35. Su, J., Lu, Y., Pan, S., Wen, B., Liu, Y.: RoFormer: enhanced transformer with rotary position embedding. arXiv:2104.09864 (2021)

36. Van Putten, M.J., Olbrich, S., Arns, M.: Predicting sex from brain rhythms with deep learning. Sci. Rep. **8**(1), 1–7 (2018)

37. Vaswani, A., et al.: Attention is all you need. In: NeurIPS, vol. 30 (2017)

38. Wang, H., Zhu, Y., Adam, H., Yuille, A., Chen, L.C.: MaX-DeepLab: end-to-end panoptic segmentation with mask transformers. In: CVPR, pp. 5463–5474 (2021)

39. Xin, J., Zhang, Y., Tang, Y., Yang, Y.: Brain differences between men and women: evidence from deep learning. Front. Neurosci. **13**, 185 (2019)

40. Yun, S., Han, D., Oh, S.J., Chun, S., Choe, J., Yoo, Y.: CutMix: regularization strategy to train strong classifiers with localizable features. In: ICCV, pp. 6023–6032 (2019)

41. Zhang, B., et al.: Co-training transformer with videos and images improves action recognition. arXiv:2112.07175 (2021)

42. Zhang, H., Cisse, M., Dauphin, Y.N., Lopez-Paz, D.: Mixup: beyond empirical risk minimization. arXiv:1710.09412 (2017)

43. Zhao, H., Jiang, L., Jia, J., Torr, P.H., Koltun, V.: Point transformer. In: ICCV, pp. 16259–16268 (2021)

44. Zhao, Q., Adeli, E., Pfefferbaum, A., Sullivan, E.V., Pohl, K.M.: Confounder-aware visualization of ConvNets. In: Suk, H.-I., Liu, M., Yan, P., Lian, C. (eds.) MLMI 2019. LNCS, vol. 11861, pp. 328–336. Springer, Cham (2019). https://doi.org/10.1007/978-3-030-32692-0_38

Intervertebral Disc Labeling
with Learning Shape Information, a Look
once Approach

Reza Azad[1]([✉]), Moein Heidari[2], Julien Cohen-Adad[3,4,5], Ehsan Adeli[6],
and Dorit Merhof[1,7]

[1] Institute of Imaging and Computer Vision, RWTH Aachen University,
Aachen, Germany
{azad,dorit.merhof}@lfb.rwth-aachen.de
[2] School of Electrical Engineering, Iran University of Science and Technology,
Tehran, Iran
moein_heidari@elec.iust.ac.ir
[3] Functional Neuroimaging Unit, CRIUGM, University of Montreal,
Montreal, Canada
[4] NeuroPoly Lab, Institute of Biomedical Engineering, Polytechnique Montreal,
Montreal, Canada
[5] Mila, Quebec AI Institute, Montrea, Canada
jcohen@polymtl.ca
[6] Stanford University, Stanford, USA
eadeli@stanford.edu
[7] Fraunhofer Institute for Digital Medicine MEVIS, Bremen, Germany

Abstract. Accurate and automatic segmentation of intervertebral discs
from medical images is a critical task for the assessment of spine-related
diseases such as osteoporosis, vertebral fractures, and intervertebral disc
herniation. To date, various approaches have been developed in the
literature which routinely rely on detecting the discs as the primary
step for detecting abnormality in intervertebral Discs. A disadvantage of
many cohort studies is that the localization algorithm also yields to false
positive detections. In this study, we aim to alleviate this problem by
proposing a novel U-Net-based structure to predict a set of candidates
for intervertebral disc locations. In our design, we integrate the image
shape information (image gradients) to encourage the model to learn
rich and generic geometrical information. This additional signal guides
the model to selectively emphasize the contextual representation and
to supress the less discriminative features. On the post-processing side,
to further decrease the false positive rate, we propose a permutation
invariant "look once" model, which accelerates the candidate recovery
procedure. In comparison with previous studies, our proposed approach
does not need to perform the selection in an iterative fashion. The proposed method was evaluated on the spine generic public multi-center
dataset and demonstrated superior performance compared to previous
work. The codes is publicly available at github.

Keywords: Deep learning · intervertebral disc labeling · look once ·
shape feature

© The Author(s), under exclusive license to Springer Nature Switzerland AG 2022
I. Rekik et al. (Eds.): PRIME 2022, LNCS 13564, pp. 49–59, 2022.
https://doi.org/10.1007/978-3-031-16919-9_5

1   Introduction

The human vertebral column consists of 33 individual vertebrae stacked on top of each other and connected through the ligaments and intervertebral discs (IVDs). The vertebral column is divided into cervical, thoracic, lumbar, sacral and caudal vertebrae [3]. Each of these regions performs a vital function in the human body including, absorbing shock, load breathing, protection of the spinal cord, controlling load through the vertebral column, and so on [1]. More precisely, the IVDs act as cushions of fibrocartilage and as principal joints between vertebrae and they absorb the stress and shock the body sustains during motion and allow the spine to be flexible while preventing the vertebrae from grinding against one another. Disruption in any of the vertebral discs through aging, degeneration, or injury will result in an alteration in the corresponding disc's properties along with flaws in mechanical functionalities of adjacent tissues [19]. As a consequence, location and segmentation of intervertebral discs is a crucial task for spine disease diagnosis and provides versatile information in the quality of treatment procedure. To this end, various semi-automated and automated techniques have been proposed in the literature. These methods can be divided into two taxonomies: hand-crafted methods and deep learning-based approaches. As an example for hand-crafted dissertations, Cheng et al. [5] proposed a two-step approach where they first localize the center of each IVD by adapting a data-driven estimation framework [6] and, then, segment IVDs by classifying image pixels around each disc center as either foreground (disc) or background. Glocker et al. [11] utilized a regression forest and a probabilistic graphical model to detect and localize intervertebral discs from CT scan images. A polynomial iterative randomized Hough transform approach to segment the spine and intervertebral discs was proposed in [4]. Irrespective of the good performance of these traditional methods, in some cases they intrinsically render poor performance when compared to deep learning-based methods [2,5]. Recent advances in deep learning have facilitated investigation of robust intervertebral disc labeling [7,8,20]. In [12] the authors proposed to use a standard CNN for IVD segmentation. Dolz et al. [10] proposed an architecture called 'IVD-Net' to leverage information from multiple image modalities for inter-vertebral disc segmentation by adopting a U-Net-like architecture. In a recent article Vania et al. [20] developed a method which builds upon mask-RCNN and formulated a multi-optimization training system at a different stage to increase the computational efficiency. In another approach [21], a cross-modality method for detecting both vertebral and intervertebral discs on volumetric data has been proposed. This approach utilizes a local entropy-based texture model to localize the sacral region. Then, using three-disc entropy models, detected positions are aligned and further refined by taking into account the intensity match between regions and a spinal column template. A transfer learning-based approach is utilized by [14]. In this work, a 2D convolutional structure is exploited to detect the lumbar disc from axial images. Their proposed network uses the strength of the U-Net structure with a VGG backbone to produce a spine segmentation mask. Then, the segmented regions are used to calculate the herniation in lumbar discs. The authors of [17] combine a fully convolutional network with inception modules to localize and label intervertebral discs. Azad et al. [3] reformulated the semantic vertebral disc labeling using pose estimation and utilized an hourglass neural network to semantically label the intervertebral discs.

The main limitation of the reviewed methods is their dependency on the regular CNN learning strategy (learning texture, shape, colour) which is not optimal for labelling anatomical structures such as intervertebral discs and usually produces both false positive (FP) and false negative (FN) detections [13]. To overcome this issue, we propose to incorporate shape information within the learning process. This additional signal guides the model to selectively emphasize the contextual representation, magnifies the structural regions and supresses the less discriminative features (e.g. color, texture).

Moreover, a principal limitation of many cohort studies is that, as they utilize the local maximum technique to locate the position of the vertebral discs in 2D space on top of the prediction masks, they encounter a substantial false positive rate. Exhaustive search tree [3], template matching [18] and point coordinate condition [17] are among the popular algorithms proposed to eliminate the FP rate. However, these approaches usually lack computational efficiency and render a poor candidate recovery. Therefore, a general method is required to handle this challenge. In this work, we propose to mitigate this limitation by bolstering the post-processing step in the intervertebral disc labeling procedure. The main idea is that, inspired by the idea of YOLO [16], we propose a permutation invariant "look once" model to increase the True Positive (TP) rate while reducing the FN detection. We re-formulate the problem by a modified version of the PointNet model [15] which is invariant to certain geometric transformations (e.g. rotation). To the best of our knowledge, this is the first post-processing algorithm that processes the whole prediction in one step without any iteration ("look once"). Our contributions are as follows:

- Adapting U-Net structure for semantic intervertebral disc labeling;
- Incorporation of shape information to further boost model performance;
- A permutation-invariant post-processing approach to reduce the FP rate;
- Publicly available implementation source code (once accepted);

2 Proposed Method

Our proposed method consists of two stages. In the first stage we utilize a U-Net-based structure to detect and predict semantic labeling for each intervertebral disc location. In the second stage, we propose a deep permutation invariant "look once" model to refine the prediction results and eliminate the FP candidates. In the next subsections, we will discuss each phase in more detail.

2.1 Semantic Intervertebral Disc Labeling

The concept of the proposed method is depicted in Fig. 1. In our novel design, we incorporate the shape information (gradient of the input image) as an additional

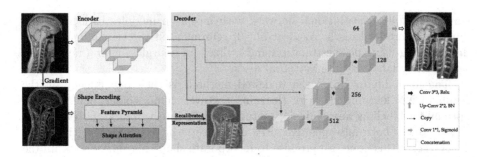

Fig. 1. Proposed method for intervertebral disc labeling with incorporating shape information.

signal to encourage the model to learn contextual and geometric information. To this end, we form a pyramid representation using the multi-level description resulting from each block of the encoder (U-Net encoder E parametrized with θ) module: $P = \{f_j = E(x, \theta), j = 0, 1, ...L\}$, where L is the number of pyramid levels. Next, we propose a shape attention module. Our attention module (Fig. 2) uses the global representation of each feature map alongside the shape description to selectively emphasize the contextual representation and supress the less discriminative features. To this end, for each level of the pyramid, we learn the channel-wise recalibration parameters (w_j^f) and spatial recalibration parameters (w_{sp}) from the shape feature description (sf):

$$w_j^f = \sigma \left(\mathbf{W}_2 \delta \left(\mathbf{W}_1 GAP_j^f \right) \right), w_{sp} = \sigma \left(\mathbf{W}_4 \delta \left(\mathbf{W}_3 GAP(sf) \right) \right) \tag{1}$$

where $W_k, k \in \{1, 2, 3, 4\}$ are the learning parameters that apply to the global representation (GAP) of each pyramid level, and δ and σ stand for the ReLU and Sigmoid activations. We form the re-calibrated description by scaling both channel and spatial dimensions: $\tilde{P}_j^f = w_{sp} \cdot (w_j^f \cdot P_j^f) + sf$. Once the re-calibration performed, we aggregate the multi-level features in a nonlinear fashion (aggregation parameter w_{prm}) to produce a shape-attenuating description:

$$f' = \sigma \left(\sum_{j=1}^{L} w_{prm}^j \tilde{P}_j^f \right) \tag{2}$$

Subsequently, the same decoder as in the regular U-Net, but with $V = 11$ output channels (we assume that the input image comprises, at most, 11 intervertebral discs according to [9]), is utilized to estimate the location of each intervertebral disc accordingly. Similarly, our ground truth mask consists of V channels, where in each channel the location of an intervertebral disc is labelled with a Gaussian kernel of radius 10. We employ the mean squared (MSE) loss to train the network.

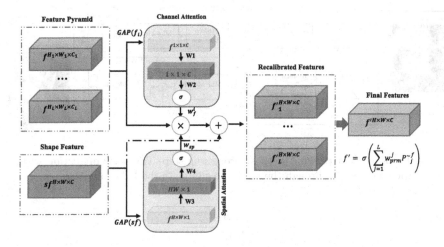

Fig. 2. Detailed structure of the proposed shape attention mechanism.

2.2 Refinement Network

Detecting intervertebral disc locations often comprises FP and FN predictions. Several post-processing approaches were proposed in the literature to overcome this problem. Rouhier et al. [17], deploys a condition-based strategy to eliminate the FP candidate generated by their countception method. In a recent article, Azad et al. [3] argues that the condition-based strategy usually fails to recover the TP candidates among the detected regions and proposes a tree-based decision space. Their approach suggests creating a search tree, where each path shows one possible combination of ordered intervertebral disc locations. Then, they calculate an error function between the general skeleton and the predicted skeleton. This iterative algorithm performs an exhaustive search and is not efficient when the number of FP is high. Template matching [18] is also another approach that seeks to reduce the FP rate by considering predefined patterns. These methods all have their assumption of particular conditions or predefined patterns in common. In addition, some of these methods perform the selection in an iterative fashion, which may not be feasible when the number of FP is high. To mitigate these issues we propose a method to 'look only once' at the noisy prediction to recover the intervertebral disc locations. To this end, we assume that, for the input image I with N intervertebral disc location, the detection model predicts a set of M intervertebral disc candidates, usually $M >= N$ and $M \in R^2$ (i.e. 2D position). Taking into further consideration in a general form, we assume that the prediction model is not able to provide any semantic labelling. Thus, the objective is to recover N points out M which best matches the ground truth intervertebral disc locations. Since the semantic information is not provided for the predicted points, we consider it as a set of M intervertebral candidates. The set is made up of unstructured data and selecting N intervertebral disc location out of M candidates requires the following processing permutations:

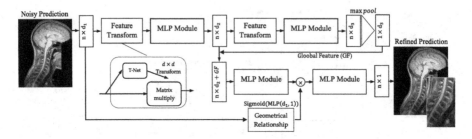

Fig. 3. Proposed structure for the post-processing step. The noisy prediction without a semantic label passes through the model to eliminate the FP candidates.

$$\frac{(M)!}{(N)!(M-N)!} \tag{3}$$

permutations. The processing time will dramatically increase if $M >> N$. To overcome this limitation, it is highly desirable that the post-processing algorithm processes the whole prediction at once without any iterations("look once"). Therefore, the deep model needs to be permutation invariant, i.e., any order of points should produce the same result. The proposed structure is depicted in Fig. 3. The proposed method consists of two data streams, where in the first stream (top), a series of feature transformation layers, followed by the multi-layer perceptron (MLP), is designed to encode the input coordinate into a high-level representational space. The objective of this representation is to create a discriminative embedding space to characterize each point by a hidden dependency underlying the input data. Intrinsically, the transformation layer in this stream assures the robustness of the representation to the noisy samples and provides a less sensitive transformation to an affine geometrical transformation (e.g. rotation). Inspired by the permutation invariance characteristics, the MLP layer deploys a shared kernel to produce a set of representations independent of their order. Eventually, in addition to the generated feature map, a symmetric function (global pooling) is utilized to capture the shared signature among all points. We concatenate the global information with the local representation of each point to describe each intervertebral disc candidate. Details on the network structure is illustrated in Table 1. This representation more or less contains the general structure of the data, however, it still requires pair-wise relational information. To include such information, we create a geometrical representation. To this end, using the fully connected layers, we learn the embedding parameters to model the long-range geometrical dependency. The main objective of this layer is to capture the geometrical relation between points and feed it to the scaler function. We include the sigmoid function on top of the generated representation to form an attention vector. This attention vector performs the re-calibration process and adaptively scales the generated feature map. The generated final representation is then fed to the single-layer perceptron model to perform the softmax operation and to classify each candidate.

Table 1. Details on network architecture for the post-processing stage. We follow [15] for the structure of the Feature Transform module (including T-Net) which simply aligns the input to a feature space using an affine transformation without changing the dimension. We refer the reader to [15] for more general expositions. Note that **n** denotes the number of vertebral discs detected.

Module	Neurons	Input-size	Output-size
MLP Module(1)	64	(nx3)	(nx64)
MLP Module(2)	128	(nx64)	(nx128)
MLP Module(3)	512	(nx128)	(nx512)
MLP Module(4)	1024	(nx512)	(nx1024)

3 Experimental Results

In this section, we first describe the datasets and metrics used throughout our experimental evaluation. Then, we provide a deep insight into the experimental results. Our analysis was based on the publicly available Spine Generic Dataset [9]. The dataset was acquired across 42 centers (with a total of 260 participants) worldwide, accommodating both T1 and T2 MRI contrasts for each subject. Images obtained from diverse institutes, considerably varying in image quality, ages and imaging devices, render a feasibly challenging benchmark for the task of intervertebral disc labelling.

3.1 Metrics

To ensure the validity of the comparison of results and to draw conclusions on the applicability of our approach, we consider different comparison metrics. In the first instance, we take into account the L2 norm by calculating the distance of the vector coordinate between each predicted intervertebral disc location and the ground truth while considering the superior-inferior axis to quantify the punctuality of our proposal. In order to gain insights into the versatility of our post-processing approach, the False Positive Rate (FPR) and False Negative Rate (FNR) were selected as the primary inclusion criteria. Similar to [3], the FPR calculates the number of predictions which are at least 5 mm away from the ground truth positions. Likewise, the FNR counts the number of predictions where the ground truth has at least 5mm distance from the predicted intervertebral position.

3.2 Comparison of Results

We train all of our models upstream using the Adam solver with the momentum in 100 epochs with the batch size 2. In our experiments, we use an initial learning rate of 0.0001 with the decay by a factor of 0.5 at every 20th epoch, respectively. We use the same setting as explained in [17] to achieve a general

Table 2. Intervertebral disc labeling results on the spine generic public dataset. Note that **DTT** indicates Distance to target

Method	T1			T2		
	DTT (mm)	FNR (%)	FPR (%)	DTT (mm)	FNR (%)	FPR (%)
Template Matching [18]	1.97(4.08)	8.1	2.53	2.05(3.21)	11.1	2.11
Countception [17]	**1.03(2.81)**	4.24	0.9	1.78(2.64)	3.88	1.5
Pose Estimation [3]	1.32(1.33)	**0.32**	0.0	1.31(2.79)	1.2	0.6
Baseline	1.45(2.70)	7.3	1.2	1.80(2.80)	5.4	1.8
Proposed	1.2(1.90)	0.7	0.0	**1.28(2.61)**	**0.9**	**0.0**

consensus in comparing our method with the literature and we report our findings in Table 2. Note: our baseline model uses the same structure as presented but without employing the proposed modules. The results show that our approach achieves a competitive result in T1 and T2 contrasts. Specifically, our proposed method shows superior performance in T2 contrast, where our approach prominently outperforms all other approaches in terms of FNR and distance to the target. Compared to the pose estimation approach [3], our method produces on T1 modality an average lower distance to the intervertebral locations, but there is only a small gap in distance variance. We also observe that, by removing the proposed modules the performance of the model slightly decreases, which highlights the importance of shape information in intervertebral disc labeling. Moreover, unlike the countception and template matching approaches, our method does not require a heavy preprocessing step for spinal cord region detection and outperforms these methods with both quantitative performance and inference time. In contrast to our proposal, the inference time in the two aforementioned approaches grows exponentially when the FP rates increases (see Table 3). In Fig. 4(a) we provide sample results of the proposed model on T2 modalities. It can be observed that the method precisely provides a semantic label for each IVD location without any FP predictions. It should be noted that our method requires less processing time even with large number of FP detection in opposite to the SOTA approaches (illustrated in Fig. 5).

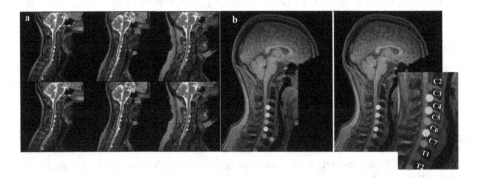

Fig. 4. (a): Intervertebral labeling results of three representative T2 images. upper row: ground truth, lower row: predictions. (b): Before (left) and after (right) applying look-once approach on the T1 generated noisy prediction.

Table 3. Performance comparison of the proposed post-processing approach vs the SOTA approach for eliminating FP detection. The experiment was done on 100 images, where for each image 20 random FP detection was added.

Method	F1	Accuracy	specificity	sensitivity	AUC
Template Matching [18]	0.850	0.881	0.891	0.902	0.890
Pose Estimation [3]	0.902	0.921	0.925	0.914	0.920
Proposed method (without geometrical relationship module)	0.914	0.932	0.941	0.917	0.929
Proposed method (Only look once)	**0.942**	**0.958**	**0.967**	**0.942**	**0.955**

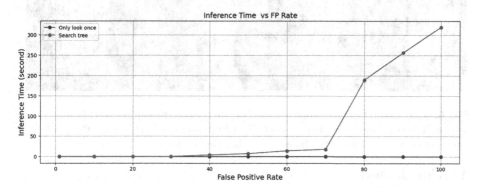

Fig. 5. Inference time of the proposed method vs the search-tree based approach [3]. Our method only looks once at the prediction to eliminate the FP samples while the search based approach uses an iterative algorithm.

3.3   Evaluation on the Noisy Prediction

To further analyze the robustness of the proposed method in the presence of noisy predictions, we attain an evaluation on the proposed "look once" post-processing method. To this end, we create a 2D Gaussian distribution around each intervertebral disc to generate new points. A sample of generated noisy image along with the model prediction is depicted in Fig. 4(b). As shown, the proposed method works well (including very fast timing) on retrieving IVD locations from the noisy prediction without relying on any predefined assumption. In addition, in our experiment (supplementary file), we observe that for the search-tree-based approach the post-processing time exponentially increased with the increase of FP rate. Similarly, the template matching method failed to recover the TP candidates in most of the cases. Whereas, our method recovered the TP samples with high precision without any iteration. Moreover, to disentangle the contribution of our proposal, we take a closer look at some additional sample detections of our method in Fig. 6 which proves its efficiency in terms of perceptual realism.

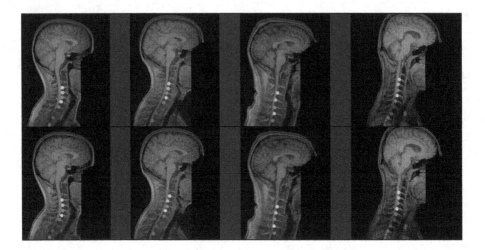

Fig. 6. More results of the proposed method for intervertebral disc labeling on T1w images. The first row shows the grand truth while the second row shows the predicted intervertebral disc along with the semantic labeling (color).

4   Conclusion

In this paper, we systematically formulate the intervertebral disc labelling problem by designing a novel method to incorporate shape information. The proposed method encourages the model to focus on learning contextual and geometrical features. Additionally, we propose a "look once" post-processing approach. Powered by this, our model alleviates the false-positive detections along with a substantial refinement in model acceleration. The results presented in this paper demonstrate the potential of our methodology across all competing methods.

References

1. Al-kubaisi, A., Khamiss, N.N.: A transfer learning approach for lumbar spine disc state classification. Electronics **11**(1), 85 (2022)
2. Ben Ayed, I., Punithakumar, K., Garvin, G., Romano, W., Li, S.: Graph cuts with invariant object-interaction priors: application to intervertebral disc segmentation. In: Székely, G., Hahn, H.K. (eds.) IPMI 2011. LNCS, vol. 6801, pp. 221–232. Springer, Heidelberg (2011). https://doi.org/10.1007/978-3-642-22092-0_19
3. Azad, R., Rouhier, L., Cohen-Adad, J.: Stacked hourglass network with a multi-level attention mechanism: where to look for intervertebral disc labeling. In: Lian, C., Cao, X., Rekik, I., Xu, X., Yan, P. (eds.) MLMI 2021. LNCS, vol. 12966, pp. 406–415. Springer, Cham (2021). https://doi.org/10.1007/978-3-030-87589-3_42
4. Badarneh, A., Abu-Qasmeih, I., Otoom, M., Alzubaidi, M.A.: Semi-automated spine and intervertebral disk detection and segmentation from whole spine MR images. Inform. Med. Unlocked **27**, 100810 (2021)
5. Chen, C., et al.: Localization and segmentation of 3D intervertebral discs in MR images by data driven estimation. IEEE Trans. Med. Imaging **34**(8), 1719–1729 (2015)

6. Chen, C., Xie, W., Franke, J., Grutzner, P., Nolte, L.P., Zheng, G.: Automatic x-ray landmark detection and shape segmentation via data-driven joint estimation of image displacements. Med. Image Anal. **18**(3), 487–499 (2014)
7. Chen, J.C., Lan, T.P., Lian, Z.Y., Chuang, C.H.: A study of intervertebral disc segmentation based on deep learning. In: 2021 IEEE 4th International Conference on Knowledge Innovation and Invention (ICKII), pp. 85–87. IEEE (2021)
8. Cheng, Y.K., et al.: Automatic segmentation of specific intervertebral discs through a two-stage multiresunet model. J. Clin. Med. **10**(20), 4760 (2021)
9. Cohen-Adad, J., et al.: Open-access quantitative MRI data of the spinal cord and reproducibility across participants, sites and manufacturers. sci. data. https://doi.org/10.1038/s41596-021-00588-0
10. Dolz, J., Desrosiers, C., Ben Ayed, I.: IVD-net: intervertebral disc localization and segmentation in MRI with a multi-modal UNet. In: Zheng, G., Belavy, D., Cai, Y., Li, S. (eds.) CSI 2018. LNCS, vol. 11397, pp. 130–143. Springer, Cham (2019). https://doi.org/10.1007/978-3-030-13736-6_11
11. Glocker, B., Feulner, J., Criminisi, A., Haynor, D.R., Konukoglu, E.: Automatic localization and identification of vertebrae in arbitrary field-of-view CT scans. In: Ayache, N., Delingette, H., Golland, P., Mori, K. (eds.) MICCAI 2012. LNCS, vol. 7512, pp. 590–598. Springer, Heidelberg (2012). https://doi.org/10.1007/978-3-642-33454-2_73
12. Ji, X., Zheng, G., Belavy, D., Ni, D.: Automated intervertebral disc segmentation using deep convolutional neural networks. In: Yao, J., Vrtovec, T., Zheng, G., Frangi, A., Glocker, B., Li, S. (eds.) CSI 2016. LNCS, vol. 10182, pp. 38–48. Springer, Cham (2016). https://doi.org/10.1007/978-3-319-55050-3_4
13. Liu, L., Wolterink, J.M., Brune, C., Veldhuis, R.N.: Anatomy-aided deep learning for medical image segmentation: a review. Phy. Med. Biol. **66**, 11TR01 (2021)
14. Mbarki, W., Bouchouicha, M., Frizzi, S., Tshibasu, F., Farhat, L.B., Sayadi, M.: Lumbar spine discs classification based on deep convolutional neural networks using axial view MRI. Interdisc. Neurosurg. **22**, 100837 (2020)
15. Qi, C.R., Su, H., Mo, K., Guibas, L.J.: Pointnet: Deep learning on point sets for 3D classification and segmentation. In: Proceedings of the IEEE Conference on Computer Vision and Pattern Recognition, pp. 652–660 (2017)
16. Redmon, J., Divvala, S., Girshick, R., Farhadi, A.: You only look once: Unified, real-time object detection. In: Proceedings of the IEEE Conference on Computer Vision and Pattern Recognition, pp. 779–788 (2016)
17. Rouhier, L., Romero, F.P., Cohen, J.P., Cohen-Adad, J.: Spine intervertebral disc labeling using a fully convolutional redundant counting model. arXiv preprint arXiv:2003.04387 (2020)
18. Ullmann, E., Pelletier Paquette, J.F., Thong, W.E., Cohen-Adad, J.: Automatic labeling of vertebral levels using a robust template-based approach. Int. J. Biomed. Imaging 2014 (2014)
19. Urban, J.P., Roberts, S.: Degeneration of the intervertebral disc. Arthritis Res Ther **5**(3), 1–11 (2003)
20. Vania, M., Lee, D.: Intervertebral disc instance segmentation using a multistage optimization mask-RCNN (mom-RCNN). J. Comput. Des. Eng. **8**(4), 1023–1036 (2021)
21. Wimmer, M., Major, D., Novikov, A.A., Bühler, K.: Fully automatic cross-modality localization and labeling of vertebral bodies and intervertebral discs in 3D spinal images. Int. J. Comput. Assist. Radiol. Surg. **13**(10), 1591–1603 (2018)

Mixup Augmentation Improves Age Prediction from T1-Weighted Brain MRI Scans

Lara Dular[(⊠)] and Žiga Špiclin

Faculty of Electrical Engineering, Laboratory of Imaging Technologies,
University of Ljubljana, Tržaška 25, 1000 Ljubljana, Slovenia
lara.dular@fe.uni-lj.si
http://lit.fe.uni-lj.si/

Abstract. Age predictions from T1-weighted (T1w) MR brain images using deep learning models have become increasingly more accurate, mainly with the construction of larger and more complex model architectures, such as cascade networks, but also with the use of larger training datasets. We adopted and evaluated a data augmentation strategy called Mixup that combines input T1w brain scans and associated output ages for the brain age regression task. On a multi-site dataset of 2504 T1w brain scans we evaluated and tested multiple mixing factor distributions, applied mixing of similar/different sample pairs based on low/high age difference, and combined mixing in auxiliary variables. We found consistent improvements in prediction accuracy with the use of Mixup augmentation, with minimal computational overhead, and, despite using a simple VGG-based deep learning model architecture, achieved a highly competitive mean absolute error as low as 2.96 years.

Keywords: Deep regression · Brain age · Mixup data augmentation

1 Introduction

Data augmentation methods that expand the sampling space by combining multiple input images and associated output annotations have been shown to significantly improve model performance on imaging datasets with little computational overhead. For instance, the Thumbnail [18] approach creates a downsampled copy of the original image and inserts it into a random location within the same (original) image, thus forcing the model to learn global features. CutMix [19] replaces a randomly-sized patch of the first image with a same-sized segment from the second image. Similarly, Mixup [20] involves linearly interpolating two input images and their corresponding one-hot encoded output labels. Improving upon the Mixup method, Manifold Mixup [17] mixes the two samples at a randomly chosen hidden layer of the neural network (not necessarily the input layer). While the aforementioned approaches were developed in the context of classification tasks, MixR [7] was designed for regression models and is based

I. Rekik et al. (Eds.): PRIME 2022, LNCS 13564, pp. 60–70, 2022.
https://doi.org/10.1007/978-3-031-16919-9_6

on the assumption that mixing continuous labels of two very different samples may result in arbitrarily-incorrect labels, and hence learns, for each example, how many nearest neighbors it should be mixed with for the best model performance.

In medical imaging, Mixup was shown to improve performance of deep nural networks for various medical imaging segmentation and classification tasks. Among others it was used for MRI segmentation of brain gliomas [4], prostate [8] and knee segmentation [12], classification of Alzheimer's disease (AD) and prediction of conversion to AD in individuals with mild cognitive impairment (MCI) [1]. Moreover, it was improved upon for classification problems on unbalanced datasets, for instance, gastrointestinal image classification and diabetic retinopathy grading [6]. To the best of our knowledge, Mixup has not yet been applied in (medical) regression tasks.

In this paper, we apply and evaluate Mixup augmentation strategy for the regression task of brain age prediction, i.e. prediction of age from T1-weighted (T1w) brain magnetic resonance images (MRI). While initially devised for classification, the Mixup augmentation naturally extends to regression, where linearly combining two scalar values results in a value in the domain space of the continuous target. In most previous studies involving Mixup in the domain of medical imaging, the Mixup was applied by considering a single sampling distribution of mixing factor or even a single fixed mixing factor. In this paper we perform an extensive experimental evaluation of Mixup augmentation hyperparameters for the brain age regression task with the aim to improve upon the existing and widely validated deep learning based age prediction models. For instance, we test multiple input/output mixing distributions and, specific to regression tasks, we consider combining pairs closer or further apart, based on their age difference, and verifying their impact on the age prediction accuracy. We also explore Mixup when using auxiliary variables, such as subject's sex that was shown to improve the brain age predictions [2], and perform an ablation study to investigate the effect of Mixup and/or sex information on brain age prediction. The training and validation of models was conducted on a large multi-site public database in a fully reproducible study design.

2   Materials and Methods

2.1   Data

Heterogeneous multi-site dataset of T1w MR images were gathered from seven public datasets, including healthy adult subjects between the age of 18 and 100 years. All T1w images underwent a visual quality check and the images with poor visual contrast, motion artifacts and/or failed preprocessing were excluded. The remaining 2504 subjects (1190 males) were split into train ($N_{tr} = 2012$), validation ($N_v = 245$) and test ($N_t = 247$) datasets. Detailed dataset information is given in Table 1.

Table 1. Age statistics, i.e. span, mean age ($\mu_{\mathbf{age}}$) and standard deviation ($\mathbf{sd_{age}}$) in *years* per dataset.

Dataset	$\mathbf{N_{samples}}$	Age span	$\mu_{\mathbf{age}} \pm \mathbf{sd_{age}}$
ABIDE I[1]	161	$18.0 - 48.0$	25.7 ± 6.4
ADNI[2]	248	$60.0 - 90.0$	76.2 ± 5.1
CamCAN [13–15][3]	624	$18.0 - 88.0$	54.2 ± 18.4
CC-359[4]	349	$29.0 - 80.0$	53.5 ± 7.8
FCON 1000[5]	572	$18.0 - 85.0$	45.3 ± 18.9
IXI[6]	472	$20.1 - 86.2$	49.0 ± 16.2
OASIS-2 [10][7]	78	$60.0 - 95.0$	75.6 ± 8.4
Total	2504	$18.0 - 95.0$	52.1 ± 19.1

[1]Data available at: http://fcon_1000.projects.nitrc.org/indi/abide/abide_I.html.
[2]Data available at: http://adni.loni.usc.edu/.
[3]Data available at: https://camcan-archive.mrc-cbu.cam.ac.uk/dataaccess/.
[4]Data available at: https://sites.google.com/view/calgary-campinas-dataset/download.
[5]Data available at: http://fcon_1000.projects.nitrc.org/indi/enhanced/neurodata.html.
[6]Data available at: https://brain-development.org/ixi-dataset/.
[7]Data available at: https://www.oasis-brains.org/.

2.2   T1w Preprocessing

Image preprocessing was conducted using a combination of publicly available and in-house software tools. The input DICOM T1w image was first converted to Nifti file format and re-oriented to a common reference space as the MNI152 nonlinear atlas, version 2009c [5], with size $193 \times 292 \times 193$ and spacing 1 mm^3. The raw T1w image was denoised using adaptive non-local means denoising[1] with spatially varying noise levels [9]. Following rigid and affine image registration of the denoised T1w image to the T1w image of the MNI152 atlas, performed using the publicly available NiftyReg software [11][2], the *sinc* resampling was applied to map the input MR image into atlas space. To improve registration accuracy, the intensity inhomogeneity correction (without mask) was applied to the denoised image using N4 algorithm [16][3], prior to running the registration. The inhomogeneity corrected image was used during registration only, while, finally, only the denoised image was *sinc* resampled using the rigid and affine registrations.

---

[1] Adaptive non-local means denoising: https://github.com/djkwon/naonlm3d.
[2] NiftyReg registration: http://cmictig.cs.ucl.ac.uk/wiki/index.php/NiftyReg.
[3] N4 bias field correction: https://manpages.debian.org/testing/ants/N4BiasFieldCorrection.1.en.html.

The registered T1w image was intensity windowed, setting grayscale outliers above 99-th and below 5-th percentile to the corresponding limiting values. Next, intensity inhomogeneity correction was applied to the T1w image, masked with MNI152 atlas mask dilated by 3 voxels, using the N4 algorithm. Finally, to remove the empty space around the head, the image was cropped to fixed size of $157 \times 189 \times 170$.

2.3   Brain Age Prediction

Model Architecture. For brain age prediction we implemented a simple VGG-based model trained on 3D T1w MRIs, proposed by Cole et al. [3]. The model was composed of five feature extracting convolutional blocks, each consisting of a convolutional layer with $3 \times 3 \times 3$ kernels, ReLU activation, convolutional layer with $3 \times 3 \times 3$ kernels, a batch normalization layer, ReLU activation and a max pooling layer with $2 \times 2 \times 2$ kernels. The number of feature maps was 8 in the fist convolutional block and doubled in each consecutive block. The output of the last block was flattened into a single fully connected layer with a linear activation function so as to output a single scalar value, i.e. age. The model architecture is depicted in Fig. 1.

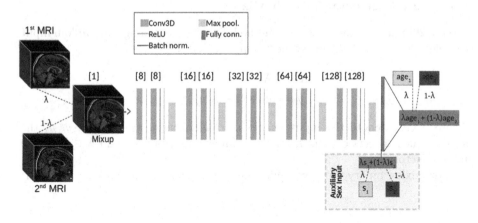

Fig. 1. Brain age model architecture with Mixup augmentation.

Loss and Performance Metrics. The loss and evaluation metric used in all experiments was the mean absolute error (MAE) between model prediction and actual age.

Baseline Model. For the baseline model as described above the hyperparameter values were chosen based on a grid search. Batch size (bs) was set to 4, 8, 16 and 24. The initial learning rate (lr) was set to 0.01, 0.001 and 0.0001 and reduced for 3% after each epoch. In each training session the L1 loss function was optimized for 110 epochs using SGD algorithm with momentum 0.9 and weight decay 5×10^{-5}. The models were trained with commonly used augmentation methods: *(i)* random shifting along all major axes with probability of 0.3 for an integer sampled form $[-5, 5]$, *(ii)* random padding with probability of 0.3 for an integer form $[0, 5]$, and *(iii)* flipping over central sagittal plane with probability of 0.5. The optimal hyperparameter values ($bs = 16$ and $lr = 0.0001$) were chosen as the values resulting in the lowest median MAE value of the last 10 epochs on the validation set. The baseline model was trained five times with the chosen hyperparameter values, of which the best run is reported.

Postprocessing. To each trained model we apply a linear bias correction step, by fitting a regression line $\hat{y} = \beta_1 y + \beta_0$ on the validation set, where y denotes true and $\hat{y}$ predicted value. The estimated coefficients β_0 and β_1 were used for correcting the predicted brain age on the test set as $y' = (\hat{y} - \beta_0)/\beta_1$. This results in an overall minor increase or decrease in MAE (from 3.26 to 3.27 years for the baseline model), but allow for a minor correction on the edges of the age interval, where regression models tend to over/underestimate.

2.4 Data Augmentation with Mixup

Mixup [20] is a data augmentation method, linearly combining two random input samples $(X_i, y_i), (X_j, y_j)$ into a new sample $(\tilde{X}, \tilde{y})$ as

$$\tilde{X} = \lambda X_i + (1 - \lambda)X_j,$$
$$\tilde{y} = \lambda y_i + (1 - \lambda)y_j,$$

where X_i, X_j denote the input images of random subjects i and j, y_i, y_j the single-valued targets coming from a continuous distribution, and $\lambda \in [0, 1]$ the mixing factor.

For mixing binary input variables, i.e. sex information in our case, we used

$$\tilde{b} = \lambda b_i + (1 - \lambda)b_j,$$

resulting in continuous variable $\tilde{b} \in [0, 1]$.

In practice, Mixup augmentation was implemented on a sample batch, by shuffling randomly (or with respect to the age) the order of scans in the batch. Such reordered batch was then linearly combined with the original sample batch, by mixing correspondingly indexed pairs of T1w scans, sex information and associated subject ages. An example of MRI Mixup is shown in Fig. 2.

3 Experiments and Results

In subsequent experimental sections we investigate the use of Mixup augmentation with respect to the baseline model and evaluate the impact of the choice of

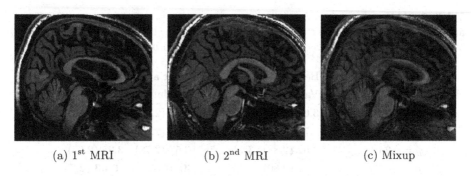

(a) 1st MRI   (b) 2nd MRI   (c) Mixup

Fig. 2. MR image Mixup for $\lambda = 0.5$.

Mixup augmentation probability, the choice of λ and/or its sample distribution, the strategy of sampling input pairs for Mixup according to the age difference, and verify the consistency of the performance gains in age prediction accuracy achieved by Mixup in combination with sex information as auxiliary input.

For all experiments and results reported in this paper, the same model architecture was trained using the same hyperparameters as for the baseline model. Results are reported for the best model in the last 10 training epochs, chosen according to the lowest MAE on validation set. Furthermore, each model underwent a linear bias correction determined using linear regression on the validation dataset.

Experiments were run using Intel Core i7-8700K CPU and three NVIDIA GeForce RTX 2080 Ti GPUs. Models were implemented in PyTorch 1.4.0 for Python 3.6.8. Each model was trained for approximately 10 h.

3.1   Mixup Probability

To find the optimal probability of Mixup augmentation during training we applied it on each batch with a certain probability p. In this experiment, the mixing parameter λ was set to a fixed value of 0.5. Additionally, we tested whether it is best to apply the Mixup before or after other image augmentation steps (e.g. padding, shifting and/or flipping).

The results in Table 2 show that the use of Mixup generally improves the model performance. Best overall improvement on validation and test set compared to the baseline was achieved when Mixup was applied after augmentation steps with probability 0.5. We chose this value for the remaining experiments.

3.2   Mixing Sample Distribution

To gain a general sense of whether a symmetrical or asymmetrical input sample mixing leads to better results, we mixed sample pairs with a fixed factor λ. We then randomized the mixing parameter by sampling from multiple $Unif([a, b])$

Table 2. MAE and standard deviation in *years* on validation and test set with Mixup applied before or after other data augmentation steps with probability p and fixed mixing factor $\lambda = 0.5$. The chosen parameters are marked in bold.

Mixup probability	Before augmentation		After augmentation	
	Validation	Test	Validation	Test
$p = 0.0$ (baseline)	3.66 (2.66)	3.29 (2.63)	3.66 (2.66)	3.29 (2.63)
$p = 0.1$	3.73 (2.70)	3.21 (2.53)	3.69 (2.52)	3.00 (2.44)
$p = 0.25$	3.52 (2.83)	3.14 (2.56)	3.57 (2.78)	3.25 (2.65)
$p = 0.5$	3.67 (2.80)	3.10 (2.69)	**3.30** (2.55)	**3.03** (2.65)
$p = 0.7$	3.33 (2.55)	3.14 (2.56)	3.41 (2.78)	3.18 (2.66)

distribution by changing the lower interval limit and keeping the upper interval limit equal to 0.5. Finally, we sampled λ from a symmetrical $Beta(\alpha, \alpha)$ distribution, as originally proposed by Zhang et al. [20].

Out of the two random distributions, the *Beta* distribution yielded better results, with $Beta(4, 4)$ resulting in the best improvement on the validation and test set (cf. Table 3). However, for both distributions the models with mixing parameters sampled closer to the value $\lambda = 0.5$ outperformed highly asymmetric mixing. The overall best result on the validation and test set was achieved by a fixed mixing parameter of 0.5 (cf. Table 3).

Table 3. MAE and standard deviation in *years* on validation and test set for different distributions of mixing parameter λ. The best results for each tested mixing distribution are marked in bold.

Fixed			Unif(a,b)			Beta(α,α)		
λ	Validation	Test	$[a, b]$	Validation	Test	α	Validation	Test
0.1	3.64 (2.66)	3.30 (2.74)	$[0.0, 0.5]$	3.69 (2.88)	3.27 (2.65)	0.1	3.60 (2.84)	3.15 (2.53)
0.2	3.74 (2.80)	3.18 (2.59)	$[0.1, 0.5]$	3.72 (2.73)	3.24 (2.66)	0.2	3.68 (2.57)	3.08 (2.68)
0.3	3.59 (2.69)	3.26 (2.70)	$[0.2, 0.5]$	**3.43** (2.75)	**3.10** (2.56)	0.4	3.55 (2.76)	3.15 (2.63)
0.4	3.53 (2.65)	3.16 (2.59)	$[0.3, 0.5]$	3.86 (2.78)	3.21 (2.71)	1	3.53 (2.84)	3.22 (2.6)
0.5	**3.30** (2.55)	**3.03** (2.64)	$[0.4, 0.5]$	3.43 (2.68)	3.32 (2.72)	2	3.56 (2.89)	3.08 (2.69)
						4	**3.35** (2.69)	**3.09** (2.5)
						8	3.55 (2.78)	3.11 (2.63)
						12	3.59 (2.76)	3.18 (2.61)

3.3 Mixing Based on Age Difference

We further inspect whether pairing of vicinal samples, i.e. samples closer or further apart in age, has an impact on brain age prediction performance. We performed two experiments: in the first one we sampled pairs similar in age, where

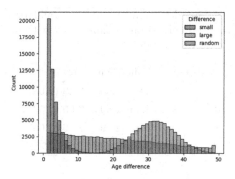

Fig. 3. Histogram of age differences between sample pairs when mixing pairs with small age difference (*blue*), large age difference (*orange*) and random age difference (*green*). (Color figure online)

the average age difference over the batches in all epochs was 2.1 ± 2.1 years; in the second one, we sampled pairs further apart in age, where the average age difference over the batches in all epochs was 31.5 ± 5.9 years. The sampling was implemented by sorting the input batch according to the age and, in first experiment, pairing samples with consecutive indices, while for the second experiment samples were paired with a fixed stride, half the batch size.

The age difference distributions emanating from the two experiments, and the age difference distribution of the random sampling based Mixup, are shown in Fig. 3. In this experiment the mixing parameter λ was sampled from $Beta(\alpha, \alpha)$ distribution, with $\alpha = 4$.

Both large age difference ($MAE_v = 3.62$, $MAE_t = 3.17$) and small age difference ($MAE_v = 3.85$, $MAE_t = 3.89$) resulted in inferior MAE results when compared to Mixup with random pair sampling ($MAE_v = 3.27$, $MAE_t = 3.03$).

3.4 Mixup with Auxiliary Input

We investigated the impact of Mixup when mixing an auxiliary binary input variable (sex) in addition to the input T1w images. The mixed sex was modeled as a linear combination, $\lambda s_1 + (1 - \lambda)s_2 \in [0, 1]$, $s_1, s_2 \in \{0, 1\}$, where 0 represents male and 1 female sex, and was concatenated with the fully connected layer preceding the linear regression output layer. In this experiment the mixing parameter λ was sampled from $Beta(\alpha, \alpha)$ distribution, with $\alpha = 4$.

Results of the ablation study are given in Table 4 and show that including both the sex information and Mixup resulted in an overall best model on validation and test set, with MAE under three years. This verified that the use of Mixup has a positive and consistent impact on the brain age prediction accuracy.

Table 4. MAE and standard deviation in *years* on validation and test set for an ablation study including sex information as input, and with or without Mixup augmentation. Best result on test set is bolded.

Mixup	Sex	Validation	Test
✗	✗	3.66 (2.66)	3.29 (2.63)
✓	✗	3.35 (2.69)	3.09 (2.50)
✗	✓	3.62 (2.79)	3.09 (2.66)
✓	✓	**3.46** (2.80)	**2.96** (2.50)

4 Discussion

Mixup augmentation was applied to the regression task of brain age prediction using a simple VGG-based CNN and was shown to consistently improve the prediction accuracy in terms of mean absolute age error (MAE). Even when introducing Mixup to auxiliary data, such as sex information, the Mixup augmentation consistently improved the age prediction accuracy.

The choice of mixing distribution and its parameters has a substantial impact on the efficacy of Mixup data augmentation. In contrary to [20], where the optimal parameter α in the *Beta* distribution for most use cases was smaller than 1, the experimental results on the brain age regression task indicated improvements when the samples were mixed with $\alpha > 1$, in which the most likely the mixing factor λ was close to the value 0.5. We argue this was due to rather homogeneous distribution of the T1w MRI data, which was extensively preprocessed, including affine registration to the MNI152 atlas and intensity corrections. Hence, the T1w images being mixed were sufficiently distinguished only for λ close to 0.5. Interestingly, α values above 1 were not tested for either the task of medical image segmentation [4] nor classification [6] and, based on our findings, thus remain an open avenue for further optimization.

Depending on the task at hand, the particular sequence of execution of the augmentation operations and the Mixup may be relevant and should be experimentally determined. In our task, the results indicate that the Mixup is marginally more effective when applied after the other augmentation steps. We argue that implementing Mixup after the other augmentation steps allows different random shifts for each image before mixing and thus prevents a complete overlap of the otherwise atlas-aligned brain structures.

Mixing randomly across the training data manifold yielded best performance. While simpler than the MixR strategy [7], our Mixup strategy controlled for pairing based on (small or large) age difference. In both controlled pairing experiments the Mixup performed worse than random pairing, which was in line with the original Mixup study [20]. We argue that the controlled pairing of individuals close in age may not fully take advantage of linear mixing across different age groups as the morphological differences due to similar age are thus not emphasized, while the inherent biological variability acts as additive input noise. In the other extreme of mixing individuals with large age differences, the model may fail to learn to model a linear transition between the adjacent age groups. We found that mixing pairs across all age intervals and age differences resulted in best age prediction accuracy.

In conclusion, we found consistent improvements of age prediction accuracy from T1w brain scans with the use of Mixup data augmentation, which had minimal computational overhead, and, despite using a simple VGG-based deep learning model architecture, achieved a highly competitive mean absolute error as low as 2.96 years.

Acknowledgements. This study was supported by the Slovenian Research Agency (Core Research Grant No. P2-0232 and Research Grants Nos. J2-2500 and J2-3059).

Data collection and sharing for this project was partially provided by:

- **Alzheimer's Disease Neuroimaging Initiative (ADNI) database (adni.loni. usc.edu).** The investigators within the ADNI contributed to the design and implementation of ADNI and/or provided data but did not participate in analysis or writing of this report. A complete listing of ADNI investigators can be found at http://adni.loni.usc.edu/wp-content/uploads/how_to_apply/ ADNI_Acknowledgement_List.pdf.
- **Cambridge Centre for Ageing and Neuroscience (CamCAN).** CamCAN funding was provided by the UK Biotechnology and Biological Sciences Research Council (grant number BB/H008217/1), together with support from the UK Medical Research Council and University of Cambridge, UK.
- **OASIS Longitudinal.** Principal Investigators: D. Marcus, R, Buckner, J. Csernansky, J. Morris; P50 AG05681, P01 AG03991, P01 AG026276, R01 AG021910, P20 MH071616, U24 RR021382.
- **ABIDE I.** Primary support for the work by Adriana Di Martino was provided by the (NIMH K23MH087770) and the Leon Levy Foundation.

References

1. Bron, E.E., et al.: Cross-cohort generalizability of deep and conventional machine learning for MRI-based diagnosis and prediction of Alzheimer's disease. NeuroImage: Clin. **31**, 102712 (2021). https://doi.org/10.1016/j.nicl.2021.102712. https://www.sciencedirect.com/science/article/pii/S221315822100156X
2. Cheng, J., et al.: Brain age estimation from mri using cascade networks with ranking loss. In: IEEE Transactions on Medical Imaging, pp. 1–1 (2021). https://doi.org/10.1109/TMI.2021.3085948
3. Cole, J.H., et al.: Predicting brain age with deep learning from raw imaging data results in a reliable and heritable biomarker. Neuroimage **163**, 115–124 (2017). https://doi.org/10.1016/j.neuroimage.2017.07.059. http://www.sciencedirect.com/science/article/pii/S1053811917306407
4. Eaton-Rosen, Z., Bragman, F., Ourselin, S., Cardoso, M.J.: Improving data augmentation for medical image segmentation. In: International Conference on Medical Imaging with Deep Learning, p. 3 (2018)

5. Fonov, V., Evans, A., McKinstry, R., Almli, C., Collins, D.: Unbiased nonlinear average age-appropriate brain templates from birth to adulthood. Neuroimage **47**, S102 (2009). https://doi.org/10.1016/S1053-8119(09)70884-5. https://www.sciencedirect.com/science/article/pii/S1053811909708845
6. Galdran, A., Carneiro, G., Ballester, M.A.G.: Balanced-MixUp for highly imbalanced medical image classification. arXiv:2109.09850 [cs] (2021). http://arxiv.org/abs/2109.09850, arXiv: 2109.09850
7. Hwang, S.H., Whang, S.E.: MixR: data mixing augmentation for regression (2021). https://doi.org/10.48550/ARXIV.2106.03374. https://arxiv.org/abs/2106.03374
8. Isaksson, L.J., et al.: Mixup (sample pairing) can improve the performance of deep segmentation networks. J. Artif. Intell. Soft Comput. Res. **12**(1), 29–39 (2022). https://doi.org/10.2478/jaiscr-2022-0003. https://www.sciendo.com/article/10.2478/jaiscr-2022-0003
9. Manjón, J.V., Coupé, P., Martí-Bonmatí, L., Collins, D.L., Robles, M.: Adaptive non-local means denoising of MR images with spatially varying noise levels. J. Magn. Reson. Imaging **31**(1), 192–203 (2010). https://doi.org/10.1002/jmri.22003
10. Marcus, D.S., Fotenos, A.F., Csernansky, J.G., Morris, J.C., Buckner, R.L.: Open access series of imaging studies: longitudinal MRI data in nondemented and demented older adults. J. Cogn. Neurosci. **22**(12), 2677–2684 (2010). https://doi.org/10.1162/jocn.2009.21407
11. Modat, M., Cash, D.M., Daga, P., Winston, G.P., Duncan, J.S., Ourselin, S.: Global image registration using a symmetric block-matching approach. J. Med. Imaging **1**(2), 1–6 (2014). https://doi.org/10.1117/1.JMI.1.2.024003. https://doi.org/10.1117/1.JMI.1.2.024003
12. Panfilov, E., Tiulpin, A., Klein, S., Nieminen, M.T., Saarakkala, S.: Improving robustness of deep learning based knee MRI segmentation: Mixup and adversarial domain adaptation. In: Proceedings of the IEEE/CVF International Conference on Computer Vision (ICCV) Workshops (2019)
13. Shafto, M.A., et al.: The Cambridge centre for ageing and neuroscience (Cam-CAN) study protocol: a cross-sectional, lifespan, multidisciplinary examination of healthy cognitive ageing. BMC Neurol. **14** (2014). https://doi.org/10.1186/s12883-014-0204-1. https://www.ncbi.nlm.nih.gov/pmc/articles/PMC4219118/
14. Taylor, J.R., et al.: The Cambridge centre for ageing and neuroscience (Cam-CAN) data repository: structural and functional MRI, MEG, and cognitive data from a cross-sectional adult lifespan sample. Neuroimage **144**(Pt B), 262–269 (2017). https://doi.org/10.1016/j.neuroimage.2015.09.018
15. The Cambridge Centre for Ageing and Neuroscience (CamCAN). http://fcon_1000.projects.nitrc.org/indi/abide/abide_I.html
16. Tustison, N.J., et al.: N4ITK: improved N3 bias correction. IEEE Trans. Med. Imaging **29**(6), 1310–1320 (2010). https://doi.org/10.1109/TMI.2010.2046908
17. Verma, V., et al.: Manifold Mixup: better representations by interpolating hidden states. In: Proceedings of the 36th International Conference on Machine Learning, pp. 6438–6447. PMLR (2019). https://proceedings.mlr.press/v97/verma19a.html
18. Xie, T., Cheng, X., Liu, M., Deng, J., Wang, X., Liu, M.: Thumbnail: a novel data augmentation for convolutional neural network. arXiv:2103.05342 [cs] (2021). http://arxiv.org/abs/2103.05342. arXiv: 2103.05342
19. Yun, S., Han, D., Oh, S.J., Chun, S., Choe, J., Yoo, Y.: CutMix: regularization strategy to train strong classifiers with localizable features. arXiv:1905.04899 [cs] (2019). http://arxiv.org/abs/1905.04899. arXiv: 1905.04899
20. Zhang, H., Cisse, M., Dauphin, Y.N., Lopez-Paz, D.: mixup: Beyond empirical risk minimization. arXiv preprint arXiv:1710.09412 (2017)

Diagnosing Knee Injuries from MRI with Transformer Based Deep Learning

Gökay Sezen[✉] and İlkay Öksüz

Computer Engineering Department, Istanbul Technical University, Istanbul, Turkey
sezengo@itu.edu.tr

Abstract. Magnetic Resonance Images (MRI) examinations are widely used for diagnosing injuries in the knee. Automatic interpretable detection of meniscus, Anterior Cruciate Ligament (ACL) tears, and general abnormalities from knee MRI is an essential task for automating the clinical diagnosis of knee MRI. This paper proposes a combination of convolution neural network and sequential network deep learning models for detecting general anomalies, ACL tears, and meniscal tears on knee MRI. We combine information from multiple MRI views with transformer blocks for final diagnosis. Also, we did an ablation study which is training with only CNN, and saw the impact of the transformer blocks on the learning. On average, we achieve a performance of 0.905 AUC for three injury cases on MRNet data.

Keywords: MRNet · Knee MRI · ACL · Abnormal · Meniscus

1 Introduction

The gold standard for diagnosing serious knee injuries is Magnetic resonance imaging (MRI). The knee receives more MRI exams than any other part of the body [1–3]. Manual analysis of knee MRI scans can be time-consuming and error-prone. Patients' MR images might differ significantly, making interpretation difficult for healthcare workers. Therefore, an automated diagnosis system for knee MRI is an essential task.

In this study, we propose a method to automatically determine whether a patient has a knee injury or not on a publicly available dataset of knee MRI scans (MRNet dataset [4]). A network structure idea is developed to perform tear detection on knees using MRNet data. Convolutional neural networks (CNN) and transformer-based networks are used and combined to utilize multiple views in combination. CNNs are used to extract image features of every single image, and transformer encoders are used to gather information between slice images for a patient.

The main contributions of this study are diagnosing the knee injuries with a network consisting of CNN and transformer-based layers and finding out the impact of transformer blocks to fuse information from multiple MRI slices. Firstly, network architecture with ResNet [5] and transformer encoder layers

I. Rekik et al. (Eds.): PRIME 2022, LNCS 13564, pp. 71–78, 2022.
https://doi.org/10.1007/978-3-031-16919-9_7

[6] are used to extract semantic features of each view, then bring together information extracted from multiple views to get global information. Secondly, we remove the transformer blocks and train the network with only ResNet layers and compare the two networks to see the effects of the transformer block on learning the MR images.

2   Related Works

Diagnosis of disease on knee MR images has been studied within the context of the MRNet dataset. Bien, N. [7] published the MRNet Dataset and stated Deep-learning-assisted diagnosis with MRNet architecture for knee magnetic resonance imaging. The article tries to diagnose three knee injuries: abnormalities, ACL tears, and meniscal tears, from magnetic resonance images with the deep learning-assisted method. An anterior cruciate ligament (ACL) injury is often a complete tear of the ligament, resulting in an unstable knee. A meniscal tear is a tear in the cartilage that supports the bones in the leg, and an abnormal exam refers to general knee disorders. MRNet includes a CNN-based network and logistic regression network at the end to predict a patient's knee injuries for all three cases. First, CNN networks are trained separately for all three planes axial, coronal, and sagittal. Then, a logistic regression network is trained to combine each plane's output to a single probability for each injury case ACL tear, abnormalities, and meniscal tear. MRNet contains AlexNet [8], which was pre-trained on the ImageNet, as a feature extractor for each MR image. Each slice is given to AlexNet separately and a global average pooling operation is performed to reduce the dimension of the feature tensor. After the classification networks are trained for each plane axial, coronal, and sagittal, a logistic regression operation is used to get the probability for each case of ACL tear, abnormalities, and meniscal tear.

Azcona et al. [9] used the MRNet dataset to perform the detection of ACL tear, abnormalities, and meniscal tear in knee MRI scans using a deep residual network with a transfer learning approach. The paper uses ResNet-18 for feature extraction (similar to the original MRNet structure) and trains all planes separately first, then combines the solutions with logistic regression.

Tsai et al. [10] proposed an Efficiently-Layered Network (ELNet) design that has been tuned for MRI-based knee diagnostics. The fundamental contribution of this paper is a novel slice feature extraction network that combines multi-slice normalization with BlurPool down-sampling. They do not use all planes of the MR images to detect the cases. The coronal images are chosen to detect meniscal tears, and the axial images to detect ACL tears and abnormalities.

Kara et al. [11] proposed a study that has a combination of 3 different network strategies to detect knee injuries from the MRNet dataset. The first network is a ResNet50 network to select eligible data from the entire dataset. They created a different number of classes based on the qualities of MR images for each plane, and train the network with these labels. Then, to select the relevant area from the eligible dataset, the second network which consists of CNN and autoencoder blocks is trained. After selecting the relevant are from MR images, the last ResNet50 network is trained to detect the injury cases.

The original MRNet architecture method [7] and the best resulting method of Azcona et al. [9] use the same approach that feeding all slices separately with a CNN feature extractor. After they get the feature tensor with dimension $s \times N$ (N is the feature length of the selected model's output), an average pooling layer is used to combine all slices and get the output with dimension N. Also, Tsai et al. and Kara et al. brought novel intuitions for diagnosing knee injury tasks. However, neither of them interpreted the information between the slices. In this way, the information between slices is lost. However, the slices belong to the same patient and they are taken sequentially, so, there can be gain helpful information by considering the combination of slices while building the model. In this study, we propose a new network architecture that consists of ResNet and transformer encoder networks by considering the relative information between slices.

3   Materials and Methods

3.1   Dataset

MRNet Dataset [7] contains 1,370 knee MRI samples. Each patient's exam has 3 different planes: axial, coronal, and sagittal. Each sample can have different numbers of slices for all planes. The slice images in these series vary in number from 17 to 61. (mean 31.48, SD 7.97). The dataset labels are binary numbers for each patient's exams in each injury case. Each exam can have multiple types of disease, and all patients that have meniscal or/and ACL tears have abnormal injury certainly.

The dataset includes;

- 1,104 (80.6%) abnormal exams
- 319 (23.3%) ACL (anterior cruciate ligament) tears
- 508 (37.1%) meniscal tears

Because patients who receive an MRI are more likely to develop a knee injury, the dataset is highly imbalanced in favor of classifications with injuries. The exams were split into a training set (1,130 exams), a validation set (120 exams), and a test set (120 exams). The test set is a closed set that can be performed in only MRNet Competition to test the performance of the models. Hence, the validation set is used as the test set in this study.

3.2   Methods

We propose a network architecture for the diagnosis of three knee injuries ACL tear, meniscal tear, and general abnormalities by using the MRNet dataset. ResNet and transformer encoder networks are used in the architecture. We utilize ResNet to extract semantic features from multiple view images. The transformer structure is a deep neural network mainly based on the self-attention mechanism

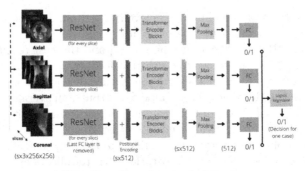

(a) ResNet+Transformer Architecture

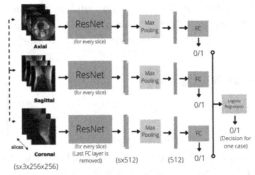

(b) ResNet Only Architecture

Fig. 1. Figure (a) represents the ResNet + Transformer structure which has ResNet34 and transformer encoder layers. Figure (b) represents the ResNet Only structure which has only the ResNet34 blocks to learn from slice images.

to extract intrinsic features of sequential data. The transformer encoder is the first part of the original transformer architecture to perform multi-headed attention networks to the input sequential set and encode to an output set.

MRNet dataset includes image slices for each patient exam at 3 different views axial, coronal, and sagittal. The slice images are consecutive and any image is significantly similar and related to the one before and after it. Therefore, the slices are considered as a sequence of images like frames of a video, and the relation between them is tried to examine with transformer-encoder blocks. After that, the transformer blocks are removed and the network is trained with only ResNet layers to see the effectiveness of the transformer blocks on the slice MR images and compare the results. The networks are trained for all planes (axial, coronal, sagittal) separately to see the results of learning the slice images in every plane. We did this operation for all cases (ACL, abnormal, sagittal).

The whole structure of the proposed network can be seen in Fig. 1. The ResNet structure which is pre-trained on the ImageNet dataset is used for the feature extraction operation. The last layer of the ResNet network is removed to obtain a proper size feature vector for each slice. The transformer part is used to consider the relative information between slices features which are extracted from ResNet and create output features.

There are three separately initialized ResNet networks in this structure for per plane axial, coronal, and sagittal. Every slice is given to the ResNet network first to extract the semantic features. At the output of ResNet, it is obtained a vector for each slice with dimension 512. Hence, there are tensors with dimensions $s \times 512$ at each plane's ResNet output. To decide about injuries by considering the relationships between slices the transformer encoder networks are used. The features of slices are thought of as sequential data and fed to the transformer encoder with positional encoding. Because the transformer has no memory mechanism, positional encoding is carry the information about the order of the sequence data. Embedding operation is not necessary for this work, as the data is already in a numerical form. After the transformer encoder; it is acquired tensors which carry not only the semantic information of each slice itself from ResNet but also the relations between the slices from the transformer encoder. These tensors are obtained for each plane with the same dimensionality with the input $s \times 512$. Then, a max-pooling operation is used to reduce the s dimensionality, and get one dimension vector for each plane. A last fully connected network is used to decide whether the slice images of specific planes have an injury case or not. For all injury cases, 3 different networks are trained separately for all planes, then combine their outputs with logistic regression to decide the probability of one case. By doing that, we can analyze the results of each plane and also each injury case. The whole procedure is executed for all knee injury cases ACL tears, abnormalities, and meniscus tears. In total, 9 different models were trained for each plane then 3 logistic regression models were trained to decide for each case.

The structure of the "ResNet Only" network can be seen in Fig. 1. We consider these networks as an ablation study to investigate the influence of transformer blocks. The whole structure and hyperparameters are exactly the same between these two networks to enable a fair comparison.

3.3 Implementation Details

ResNet34 structure is used as the backbone of the networks. The transformer has 2 encoder blocks with 8 heads. The dropout value is set as 0.1. Augmentation strategy is used whenever a training example occurred in training. The exams were rotated randomly between -25 and $25°$, moved randomly between -25 and 25 pixels, and flipped horizontally with a 50% probability. The networks are trained with a single batch because the number of slices can vary for each exam and plane. Hence, it cannot be combined with multiple tensors of image samples. The slice images are given to the network's backbone separately, then combined with the transformer layers. The learning rate is set $1e-5$ at the beginning of training and configured with a learning rate optimization to arrange the learning rate while training. Binary cross-entropy loss and Adam optimizer are used. The loss is also scaled inversely proportionally to the number of samples of that class in the dataset to handle the imbalanced dataset. The default maximum number of epochs is 50; however, an early stopping technique is used, where the validation AUC score is monitored for 7 epochs, and the training is stopped if no improvement is observed. Nvidia Tesla T4 GPU is used to train all models.

Table 1. Comparison of AUC scores of proposed networks for all injury cases and planes. Almost all AUC scores of the ResNet+Transformer networks are higher than the ResNet Only networks.

		ResNet Only	ResNet+Transformer
ACL	axial	0.937	**0.951**
	coronal	0.839	**0.928**
	sagittal	0.841	**0.933**
	log.reg.	0.838	**0.952**
Abnormal	axial	0.718	**0.913**
	coronal	**0.898**	0.871
	sagittal	0.831	**0.891**
	log.reg.	0.882	**0.914**
Meniscus	axial	0.735	**0.820**
	coronal	0.818	**0.847**
	sagittal	0.652	**0.730**
	log.reg	0.817	**0.850**

4   Results

4.1   Experimental Results

The performance criterion of MRNet competition [4] is mainly the AUC score in ROC curves. We report the AUC score of all trained models on the validation dataset. Table 1 shows the AUC scores of both ResNet+Transformer and ResNet Only models. The first column represents the injury cases. The second column is for slice planes and the combined logistic regression score for three planes. The third and fourth columns represent the AUC scores of ResNet Only and ResNet+Transformer models.

In Table 1, the AUC scores of the network with transformer encoder blocks surpass the AUC scores of the ResNet Only network in almost every injury case, plane, and combined logistic regression result. Figure 1 shows the ROC curves of the networks for three injury cases. As can be seen in the figures most parts of the ROC curves the ResNet+Transformer network method is ahead of the ResNet Only method. It can be said that the transformer encoder blocks can help to learn better the relationship between MRI slices and make more precise decisions about the injury cases. By looking at these results, the transformer encoder blocks can be used with convolutional neural networks to learn better inference about sliced or multiple viewed datasets.

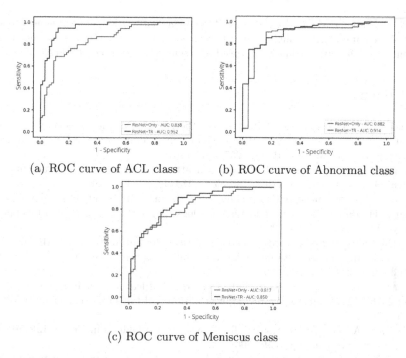

(a) ROC curve of ACL class   (b) ROC curve of Abnormal class

(c) ROC curve of Meniscus class

Fig. 2. (a), (b), and (c) figures represent the comparison ROC curve of the ResNet Only and ResNet+Transformer method in ACL, abnormal, and meniscus tasks respectively. The ResNet+Transformer generates better results compared to the ResNet-only in terms of AUC scores.

5 Conclusions

In this study, a network structure to address the problem of diagnosing the three knee injuries ACL tear, general abnormalities, and meniscal tears is proposed. We aimed to interpret both individual semantic information of the MR image slices themselves and the common information of a combination of slices for all injury cases. ResNet and transformer encoder networks are combined and used to perform this task. Also, another network consisting of just ResNet blocks is trained for all scenarios to perform an ablation study and compare it with the proposed architecture. We validate the usage of transformer blocks when used with CNN layers to learn from multiple slices or multiple view data in classification tasks.

In the future, we aim to apply our model to medical image classification tasks, where sequential information can be utilized (e.g. stroke detection in 3D brain MRI). Besides, we aim to utilize advanced transformer structures with multiple parameters to boost the classification performance further.

Acknowledgments. This paper has been produced benefiting from the 2232 International Fellowship for Outstanding Researchers Program of TUBITAK (Project No:

118C353). However, the entire responsibility of the publication/paper belongs to the owner of the paper. The financial support received from TUBITAK does not mean that the content of the publication is approved in a scientific sense by TUBITAK.

References

1. Nacey, N.C., Geeslin, M.G., Miller, G.W., Pierce, J.L.: Magnetic resonance imaging of the knee: an overview and update of conventional and state of the art imaging. J. Mag. Reson. Imaging **45**(5), 1257–1275 (2017)
2. Naraghi, A.M., White, L.M.: Imaging of athletic injuries of knee ligaments and menisci: sports imaging series. Radiology **281**(1), 23–40 (2016)
3. Helms, C.A.: Magnetic resonance imaging of the knee. In: Brant, W.E., Helms, C.A. (eds.) Fundamentals of Diagnostic Radiology, pp. 1193–204. Lippincott Williams & Wilkins, Philadelphia (2007)
4. MRNet: a dataset of knee MRIs and competition for automated knee MRI interpretation (n.d.). https://stanfordmlgroup.github.io/competitions/mrnet/. Accessed 20 June 2022
5. He, K., Zhang, X., Ren, S., Sun, J.: Deep residual learning for image recognition. In: 2016 IEEE Conference on Computer Vision and Pattern Recognition (CVPR), 770–778 (2016)
6. Vaswani, A., et al: Attention is all you need. In: Advances in Neural Information Processing Systems, pp. 5998–6008 (2017)
7. Bien, N., et al.: Deep-learning-assisted diagnosis for knee magnetic resonance imaging: development and retrospective validation of MRNet. PLoS Medicine **15**(11), e1002699 (2018)
8. Krizhevsky, A., Sutskever, I., Hinton, G.E.: ImageNet classification with deep convolutional neural networks. Adv. Neural. Inf. Process. Syst. **25**, 1097–1105 (2012)
9. Azcona, D., McGuinness, K., Smeaton, A.F.: A comparative study of existing and new deep learning methods for detecting knee injuries using the MRNet dataset. In: 2020 International Conference on Intelligent Data Science Technologies and Applications (IDSTA), pp. 149–155. IEEE (2020)
10. Tsai, C. H., Kiryati, N., Konen, E., Eshed, I., Mayer, A.: Knee injury detection using MRI with efficiently-layered network (ELNet). In: Medical Imaging with Deep Learning, pp. 784–794. PMLR (2020)
11. Kara, A.C., Hardalaç, F.: Detection and classification of knee injuries from MR images using the MRNet dataset with progressively operating deep learning methods. Mach. Learn. Knowl. Extr. **3**(4), 1009–1029 (2021)

MISS-Net: Multi-view Contrastive Transformer Network for MCI Stages Prediction Using Brain ^{18}F-FDG PET Imaging

Anouar Kherchouche[1,3(✉)], Olfa Ben-Ahmed[1,3], Carole Guillevin[2,3],
Benoit Tremblais[1,3], Christine Fernandez-Maloigne[1,3], Rémy Guillevin[2,3],
For Alzheimer's Disease Neuroimaging Initiative

[1] XLIM Research Institute, URM CNRS 7252, University of Poitiers, Poitiers, France
{anouar.kherchouche,olfa.ben-ahmed,benoit.tremblais,
christine.fernandez-maloigne}@univ-poitiers.fr
[2] DACTIM-MIS, LMA, URM CNRS 7348, University and Hospital of Poitiers,
Poitiers, France
{carole.guillevin,remy.guillevin}@chu-poitiers.fr
[3] I3M, Common Laboratory CNRS-Siemens-Healthineers,
University and Hospital of Poitiers, Poitiers, France

Abstract. Mild Cognitive Impairment (MCI) is the transitional stage between healthy aging and dementia. MCI patients are characterized by very subtle changes in the brain. These changes with disease progression might assist the more precise dementia staging, which can reduce the number of Alzheimer's Disease (AD) patients through early intervention. Indeed, subjects diagnosed with MCI could be further divided into sub-categories (stable MCI and progressive MCI) and only part of them will convert to dementia. In this paper, we propose a multi-view contrastive transformer network for MCI sub-categories detection with the aim of early AD conversion prediction. The proposed method is based on a two-stage learning scheme that optimally captures local and global information from [18]F FluoroDeoxyGlucose Positron Emission Tomography (^{18}F-FDG PET) images. The proposed approach optimally exploits the complementary of the three image projections (axial, sagittal, and coronal), through contrastive learning, for efficient multi-view clinical pattern (embedding) learning. The proposed method has been evaluated on a subset of the ADNI dataset. Obtained results outperform recent uni-modal and multi-modal state-of-the-art approaches in (sMCI) vs. (pMCI) detection. We report an average accuracy, sensitivity, and sensitivity of respectively 87.13%, 90.61%, and 83.65%.

Keywords: Alzheimer's disease · Stable MCI · Progressive MCI · Prediction · Transformer · Contrastive learning · ^{18}F-FDG PET

© The Author(s), under exclusive license to Springer Nature Switzerland AG 2022
I. Rekik et al. (Eds.): PRIME 2022, LNCS 13564, pp. 79–90, 2022.
https://doi.org/10.1007/978-3-031-16919-9_8

1   Introduction

Alzheimer's Disease (AD) is a dominant degenerative brain disease among elderly people [1]. To date, there is no efficient cure available when the subject is once diagnosed with AD, which is in the later disease stage. Mild Cognitive Impairment (MCI) is considered a transitional stage between aging and AD. Clinical studies have shown that the detection and the therapeutic intervention at the MCI stage are promising to prevent dementia and hence can lead to social and financial benefits [2]. Indeed, the MCI group can be categorized into two subtypes[1], early/stable MCI (sMCI), and late/progressive MCI (pMCI) known respectively as non-converter and converter MCI in different studies. The sMCI is considered as the earlier point in the clinical spectrum of AD while pMCI is at the later point to progress to disease. Patients diagnosed as sMCI, had a lower risk of conversion to AD, while subjects predicted as pMCI have a higher risk to develop dementia in a short period. Therefore, MCI subtypes detection is of vital importance for an early AD conversion prediction.

Several medical imaging modalities have been investigated with deep learning techniques for early AD detection. However, few works have addressed the (sMCI vs. pMCI) prediction problem [3] due to the challenge of learning a discriminating disease signature for these groups. In this context, the most used technique is the MRI (structural MRI and functional MRI) which captures the MCI-related alterations in the brain anatomy and functions [4–6]. Moreover, Diffusion Tensor Imaging (DTI) have been recently used for MCI subtypes prediction [7,8]. However, the morphological and functional differences in the brain lesions, detected with sMRI, fMRI, and DTI, in the intermediate stages of MCI are very small [9]. Yet, ^{18}F-FluoroDeoxyGlucose Positron Emission Tomography (^{18}F-FDG PET) which measures cerebral glucose metabolism in the brain has been reported as a powerful MCI biomarker [10]. Recently, various deep-learning-based approaches for early AD prediction [9,11,12] showed the effectiveness of biomarkers derived from (^{18}F-FDG PET) versus other imaging modalities. Moreover, adding (^{18}F-FDG PET) with others modalities boost the classification performance (e.g., MRI+PET) [11,13,14]. However, existing FDG-PET-based approaches present several limitations for efficient sMCI and pMCI detection. First, most of the existing works used 2-Dimensional Convolutional Neural Networks (2D-CNN), which lack the ability to build explicit long-range semantic dependencies present in 3D medical images. More precisely, the convolutional operations attend to only a local subset from neighborhood pixels and force the network to focus on local patterns rather than the inter-slice medical information. Moreover, traditional approaches use late or early fusion to combine information derived from the three image projections (axial, sagittal coronal) which are not optimal to exploit the complementary of these projections for atrophy detection [15]. To deal with these issues, some works proposed 3D-CNN [5] or combined 2D-CNN with Recurrent Neural Network (RNN) [16]. However, these approaches suffer from overfitting and the vanishing gradient problem. Finally, most of the existing approaches include pre-processed images to augment their dataset, which may bias the prediction results by including images of the same patient.

---

[1] Based on the WMS-R Logical Memory II Story A score.

Recently, transformer-based models [17] have been shown their ability to solve the CNN issue by dealing with long-range dependencies. Transformers are built using a self-attention mechanism, enabling the model to capture the relations between associative features. Different from previous CNN-based methods, transformers can achieve excellent results by modeling the global context in computer vision tasks [17]. Transformers have also been successfully applied to full-stack clinical applications, including image reconstruction, registration, segmentation, detection, and diagnosis [18]. However, their investigation for early AD detection is under-explored. Indeed, for AD disease detection local and global information is important, i.e., intra-slice and inter-slices details are pertinent to building a discriminating atrophy description. More additionally, modeling the local features of medical image data (e.g., 3D PET scan) which contains three projections beyond 2D, is also challenging as shown in [19] since the local structure is lost after splitting the image into patches to train the transformer. Therefore, motivated by the proprieties of transformers in modeling long-range semantic dependencies [20], we propose to design a transformer-based approach that can exploit the local and global multi-view dependencies from 3D images for efficient early disease signature learning.

In this paper, we propose a multi-view contrastive transformer network for MCI stages prediction. The proposed method is based on a two-stage learning scheme that optimally captures local and global information from the three ^{18}F-FluoroDeoxyGlucose Positron Emission Tomography (^{18}F-FDG PET) image's views. To the best of our knowledge, this is the first work that exploits long-range semantic dependencies through transformers and contrastive learning for efficient ^{18}F-FDG PET multi-view embedding learning. The main contributions of this work can be summarized as follows:

- We propose a simple yet efficient transformer-based network to model the long-range semantic dependencies within the 3D PET images (intra-slice and inter-slices metabolic features);
- A two-stage training framework that uses supervised contrastive learning for efficient multi-view clinical pattern (embedding) learning is proposed. The learned features are used in the second step for MCI subtypes detection;
- The proposed approach exploits the complementary of the three projections (axial, sagittal, and coronal) for better embedding learning;
- Contrary to existing works that augment the data with longitudinal and pre-processed images from the same patients, we evaluate the proposed approach using one image per patient demonstrating the efficiency of the proposed method when learning from small and non-biased data;

The remaining of this paper is structured as follows: First, Sect. 2 describes the proposed framework. Then, experiments and results are presented and analyzed in Sect. 3. Finally, Sect. 4 concludes the paper and opens new perspectives.

2   Proposed Approach

The proposed strategy is a **M**ulti v**I**ew contra**S**tive tran**S**former **Net**work (MISS-Net) with Supervised Contrastive Learning (SCL) [21] for the prediction

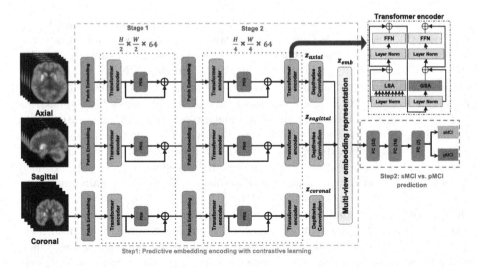

Fig. 1. Two-stage (step1 and step2) training network with transformer-based encoders for Multi-view embedding learning and sMCI vs pMCI prediction.

of MCI conversion to AD, in which axial, sagittal and coronal views can give complementary information owing to the separability of the proposed method, as shown in Fig. 1. Briefly, we propose spatial transformer block for each projection to map the view v to a vector $z = \mathrm{Proj}(v) \in \mathcal{R}^{D_P}$, where D_p is the vector size. Afterward, a linear concatenation is made with the vectors from each projection to build a multi-view embedding representation. These embeddings are pulled closer for the same class and far away from different classes. A Multi-Layer Perceptron (MLP) is added to the model followed by a softmax function to give a prediction. Finally, the model is fine-tuned by blocking gradient propagation from the MLP back to the model projectors.

2.1 Network Architecture

In this section, we introduce the proposed MISS-Net method in details, mainly including the spatial vision transformer exploited for each view to encode the images, which is then followed by a depth-wise convolutional layer to process the spatial resolution and also not increase computational cost rather than applying the commonly used 3D convolutions for medical imaging data.

Vision Transformer-Based Image Encoding The traditional self-attention used in transformers suffers from the heavy computational complexity in neuroimaging data. For a given view of $H \times W$ resolution, the self-attention complexity of dimension d is $\mathcal{O}\left(H^2W^2d\right)$. The spatial vision transformer relies on the spatial self-attention mechanism [20] aiming to diminish the complexity and improve the results. In fact, this mechanism uses a scheme of alternated local and global attention, allowing to capture both short and long-range relations. We adapt this idea to resolve the sMCI vers pMCI prediction task, where a locally-grouped self-attention (LSA) is computed for each feature map, which is spatially divided equally into $k_1 \times k_2$ non-overlapping local windows, we assume $H\%k_1 = 0$ and $W\%k_2 = 0$. Specifically, at this stage, the LSA is computed for each sub-window separately. Thus, the complexity will decrease to $\mathcal{O}\left(\frac{H^2W^2}{k_1k_2}d\right)$. However, the non-overlapping division abstains the communication between sub-windows. Thus, Global sub-sampled attention (GSA) comes into play to handle this issue. Through a convolution operation, we represent each sub-window by single key information. Then, a self-attention mechanism is applied to these key representations to capture the global important features per view with a complexity of $\mathcal{O}(k_1k_2HWd)$. Consequently, the alternated complexity of local and global attention is $\mathcal{O}\left(\frac{H^2W^2}{k_1k_2}d + k_1k_2HWd\right) \leq \mathcal{O}\left(\frac{H^2W^2}{2}d\right)$ for $k_1 \leq \frac{H}{2}$ and $k_2 \leq \frac{W}{2}$, which is significantly more efficient than the traditional self-attention. Furthermore, the succession of both attentions respectively is a kind of spatial-wise convolution aiming to retain distinctive patterns and point-wise convolution which learns significant representations among slices. The architecture is constructed by stacking a series of stages that can be represented formally as:

$$
\begin{aligned}
\hat{\mathbf{z}}_{ijk}^l &= \text{LSA}\left(\text{LayerNorm}\left(\mathbf{z}_{ijk}^{l-1}\right)\right) + \mathbf{z}_{ijk}^{l-1}, \\
\mathbf{z}_{ijk}^l &= \text{FFN}\left(\text{LayerNorm}\left(\hat{\mathbf{z}}_{ijk}^l\right)\right) + \hat{\mathbf{z}}_{ijk}^l, \\
\hat{\mathbf{z}}_k^{l+1} &= \text{GSA}\left(\text{LayerNorm}\left(\mathbf{z}_k^l\right)\right) + \mathbf{z}_k^l, \\
\mathbf{z}_k^{l+1} &= \text{FFN}\left(\text{LayerNorm}\left(\hat{\mathbf{z}}_k^{l+1}\right)\right) + \hat{\mathbf{z}}_k^{l+1}, \\
&i \in \{1,2,\ldots,k_1\}, j \in \{1,2,\ldots,k_2\} \ and \ k \in \{1,2,3\}
\end{aligned}
\tag{1}
$$

where residual connections and layer normalization are included at each step. $\hat{\mathbf{z}}_{ijk}^l \in \mathcal{R}^{\frac{H}{k_1} \times \frac{W}{k_2} \times C}$ is a sub-window of the lth layer from the kth view (i.e., axial, sagittal or coronal) and C is its number of channels. Finally, after the first transformer block of each stage, the Position Encoding Generator (PEG) is added to dynamically generates the Conditional Position Encodings (CPE) using a 2D depth-wise convolution (i.e., based on the local neighbors of each slice). These conditional position encodings are able to handle the sequence longer than the absolute one as shown in [20], which is suitable for our medical data.

View Projection. At the bottleneck of the model (i.e., output of transformer's last layer of the last stage), [20] applied Global Average Pooling (GAP) replacing the fully connected layers to make a classification. Although this layer reduces the cost computation by averaging the feature map elements, it decreases the model accuracy due to the spatial loss information, especially when the size of a feature map is higher. To deal with this issue, inspired from [22], a 2D depth-wise convolution layer is applied at the last layer of the transformer encoder. The main intuition is to learn how to reduce the cost without losing spatial information. In fact, using this convolution operation will make the model capable to learn a matrix of different weights per feature map that have the same size $n \times m$.

Thus, instead of calculating the average sum per feature map, each element has a weight that represents its importance in global information. We calculate the weighted-average-sum per channel σ_c as follows:

$$\sigma_c = \frac{1}{n \times m} \sum_{i=1}^{n} \sum_{j=1}^{m} w_{cij} a_{cij}$$
$$c = 1, 2, \ldots, D_p \tag{2}$$

where D_p is the total number of channels, w_{cij} and a_{cij} are the elements of the weight matrix and the feature map respectively from the (i, j) position of the cth channel. Therefore, each view is projected by a vector $z_v = [\sigma_1, \sigma_2, \ldots, \sigma_{D_p}]$, with $v \in \{axial, sagittal, coronal\}$.

Combination and Fully-Connected Layer. After the projection step, the three projected views are linearly concatenated to get the multi-view embedding representation $z_{emb} = conct\,(z_{axial}, z_{sagittal}, z_{coronal})$. Then, we fed z_{emb} into Fully-Connected (FC) layers followed by Relu as activation function except for the last layer with 2 neurons which is delivered by a softmax function to make a prediction.

2.2   Two-Stage Training Approach for sMCI vs. pMCI Prediction

Predictive Embedding Encoding with Contrastive Learning. In order to learn a disease-related embedding able to discriminate between sMCI and pMCI, we use supervised contrastive learning [21]. The supervised contrastive coding gives a promising performance by using label information in pulling the samples belonging to the same class in the embedding space while pushing apart the samples from different classes in another embedding space. For a given batch of N samples, we randomly apply data augmentation twice on that batch (for each view) using flipping and rotations $\theta \in \{45°, 135°, 225°, 315°\}$. The data augmentation strategy did not deform the medical information and helps in learning more efficient embedding. Then, all the inputs are propagated through the encoder block (i.e., the transformer encoder) to get the embeddings z_{emb}. The supervised contrastive loss is computed on these outputs embeddings as follows:

$$\mathcal{L}_{out} = \sum_{i \in I} \frac{-1}{|P(i)|} \sum_{p \in P(i)} \log \frac{\exp\left(z_{emb}^{(i)} \cdot z_{emb}^{(p)}/\tau\right)}{\sum_{a \in A(i)} \exp\left(z_{emb}^{(i)} \cdot z_{emb}^{(a)}/\tau\right)} \tag{3}$$

Here, the $\cdot$ symbol denotes the inner (dot) product, $\tau \leq 1 \in \mathcal{R}^+$ is a scalar temperature parameter. $i \in I \equiv \{1 \ldots 2N\}$ are the indexes of the augmented data and $A(i) \equiv I \backslash \{i\}$ is all the samples beside i which is the *anchor*. $P(i) \equiv \{p \in A(i) : y_p = y_i\}$ is the set of all the positive samples of label y_p distinct from i of label y_i and $|P(i)|$ is its cardinally. The embedding learning is performed by minimizing $\mathcal{L}_{out}$, using n iterations.

sMCI vs. pMCI Prediction. The contrastive learning strategy could help in building a disease-related discriminating signature by integrating the complementary of the three projections in the embedding learning step. In a second stage, we freeze the trained encoder (transformer) for each view and we train only the MLP classifier on the z_{emb}. The training is done by minimizing the binary cross-entropy loss using the same number of epochs (i.e., n iterations).

3   Experiments and Results

3.1   Dataset Selection and Pre-processing

Data Samples Selection. In this work, we select our ^{18}F-FDG data from the publicly available Alzheimer's Disease Neuroimaging Initiative (ADNI) database [23]. As the main objective is to predict the MCI conversion to AD, we choose subjects diagnosed as MCI at the baseline, (1) then progress and stay with AD for pMCI and (2) stay in the MCI stage or even revert to Normal Control (NC) for sMCI. We collect a cohort of subjects for both stages (i.e., sMCI and pMCI), where we select only the original images without any pre-processing. Finally, the obtained data are checked manually to remove the images that fail in the pre-processing step (described in the next paragraph). The dataset includes 50 ^{18}F-FDG images per class having a demographic characteristics listed in Table 1, where MMSE is the Mini-Mental State Examination.

Table 1. Subject's demographic information.

Characteristics	# of Subjects	Male/Female	Age	MMSE
sMCI	50	21/29	71.44 ± 6.69	28.47 ± 1.24
pMCI	50	32/18	72.65 ± 4.75	27.11 ± 1.64

Data Pre-processing Data are pre-processed using the SPM12 [24] software. First, spatial normalization is done based on the template of the Montreal Neurological Institute (MNI) to put the images in the same standardized space of $91 \times 109 \times 91$ with a voxel size of $2 \times 2 \times 2\,mm^3$. Second, images are smoothed using a Gaussian filter of $8\,mm$ Full Width at Half-Maximum (FWHM).

Technically, the transformer encoder architecture requires a divisible resolution to build the LSA and GSA [20] (i.e., $H\%k_1 = 0$ and $W\%k_2 = 0$, where $H = \{91, 109\}$ and $W = \{91, 109\}$ depending on the image view). A slice selection step is mandatory. Hence, in order to improve the image content quality and to respond to the transform's input resolution requirement, we removed the first and the last α_v brain slices for each view v. These α_v values are chosen by checking the intensity's histogram of slices for each view of all the samples [25]. We hypothesize that slices with small content/lower intensity values are not pertinent for diagnosis. By browsing the slices from the two extremities and automatically checking the pixels intensity distribution, we remove slices (only the first and the last slices) in which we found 75% pixels with an intensity I lower than 150, with $I \in [0 \ldots 255]$. At the end, we obtain $\alpha_{axial} = \alpha_{sagittal} = 7$ and $\alpha_{coronal} = 15$, where we get a volume of $77 \times 79 \times 77$ per sample. We add the last removed $3, 1$ and 3 slices for the axial, sagittal and coronal views respectively to get a divisible size volume $80 \times 80 \times 80$.

3.2   Network Training Parameters and Implementation Details

For each view, the transformer encoder includes two stages (green color in Fig. 1) with a variable resolution to better tackle our dense prediction. The first stage has a resolution of $\frac{H}{2} \times \frac{W}{2}$ and a sub-windows of size (8×8) (i.e., $\frac{H}{k_1} = \frac{W}{k_2} = 8$), while for the remaining we fix the sub-windows size to (5×5) with a feature map of size $\frac{H}{4} \times \frac{W}{4}$. More additionally, the number of channels is 64 for both stages. Thus, the output vector of each view has a size of $D_p = 64$, which gives a multi-view embedding representation of size $z_{emb} = 64 \times 3 = 192$. Then, supervised contrastive loss is used to minimize the distance between the embedding of the augmentation-based sample and any sample that belongs to the same class. We trained our encoder blocks for $n = 150$ epochs with a batch size of 4 using Adam as an optimizer with $\beta_1 = 0.9$ and $\beta_2 = 0.999$. The initial learning rate is set to $2e - 3$ and decayed to $3e - 5$ within 150 iterations. Afterward, we train an MLP to build on the top of the encoder's frozen blocks, including 03 FC layers of 32, 16, and 02 neurons to make the predictions. The latter are trained for the same number of iterations (i.e., $n = 150$) with the same hyper-parameters as previously, except for the learning rate which is fixed to $1e - 3$. Finally, due to the limited number of samples, our model is validated on a fixed test set. Thus, we evaluate MISS-Net on different data splits (cross-validation) using 05 fold to test its generalization ability. Note that all the chosen parameters are based on the best performances. We implement the proposed framework using PyTorch 1.9 on a single $32G$ Tesla $V100$ GPU.

3.3   Results and Evaluation

Performance of Single View The proposed model architecture is built along three views to make a prediction between (sMCI vs. pMCI) and the final result is given by taking into consideration all the views jointly. To showcase the performance and validate the efficiency of the proposed combination compared to each view separately in prediction, we build a separate model based only on the axial, sagittal, or coronal view using the same hyper-parameters. In Fig. 2, we report the results in terms of accuracy (ACC), sensitivity (SEN), specificity (SPEC), and the area under the curve (AUC) for each view (namely axial, sagittal and coronal) and the concatenation of them. It can be seen from Fig. 2, that the axial view reports the best performances compared to the remaining views, especially in detecting the pMCI stage (i.e., specificity) with an average precision of 83.57%. Moreover, our MISS-Net model which uses the multi-view information improves the diagnostic accuracy by $\approx 2\%$.

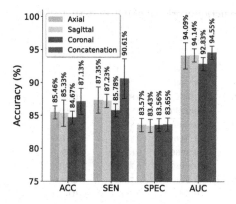 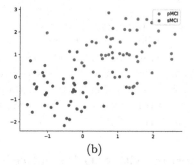

Fig. 2. Performance of each view and the concatenation of them for sMCI vs. pMCI(%).

Fig. 3. Results of the ablation studies of our MISS-Net for sMCI vs. pMCI(%).

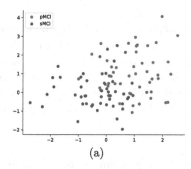

Fig. 4. Feature visualization via t-SNE of the Multi-view embedding representation. (a) without contrastive learning. (b) with contrastive learning.

Ablation Study. In order to study the effect of the 2D depth-wise convolution layer and the contrastive learning process in learning the multi-view embedding, we conduct two independent sets of experiments. First, we replace the 2D depth-wise convolution layer with a GAP layer and we train the network following the same training steps as the proposed method. Figure 3 presents the obtained classification results for both layers. We can see, that the 2D depth-wise convolution layer improves the prediction diagnosis with ≈5% in terms of accuracy, especially in detecting the pMCI stages compared to the use of the GAP layer, which proves that pertinent information in medical images are localized. Second, we omit the contrastive learning step and we train directly the model using only the binary cross-entropy loss function while keeping the same hyper-parameters on the same architecture. Figure 3 represents the classification results with and without SCL. We note that the contrastive learning step boosts the accuracy and the AUC metrics by respectively 5.57% and 5.63%. Furthermore, the SCL step boosts the sensitivity with an average precision of 90.61%, which raises the

Table 2. Results compared to SOTA prediction works of sMCI vs. pMCI (%).

Method	Modality	Data	ACC	SEN	SPEC	BAC	AUC
[7]2020	fMRI	44/38	0.7805	0.7368	0.8182	0.7775	0.8571
	DTI		0.5366	0.5789	0.5000	0.5390	0.5260
[8]2021	fMRI	44/38	0.7926	0.8421	0.7500	0.7960	0.9067
	DTI		0.8292	**0.9473**	0.7272	0.8373	0.9414
[4]2022	MRI	145/104	0.8330	0.7270	**0.9230**	0.8250	0.8880
[5]2021	MRI	232/172	0.8210	0.8120	0.8090	0.8105	0.9200
[6]2022	MRI	296/302	0.8300	0.9000	0.7600	0.8300	0.8700
[13]2020	PET+MRI	297/196	0.8333	08235	**0.8966**	0.8600	0.8947
[14]2021	PET+MRI	59/55	0.7870	0.7730	0.8000	0.7865	0.7756
[11]2020	PET+MRI	273/187	0.7387	0.9055	0.4952	0.7003	0.7000
	PET		0.6496	0.7817	0.4440	0.6128	0.6300
[9]2022	PET	290/147	0.8409	0.8235	**0.9000**	0.8617	0.8889
[12]2020	PET	360/166	0.8305	0.7576	**0.8750**	0.8163	0.8680
MISS-Net	PET	50/50	**0.8713 ±0.02**	0.9061 ±0.03	0.8365 ±0.01	**0.8713 ±0.02**	**0.9455 ±0.01**

correctly detected samples of sMCI stage, making the model more adequate for the early prediction of AD conversion. Figure 4, represents the learned feature (multi-view embedding representation z_{emb}) visualization with and without the SCL step. Here, we use the t-distributed Stochastic Neighbor Embedding (t-SNE) technique [26] for features visualization. We can conclude that the SCL step improves the embedding representation quality by optimally exploiting the complementarity of the three views.

Comparison with SOTA Approaches. We also compare our method with several recent SOTA works aiming to predict the MCI conversion including different modalities. We add the balance accuracy (BAC) as a metric to make a fair comparison since the data are not balanced for the SOTA works. From Table 2, our method outperforms those based on ^{18}F-FDG imaging data [9,11,12]. Specifically, we surpass them with more than 3% in terms of accuracy and $\approx 1\%$ in terms of (BAC). In addition, compared to the works that used MRI data [4–6], fMRI and DTI [7,8] our method also achieves an improvement in most metrics. More additionally, even fusionning PET and MRI data to get complementary information [11,13,14], the MISS-Net has dominant performance compared to them. Thanks to the multi-view embedding representation which helps to get such effectiveness.

4   Conclusion

We propose a novel framework for predicting the transitional phases of AD with FDG-PET. MISS-Net captures the local and inter slices information for each view and takes into consideration all the views jointly to make a prediction. Our method with supervised contrastive learning achieves promising prediction performance of sMCI vs. pMCI with small data. Obtained results outperform recent state-of-the-art results with FDG-PET as well as with multi-modal data. In future work, we aim to extend the proposed work to deal with multi-modal data and to evaluate it on others diagnosis problems that use 3D medical imaging.

References

1. Mayeda, E.R.: Inequalities in dementia incidence between six racial and ethnic groups over 14 years. Alzheimer's & Dementia **12**(3), 216–224 (2016)
2. López, C., Sánchez, J.L., Martín, J.: The effect of cognitive stimulation on the progression of cognitive impairment in subjects with alzheimer's disease. Appl. Neuropsychol.: Adult **29** 1–10 (2020)
3. Lisowska, A., et al.: Joint pairing and structured mapping of convolutional brain morphological multiplexes for early dementia diagnosis. Brain Connectivity **9**(1), 22–36 (2019)
4. Zheng, G., et al: A transformer-based multi-features fusion model for prediction of conversion in mild cognitive impairment. Methods **204**, 241–248 (2022)
5. Zhang, X., Han, L., Zhu, W., Sun, L., Zhang, D.: An explainable 3D residual self-attention deep neural network for joint atrophy localization and Alzheimer's disease diagnosis using structural MRI. IEEE J. Biomed. Health Inf. (2021)
6. Zhang, F., et al: A single model deep learning approach for Alzheimer's disease diagnosis. Neuroscience **491**, 200–214 (2022)
7. Lei, B., et al: Self-calibrated brain network estimation and joint non-convex multi-task learning for identification of early Alzheimer's disease. Med. Image Anal. **61**, 101652 (2020)
8. Song, X., et al: Graph convolution network with similarity awareness and adaptive calibration for disease-induced deterioration prediction. Med. Image Anal. **69**, 101947 (2021)
9. Cui, W., et al: BMNet: a new region-based metric learning method for early Alzheimer's disease identification with FDG-PET images. Front. Neurosci. **16** (2022)
10. Rubinski, A., Franzmeier, N., Neitzel, J., Ewers, M.: FDG-PET hypermetabolism is associated with higher tau-PET in mild cognitive impairment at low amyloid-PET levels. Alzheimer's research & therapy **12**(1), 1–12 (2020). https://doi.org/10.1186/s13195-020-00702-6
11. Hao, X., et al: Multi-modal neuroimaging feature selection with consistent metric constraint for diagnosis of Alzheimer's disease. Med. Image Anal. **60**, 101625 (2020)
12. Pan, X., et al.: Multi-view separable pyramid network for AD prediction at MCI stage by 18 F-FDG brain PET imaging. IEEE Trans. Med. Imaging **40**(1), 81–92 (2020)
13. Fang, C., et al.: Gaussian discriminative component analysis for early detection of Alzheimer's disease: a supervised dimensionality reduction algorithm. J. Neurosci. Methods **344**, 108856 (2020)
14. Shen, H.T., et al: Heterogeneous data fusion for predicting mild cognitive impairment conversion. Inf. Fusion **66**, 54–63 (2021)
15. Ben-Ahmed, O., Lecellier, F., Paccalin, M., Fernandez-Maloigne, C.: Multi-view visual saliency-based MRI classification for Alzheimer's disease diagnosis. In: 2017 Seventh International Conference on Image Processing Theory, Tools and Applications (IPTA), pp. 1–6. IEEE (2017)

16. Li, F., Liu, M., Initiative, A.D.N., et al.: A hybrid convolutional and recurrent neural network for hippocampus analysis in Alzheimer's disease. J. Neurosci. Methods **323**, 108–118 (2019)
17. Khan, S., Naseer, M., Hayat, M., Zamir, S.W., Khan, F.S., Shah, M.: Transformers in vision: a survey. ACM Comput. Surv. (CSUR) (2021)
18. Wyburd, M.K., Dinsdale, N.K., Namburete, A.I.L., Jenkinson, M.: TEDS-Net: enforcing diffeomorphisms in spatial transformers to guarantee topology preservation in segmentations. In: de Bruijne, M., et al. (eds.) MICCAI 2021. LNCS, vol. 12901, pp. 250–260. Springer, Cham (2021). https://doi.org/10.1007/978-3-030-87193-2_24
19. Yuan, L., ET AL: Tokens-to-token ViT: training vision transformers from scratch on imagenet. In: Proceedings of the IEEE/CVF International Conference on Computer Vision, pp. 558–567 (2021)
20. Chu, X., et al: Twins: revisiting the design of spatial attention in vision transformers. In: Advances in Neural Information Processing Systems, vol. 34 (2021)
21. Khosla, P., et al.: Supervised contrastive learning. Adv. Neural. Inf. Process. Syst. **33**, 18661–18673 (2020)
22. Rahimzadeh, M., Parvin, S., Safi, E., Mohammadi, M.R.: Wise-SrNet: a novel architecture for enhancing image classification by learning spatial resolution of feature maps. arXiv preprint arXiv:2104.12294 (2021)
23. Jack Jr, C.R., et al: The Alzheimer's disease neuroimaging initiative (ADNI): MRI methods. J. Magn. Reson. Imaging: Official J. Int. Soc. Magn. Reson. Med. **27**(4), 685–691 (2008)
24. Penny, W.D., Friston, K.J., Ashburner, J.T., Kiebel, S.J., Nichols, T.E.: Statistical Parametric Mapping: The Analysis of Functional Brain Images. Elsevier, Amsterdam (2011)
25. Shakarami, A., Tarrah, H., Mahdavi-Hormat, A.: A cad system for diagnosing alzheimer's disease using 2d slices and an improved alexnet-svm method. Optik **212**, 164237 (2020)
26. Van der Maaten, L., Hinton, G.: Visualizing data using t-SNE. J. Mach. Learn. Res. **9**(11) (2008)

TransDeepLab: Convolution-Free Transformer-Based DeepLab v3+ for Medical Image Segmentation

Reza Azad[1]([✉]), Moein Heidari[2], Moein Shariatnia[3],
Ehsan Khodapanah Aghdam[4], Sanaz Karimijafarbigloo[1], Ehsan Adeli[5],
and Dorit Merhof[1,6]

[1] Institute of Imaging and Computer Vision, RWTH Aachen University,
Aachen, Germany
{azad,dorit.merhof}@lfb.rwth-aachen.de
[2] School of Electrical Engineering, Iran University of Science and Technology,
Tehran, Iran
[3] School of Medicine, Tehran University of Medical Sciences, Tehran, Iran
[4] Department of Electrical Engineering, Shahid Beheshti University, Tehran, Iran
[5] Stanford University, Stanford, USA
[6] Fraunhofer Institute for Digital Medicine MEVIS, Bremen, Germany

Abstract. Convolutional neural networks (CNNs) have been the de facto standard in a diverse set of computer vision tasks for many years. Especially, deep neural networks based on seminal architectures such as U-shaped model with skip-connections or atrous convolution with pyramid pooling have been tailored to a wide range of medical image analysis tasks. The main advantage of such architectures is that they are prone to detaining versatile local features. However, as a general consensus, CNNs fail to capture long-range dependencies and spatial correlations due to the intrinsic property of confined receptive field size of convolution operations. Alternatively, Transformer, profiting from global information modeling that stems from the self-attention mechanism, has recently attained remarkable performance in natural language processing and computer vision. Nevertheless, previous studies prove that both local and global features are critical for a deep model in dense prediction, such as segmenting complicated structures with disparate shapes and configurations. This paper proposes TransDeepLab, a novel DeepLab-like pure Transformer for medical image segmentation. Specifically, we exploit hierarchical Swin-Transformer with shifted windows to extend the DeepLabv3 and model the Atrous Spatial Pyramid Pooling (ASPP) module. A thorough search of the relevant literature yielded that we are the first to model the seminal DeepLab model with a pure Transformer-based model. Extensive experiments on various medical image segmentation tasks verify that our approach performs superior or on par with most contemporary works on an amalgamation of Vision Transformer and CNN-based methods, along with a significant reduction of model complexity. The codes and trained models are publicly available at github.

Keywords: Deep learning · Transformer · DeepLab · Medical image segmentation

© The Author(s), under exclusive license to Springer Nature Switzerland AG 2022
I. Rekik et al. (Eds.): PRIME 2022, LNCS 13564, pp. 91–102, 2022.
https://doi.org/10.1007/978-3-031-16919-9_9

1   Introduction

Automatic and accurate medical image segmentation, which consists of automated delineation of anatomical structures and other regions of interest (ROIs), plays an integral role in the assessment of computer-aided diagnosis (CAD) [4,16]. As a flagship of deep learning, convolutional neural networks (CNNs) have scattered existing contributions in various medical image segmentation tasks for many years [21,24]. Among diverse CNN variants, the widely acknowledged symmetric Encoder-Decoder architecture nomenclature as U-Net [24] has demonstrated eminent segmentation potential. It mainly consists of a series of continuous convolutional and down-sampling layers to capture contextual semantic information through the contracting path. Then in the decoder, using lateral connections from the encoder, the coarse-grained deep features, and fine-grained shallow feature maps are up-sampled to generate a precise segmentation map. Following this technical route, many U-Net variants such as U-Net++ [30] and Res-UNet [29] have emerged to improve the segmentation performance. A paramount caveat of such architectures is the gap of restricted receptive field size, which makes the deep model unable to capture sufficient contextual information, causing the segmentation to fail in complicated areas such as boundaries. To mitigate this problem, the notable DeepLab [5] work was exhibited, triggering broad interest in the image segmentation era. The authors established remarkable contributions which experimentally proved to have substantial practical merit. First, they introduced a novel convolution operation with up-sampled filters called 'Atrous Convolution', which allows enlarging the field of view of filters to absorb larger contexts without imposing the burden of the high amount of computation or increasing number of parameters. Second, to incorporate smoothness terms enabling the network to capture fine details, they exploit a fully connected Conditional Random Field (CRF) to refine the segmentation results. Following the pioneering work, extended versions were employed to accommodate further performance boosts. As such, the DeepLabv2 [6] was proposed to conquer the challenge of the existence of objects at multiple scales. To this end, they propose the atrous spatial pyramid pooling (ASPP) module to segment objects at multiple scales robustly. ASPP probes a feature map with multiple atrous convolutions with different sampling rates to obtain multi-scale representation information. Afterward, the DeepLabv3 [7] designed an Encoder-Decoder architecture with atrous convolution to attain sharper object boundaries, where they utilized depth-wise separable convolution to increase computational efficiency. Ultimately, Chen et al. [8] proposed the DeepLabv3+ that extends DeepLabv3 by adding a simple yet effective decoder module to facilitate the segmentation performance. Despite all the efforts, the shortcomings of CNNs are also very prominent as they inevitably have constraints in learning long-range dependency and spatial correlations due to their inductive bias of locality and weight sharing [28] that results in sub-optimal segmentation of complex structures. Recently, the novel architecture Transformer [26] has sparked discussions in computer vision era [11,12] due to its elegant design and existence of attention mechanism. Indeed, it has been witnessed as capable of learning long-term features and felicitously modeling global information. The pioneering Vision Transformer (ViT) [11] was the major step toward adapting Transformers for vision tasks which accomplished satisfactory results in image classification. It mainly proposed to split the input image into patches and consider them as the source of information for the Transformer module. Despite being feasibly designed, the drawbacks of this scenario are noticeable and profound [3]. First, Transformers impose a quadratic computational load, making it intolerable for dense prediction with high-resolution image tasks. Moreover, despite being a good design choice for capturing explicit global context and long-range relations, Transformers are weak in capturing low-level pixel information, which is indisputably crucial in developing accurate segmentation. Thus, to circumvent the high memory demand in Transformers, the Swin-Transformer [19] proposed a hierarchical ViT with local computing of self-attention with non-overlapping windows, which achieved a linear complexity as opposed to ViT. Recently, faced with the dilemma between efficient CNNs and powerful ViT, crossovers between the two areas have emerged where most try to model a U-Net-like architecture with Transformers. Examples of such are Trans-UNet [4], Swin-UNet [3], and DS-TransUNet [17]. Inspired by the breakthrough performance of DeepLab models with attention mechanism in segmentation tasks [2], in this paper, we propose TransDeepLab, a DeepLab-like pure Transformer for medical image segmentation. Akin to the recently proposed Swin-UNet that models a U-Net structure with a Transformer module, we aim to imitate the seminal DeepLab with Swin-Transformer. The intuition behind our choice is that we intend to facilitate the efficient deployment of Swin-Transformer to restrain the hinder of computational demand of ViT. Moreover, applying the Swin-Transformer module with multiple window sizes can make it a lightweight yet suitable design choice for multi-scale feature fusion, which is a particularly critical equipment in segmentation tasks. In particular, we aim to substitute the ASPP module of the DeepLabv3+ model with the aforementioned hierarchical design. All these lead us to the fact that the proposed TransDeepLab can be the optimal design that is able to efficiently compensate for the mediocre design flaws of DeepLab. The proposed method acquires a significant parameter decrease compared to the cohort study. We will elaborate on the details of our proposal by pinpointing the scope and contributions of this paper in Sect. 2. Our contributions are as follows: (1) By incorporating the advantages of hierarchical Swin-Transformer into the encoder, decoder, and ASPP module of DeepLab, the proposed TransDeepLab can effectively capture long-range and multi-scale representation. (2) The cross-contextual attention to adaptively fuse multi-scale representation. (3) To the best of our knowledge, this work is the first attempt to combine the Swin-Transformer with DeepLab architecture for medical image segmentation.

2   Proposed Method

We propose the TransDeepLab model (Fig. 1), a pure Transformer-based DeepLabv3+ architecture, for medical image segmentation. The network utilizes the strength of the Swin-Transformer block [19] to build hierarchical representation. Following the original architecture of the DeepLab model, we utilize a series of Swin-Transformer blocks to encode the input image into a high-representational space. More specifically, the encoder module splits the input medical image into non-overlapping patches of size 4×4, resulting in $4 \times 4 \times 3 = 48$ as the feature dimension of each patch (signified as C) and applies the Swin-Transformer block to encode both local semantic and long-range contextual representation. To model Atrous Spatial Pyramid Pooling (ASPP), a pyramid of Swin-Transformer blocks with varying window sizes is designed. The main idea of the Swin pyramid is to capture multi-scale information by exploiting different window sizes. The obtained multi-scale contextual representation is then fused into the decoder module using a Cross-Contextual attention mechanism. The attention block applies two-level attention (e.g., channel and spatial attention) on the tokens (derived from each level of the pyramid) to formulate the multi-scale interaction. Finally, in the decoding path, the extracted multi-scale features are first bilinearly upsampled and then concatenated with the low-level features from the encoder to refine the feature representation. The details of each component of the proposed network will be elaborated on in the subsequent sections.

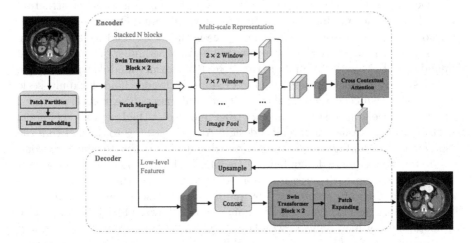

Fig. 1. The architecture of TransDeepLab, which extends the encoder-decoder structure of DeepLabv3+. Encoder and decoder are all constructed based on Swin-Transformer blocks.

2.1 Swin-Transformer Block

Based on the fact that typical vision Transformers implement the self-attention on a global receptive field, they endure quadratic computational complexity to the number of tokens. To mitigate this, the Swin-Transformer has been devised whose key design characteristic is its shifting of the window partitioner between consecutive self-attention layers constructed by designing a module based on shifted windows as a surrogate for the multi-head self-attention (MSA) module in a Transformer block. Thus, a Swin-Transformer block comprises a shifted window-based MSA module, LayerNorm (LN) layer, a two-layer MLP, and GELU nonlinearity. The window-based multi-head self-attention (W-MSA) module and the shifted window-based multi-head self-attention (SW-MSA) module are applied in the Transformer blocks in tandem. With such shifted window partitioning scheme, consecutive Swin-Transformer blocks can be formulated as:

$$\hat{z}^l = \text{W-MSA}\left(\text{LN}\left(z^{l-1}\right)\right) + z^{l-1}$$
$$z^l = \text{MLP}\left(\text{LN}\left(\hat{z}^l\right)\right) + \hat{z}^l$$
$$\hat{z}^{l+1} = \text{SW-MSA}\left(\text{LN}\left(z^l\right)\right) + z^l$$
$$z^{l+1} = \text{MLP}\left(\text{LN}\left(\hat{z}^{l+1}\right)\right) + \hat{z}^{l+1}, \tag{1}$$

where $\hat{z}^l$ and z^l denote the outputs of W-MSA and SW-MSA module of the lth block, respectively. Following [13,14] the self-attention is computed according to:

$$\text{Attention}(Q, K, V) = \text{SoftMax}\left(\frac{QK^T}{\sqrt{d}} + B\right)V, \tag{2}$$

where $Q, K, V \in \mathbb{R}^{M^2 \times d}$ are the query, key and value matrices; d is the query/key dimension, and M^2 is the number of patches in a window and B indicates the bias matrix whose values are acquired from $\hat{B} \in \mathbb{R}^{(2M-1) \times (2M+1)}$.

2.2 Encoder

Inspired by the low computation burden of the Swin-Transformer [19] block (contrary to the quadratic computation of the Vision Transformer [11]) and its strength in modeling long-range contextual dependency (unlike regular CNNs), we model our encoder model using the stacked Swin-Transformer module. Our TransDeepLab encoder first feeds the C-dimensional tokenized input with the resolution of $\frac{H}{4} \times \frac{W}{4}$ into two successive Swin-Transformer blocks to produce a hierarchical representation while keeping the resolution unchanged. Then, it applies a series of stacked Swin-Transformer blocks to gradually reduce the spatial dimension (similar to a CNN encoder) of the feature map and increase the feature dimension. The resulted mid-level representation is then fed to the Swin Spatial Pyramid Pooling (SSPP) block to capture multi-scale representation.

2.3 Swin Spatial Pyramid Pooling

The spatial resolution of the deep features extracted by the encoder module is considerably decreased due to the stacked Swin-Transformer blocks followed by the patch merging layers (similar to the consecutive down-sampling operation in a CNN encoder). Thus, to compensate for the spatial representation and produce a multi-scale representation, the DeepLab model utilizes an ASPP module, which replaces the pooling operation with atrous convolutions [6]. Concretely, DeepLab aims to form a pyramid representation by applying parallel convolution operations with multiple atrous rates. To model such an operation in a pure Transformer fashion, we create a Swin Spatial Pyramid Pooling (SSPP) block with varying window sizes to capture multi-scale representation. In our design, the smaller window size aims to capture local information while the larger windows are included to extract global information. The resulted multi-scale representation is then fed to a cross-contextual attention module to fuse and capture a generic representation in a non-linear technique.

2.4 Cross-Contexual Attention

In the DeepLabv3+ model, the feature vectors resulting from each level of the pyramid are concatenated and fed to the depthwise separable convolution to perform the fusion operation. This operation performs the convolution for each channel separately and is thus unable to model the channel-wise dependency among pyramid levels. In our design, to model the multi-scale interaction and fuse the pyramid features, we propose a cross-attention module. To this end, we assume that each level of the pyramid ($\mathbf{z}_m^{P \times C}$, P and C indicate the number of token and embedding dimension, respectively) represents the object of interest in different scales, thus, by concatenating all these features in a new dimension we create a multi-scale representation $\mathbf{z}_{all}^{P \times MC} = [\mathbf{z}_1 \| \mathbf{z}_2 ... \| \mathbf{z}_M]$, where $\|$ shows the concatenation operation. Next, to adaptively emphasize the contribution of each feature map and surpass the less discriminative features, we propose a scale attention module. Our attention module takes into account the global representation of each channel and applies the MLP layer to produce the scaling coefficients (w_{scale}) to selectively scale the channel representation among pyramid levels:

$$w_{\text{scale}} = \sigma \left(\mathbf{W}_2 \delta \left(\mathbf{W}_1 GAP_{z_{all}} \right) \right), z'_{all} = w_{\text{scale}} \cdot z_{all} \tag{3}$$

where W_1 and W_2 indicate the learnable MLP parameters and δ and σ show the ReLU and Sigmoid activations, and the GAP indicates the global average pooling. In the second attention level, we learn scaling parameters to highlight the informative tokens. To do so, we apply the same strategy:

$$w_{\text{tokens}} = \sigma \left(\mathbf{W}_3 \delta \left(\mathbf{W}_4 GAP_{z'_{all}} \right) \right), z''_{all} = w_{\text{tokens}} \cdot z'_{all} \tag{4}$$

2.5 Decoder

In the decoder, the acquired features (z''_{all}) corresponding to the attention module are first passed through the Swin-Transformer block with a patch-expanding operation to be upsampled by a factor of 4 and then concatenated with the low-level features. The scheme of concatenating the shallow features and the deep features together helps in reducing the loss of spatial details by the virtue of down-sampling layers. Finally, a series of cascaded Swin-Transformer blocks with path-expanding operations are applied to reach the full resolution of $H \times W$.

3   Experiments

3.1   Datasets

Synapse Multi-organ Segmentation. This dataset includes 30 abdominal CT scans with 3779 axial contrast-enhanced clinical images in total. Each CT posess volumes in range of 85–198 slices of 512×512 pixels, with a voxel spatial resolution of $([0.54-0.54] \times [0.98-0.98] \times [2.5-5.0])$ mm^3. We follow [4] in data partitioning and reporting the quantitative results.

Skin Lesion Segmentation. Our analysis for skin lesion segmentation was based on the ISIC 2017 [10], ISIC 2018 [9] and PH^2 [20] datasets. The ISIC datasets were collected by the International Skin Imaging Collaboration (ISIC) as a large-scale dataset of dermoscopy images along with their corresponding ground truth annotations. Furthermore, we exploit the PH^2 dataset and pursue the experimental setting used in [18] for splitting the data.

3.2   Implementation Details

Turning to implementation aspects, the proposed TransDeepLab is implemented based on the PyTorch library and trained on a single Nvidia RTX 3090 GPU. We train all of our models upstream using the SGD solver in 200 epochs using a batch size of 24. The softmax Dice loss and cross-entropy loss are employed as objective functions, and L2 Norm is also adopted for model regularization. Rotation and flipping techniques are used as data augmentation methods with the aim of diversifying the training set and obtaining an unbiased training strategy. An initial learning rate of 0.05 with an adaptive decay value is used to train the model. In addition, we use the pre-trained weights on ImageNet for the Swin-Transformer module to initialize their parameters. We embraced a task-specific approach to the scope of evaluation metrics aiming to trigger a fair comparison with respect to each experiment. These metrics include: 1) Dice Similarity Score, 2) Hausdorff Distance, 3) Sensitivity and Specificity, 4) Accuracy.

3.3   Evaluation Results

In this section, we conduct experiments to evaluate our proposed model and compare it with SOTA methods on the two aforementioned medical image segmentation tasks. Notably, we assess TransDeepLab in two distinct ways in our experiments, i.e., quantitative analysis and along with selected visualization results.

Results of Synapse Multi-organ Segmentation. Experiment on Synapse multi-organ CT dataset (Table 1) exhibit the effectiveness and generalization potential of our method, achieving the best performance with segmentation accuracy of 80.16% (DSC ↑) and 21.25% (HD ↓). Indicatively, we attain the best performance on Kidney(L) with 84.08%, Pancreas with 61.19%, and Stomach with 78.40% dice score. A sample of segmentation results of synapse multi-organ is presented in Fig. 2. The organ instances are all detected and classified correctly with slight variations in segmentation contours. Compared to the CNN-based DeepLab model, our approach produces better segmentation results. All in all, these results support our ultimate motivation of modeling both local and global contextual representation with a pure Transformer-based method along with providing a significant performance boost in the field of segmentation, where maintaining rich semantic information is crucial.

Table 1. Comparison results of the proposed method on the Synapse dataset.

Methods	DSC ↑	HD ↓	Aorta	Gallbladder	Kidney(L)	Kidney(R)	Liver	Pancreas	Spleen	Stomach
V-Net [21]	68.81	–	75.34	51.87	77.10	**80.75**	87.84	40.05	80.56	56.98
R50 U-Net [4]	74.68	36.87	87.74	63.66	80.60	78.19	93.74	56.90	85.87	74.16
U-Net [24]	76.85	39.70	89.07	**69.72**	77.77	68.60	93.43	53.98	86.67	75.58
R50 Att-UNet [4]	75.57	36.97	55.92	63.91	79.20	72.71	93.56	49.37	87.19	74.95
Att-UNet [22]	77.77	36.02	**89.55**	68.88	77.98	71.11	93.57	58.04	87.30	75.75
R50 ViT [4]	71.29	32.87	73.73	55.13	75.80	72.20	91.51	45.99	81.99	73.95
TransUnet [4]	77.48	31.69	87.23	63.13	81.87	77.02	94.08	55.86	85.08	75.62
SwinUnet [3]	79.13	21.55	85.47	66.53	83.28	79.61	**94.29**	56.58	**90.66**	76.60
DeepLabv3+ (CNN) [6]	77.63	39.95	88.04	66.51	82.76	74.21	91.23	58.32	87.43	73.53
Proposed method	**80.16**	**21.25**	86.04	69.16	**84.08**	79.88	93.53	**61.19**	89.00	**78.40**

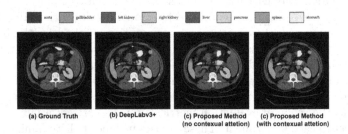

(a) Ground Truth   (b) DeepLabv3+   (c) Proposed Method (no contexual attetion)   (c) Proposed Method (with contexual attetion)

Fig. 2. Visualization result of the proposed method on the Synapse dataset.

Results of Skin Lesion Segmentation. The results are summarized in Table 2. Our TransDeepLab performs better than other competitors w.r.t. most of the evaluation metrics. We also show some samples of the skin lesion segmentation obtained by the suggested network in Fig. 3. It is evident from Fig. 3 that TransDeepLab exhibits higher boundary segmentation accuracy together with a performance boost in capturing the fine-grained details.

Table 2. Performance comparison of the proposed method against the SOTA approaches on skin lesion segmentation benchmarks.

Methods	ISIC 2017				ISIC 2018				PH2			
	DSC	SE	SP	ACC	DSC	SE	SP	ACC	DSC	SE	SP	ACC
U-Net [24]	0.8159	0.8172	0.9680	0.9164	0.8545	0.8800	0.9697	0.9404	0.8936	0.9125	0.9588	0.9233
Att U-Net [22]	0.8082	0.7998	0.9776	0.9145	0.8566	0.8674	0.9863	0.9376	0.9003	0.9205	0.9640	0.9276
DAGAN [15]	0.8425	0.8363	0.9716	0.9304	0.8807	0.9072	0.9588	0.9324	0.9201	0.8320	0.9640	0.9425
TransUNet [4]	0.8123	0.8263	0.9577	0.9207	0.8499	0.8578	0.9653	0.9452	0.8840	0.9063	0.9427	0.9200
MCGU-Net [1]	0.8927	0.8502	0.9855	0.9570	0.895	0.848	0.986	0.955	0.9263	0.8322	0.9714	0.9537
MedT [25]	0.8037	0.8064	0.9546	0.9090	0.8389	0.8252	0.9637	0.9358	0.9122	0.8472	0.9657	0.9416
FAT-Net [27]	0.8500	0.8392	0.9725	0.9326	0.8903	**0.9100**	0.9699	0.9578	0.9440	**0.9441**	0.9741	**0.9703**
TMU-Net [23]	0.9164	**0.9128**	0.9789	0.9660	0.9059	0.9038	0.9746	0.9603	0.9414	0.9395	0.9756	0.9647
Swin U-Net [3]	0.9183	0.9142	0.9798	0.9701	0.8946	0.9056	0.9798	0.9645	0.9449	0.9410	0.9564	0.9678
DeepLabv3+ (CNN) [6]	0.9162	0.8733	**0.9921**	0.9691	0.882	0.856	0.977	0.951	0.9202	0.8818	0.9832	0.9503
Proposed method	**0.9239**	0.8971	0.9886	**0.9705**	**0.9122**	0.8756	**0.9889**	**0.9654**	**0.9456**	0.9161	**0.9896**	0.9657

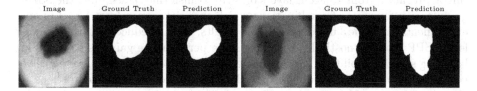

Image   Ground Truth   Prediction   Image   Ground Truth   Prediction

Fig. 3. Segmentation results of the proposed method on the skin lesion segmentation.

Model Complexity. Last but not least, we analyze the training parameters of the proposal, as heavy deep nets with small medical image datasets are usually prone to overfitting. TransDeepLab is essentially a lightweight model with only 21.14M parameters. Compared with Swin-UNet [3], the original DeepLab model [6], and Trans-UNet [4] which have 27.17M, 54.70M, and 105M parameters respectively, our lightweight TransDeepLab shows great superiority in terms of model complexity whilest being dominant in terms of evaluation metrics.

3.4 Ablation Study

CNN vs Transformer Encoder. The ablation experiment is conducted to explore the Transformer's replacement design. In particular, we employed the same decoder and SSPP module as our baseline, but replaced the encoder with a CNN backbone (e.g., ResNet-50) model (denoted as *CNN as Encoder* in Table 3). Judging from the results of Table 3, we perceive that a solitary CNN-based encoder yields a sub-optimal performance. Literally, the Transformer module indeed helps TransDeepLab to do segmentation to a certain degree.

Attention Strategy. Then, we compared the policy of fusing each level of the Swin-Transformer resulting in multi-scale representation. Concretely, we compare the proposed cross-attention module with a basic scale fusion method, concatenating the feature maps and applying a fully connected layer to fuse them (denoted as *Basic Scale Fusion* in Table 3). Judging from Table 3, we deduce that the cross-attention module confirms our intuition of capturing the interaction of feature levels in terms of informativeness of the tokens in different scales. Moreover, as for perceptual realism, we have provided sample segmentation results in Fig. 2 which indicate that by using the cross contextual attention mechanism we attain closer to the ground truth results, in line with the real situation. This visualization divulges the effect of a multi-scale Transformer module for long-range contextual dependency learning leading to precise localization abilities, especially in boundary areas, a substantial caveat in the image segmentation.

SSPP Influence. As discussed above, the SSPP module improves the representation ability of the model in context patterning by probing features at multiple scales to attain multi-scale information. We conduct an inquiry into the feature aggregation from adjacent layers of Swin-Transformer assembling the SSPP module with four sets of combinations which explicitly range from 1 to 4 in our experiments. In Table 3 by comparing the results, we can deduce that using a two-level SSPP module mostly leads to dice score performance gains as it assists in handling scale variability in medical image segmentation. Moreover, we perceive that a three-level SSPP module brings along a notable performance in terms of Hausdorff distance. However, to attain more efficiency, the resolution of the input image should be in compliance with the SSPP level, signifying that increasing the number of SSPP levels should follow a higher resolution image. The results also corroborate the propensity of Transformer in incorporating global context information into the model than its CNN counterpart. While one might speculate that thoroughly modeling a CNN-based network using Transformer would cause model complexity, it is worth mentioning that we aim to overcome this issue by exploiting the Swin-Transformer instead of a typical ViT.

Table 3. Ablation study on the impact of modifying modules inside the proposed method. We report our results using the Synapse dataset.

Setting	DSC ↑	HD ↓	Aorta	Gallbladder	Kidney(L)	Kidney(R)	Liver	Pancreas	Spleen	Stomach
CNN as encoder	75.89	28.87	85.03	65.17	80.18	76.38	90.49	57.29	85.68	69.93
Basic scale fusion	79.16	22.14	85.44	68.05	82.77	80.79	93.80	58.74	87.78	75.96
SSPP level 1	79.01	26.63	85.61	68.47	82.43	78.02	94.19	58.52	88.34	76.46
SSPP level 2	80.16	21.25	86.04	69.16	84.08	79.88	93.53	61.19	89.00	78.40
SSPP level 3	79.87	18.93	86.34	66.41	84.13	82.40	93.73	59.28	89.66	76.99
SSPP level 4	79.85	25.69	85.64	69.36	82.93	81.25	93.09	63.18	87.80	75.56

4   Conclusion

In this paper, we present TransDeepLab, a pure Transformer-based architecture for medical image segmentation. Specifically, we model the encoder-decoder DeepLabv3+ model and leverage the potential of Transformers by using the

Swin-Transformer as the fundamental component of the architecture. Showcased on a variety of medical image segmentation tasks, TransDeepLab has shown the potential to effectively build long-range dependencies and outperforms other SOTA Vision Transformers in our experiments.

References

1. Asadi-Aghbolaghi, M., Azad, R., Fathy, M., Escalera, S.: Multi-level context gating of embedded collective knowledge for medical image segmentation. arXiv preprint arXiv:2003.05056 (2020)
2. Azad, R., Asadi-Aghbolaghi, M., Fathy, M., Escalera, S.: Attention Deeplabv3+: multi-level context attention mechanism for skin lesion segmentation. In: Bartoli, A., Fusiello, A. (eds.) ECCV 2020. LNCS, vol. 12535, pp. 251–266. Springer, Cham (2020). https://doi.org/10.1007/978-3-030-66415-2_16
3. Cao, H., et al.: Swin-Unet: Unet-like pure transformer for medical image segmentation. arXiv preprint arXiv:2105.05537 (2021)
4. Chen, J., et al.: TransUNet: transformers make strong encoders for medical image segmentation. arXiv preprint arXiv:2102.04306 (2021)
5. Chen, L.C., Papandreou, G., Kokkinos, I., Murphy, K., Yuille, A.L.: Semantic image segmentation with deep convolutional nets and fully connected CRFs. arXiv preprint arXiv:1412.7062 (2014)
6. Chen, L.C., Papandreou, G., Kokkinos, I., Murphy, K., Yuille, A.L.: DeepLab: semantic image segmentation with deep convolutional nets, atrous convolution, and fully connected CRFs. IEEE Trans. Pattern Anal. Mach. Intell. 40(4), 834–848 (2017)
7. Chen, L.C., Papandreou, G., Schroff, F., Adam, H.: Rethinking atrous convolution for semantic image segmentation. arXiv preprint arXiv:1706.05587 (2017)
8. Chen, L.-C., Zhu, Y., Papandreou, G., Schroff, F., Adam, H.: Encoder-decoder with atrous separable convolution for semantic image segmentation. In: Ferrari, V., Hebert, M., Sminchisescu, C., Weiss, Y. (eds.) ECCV 2018. LNCS, vol. 11211, pp. 833–851. Springer, Cham (2018). https://doi.org/10.1007/978-3-030-01234-2_49
9. Codella, N., et al.: Skin lesion analysis toward melanoma detection 2018: a challenge hosted by the international skin imaging collaboration (ISIC). arXiv preprint arXiv:1902.03368 (2019)
10. Codella, N.C., et al.: Skin lesion analysis toward melanoma detection: a challenge at the 2017 international symposium on biomedical imaging (ISBI), hosted by the international skin imaging collaboration (ISIC). In: 2018 IEEE 15th International Symposium on Biomedical Imaging (ISBI 2018), pp. 168–172. IEEE (2018)
11. Dosovitskiy, A., et al.: An image is worth 16x16 words: transformers for image recognition at scale. arXiv preprint arXiv:2010.11929 (2020)
12. Hatamizadeh, A., et al.: UNETR: transformers for 3D medical image segmentation. In: Proceedings of the IEEE/CVF Winter Conference on Applications of Computer Vision, pp. 574–584 (2022)
13. Hu, H., Gu, J., Zhang, Z., Dai, J., Wei, Y.: Relation networks for object detection. In: Proceedings of the IEEE Conference on Computer Vision and Pattern Recognition, pp. 3588–3597 (2018)
14. Hu, H., Zhang, Z., Xie, Z., Lin, S.: Local relation networks for image recognition. In: Proceedings of the IEEE/CVF International Conference on Computer Vision, pp. 3464–3473 (2019)

15. Lei, B., et al.: Skin lesion segmentation via generative adversarial networks with dual discriminators. Med. Image Anal. **64**, 101716 (2020)
16. Li, S., Sui, X., Luo, X., Xu, X., Liu, Y., Goh, R.: Medical image segmentation using squeeze-and-expansion transformers. arXiv preprint arXiv:2105.09511 (2021)
17. Lin, A., Chen, B., Xu, J., Zhang, Z., Lu, G.: DS-TransUNet: dual swin transformer U-Net for medical image segmentation. arXiv preprint arXiv:2106.06716 (2021)
18. Liu, X., Hu, G., Ma, X., Kuang, H.: An enhanced neural network based on deep metric learning for skin lesion segmentation. In: 2019 Chinese Control and Decision Conference (CCDC), pp. 1633–1638. IEEE (2019)
19. Liu, Z., et al.: Swin transformer: hierarchical vision transformer using shifted windows. In: Proceedings of the IEEE/CVF International Conference on Computer Vision, pp. 10012–10022 (2021)
20. Mendonça, T., Ferreira, P.M., Marques, J.S., Marcal, A.R., Rozeira, J.: PH^2 - a dermoscopic image database for research and benchmarking. In: 2013 35th Annual International Conference of the IEEE Engineering in Medicine and Biology Society (EMBC), pp. 5437–5440. IEEE (2013)
21. Milletari, F., Navab, N., Ahmadi, S.A.: V-net: fully convolutional neural networks for volumetric medical image segmentation. In: 2016 Fourth International Conference on 3D Vision (3DV), pp. 565–571. IEEE (2016)
22. Oktay, O., et al.: Attention U-Net: learning where to look for the pancreas. arXiv preprint arXiv:1804.03999 (2018)
23. Reza, A., Moein, H., Yuli, W., Dorit, M.: Contextual attention network: transformer meets U-Net. arXiv preprint arXiv:2203.01932 (2022)
24. Ronneberger, O., Fischer, P., Brox, T.: U-Net: convolutional networks for biomedical image segmentation. In: Navab, N., Hornegger, J., Wells, W.M., Frangi, A.F. (eds.) MICCAI 2015. LNCS, vol. 9351, pp. 234–241. Springer, Cham (2015). https://doi.org/10.1007/978-3-319-24574-4_28
25. Valanarasu, J.M.J., Oza, P., Hacihaliloglu, I., Patel, V.M.: Medical transformer: gated axial-attention for medical image segmentation. In: de Bruijne, M., et al. (eds.) MICCAI 2021. LNCS, vol. 12901, pp. 36–46. Springer, Cham (2021). https://doi.org/10.1007/978-3-030-87193-2_4
26. Vaswani, A., et al.: Attention is all you need. In: Advances in Neural Information Processing Systems 30 (2017)
27. Wu, H., Chen, S., Chen, G., Wang, W., Lei, B., Wen, Z.: FAT-Net: feature adaptive transformers for automated skin lesion segmentation. Med. Image Anal. **76**, 102327 (2022)
28. Xie, Y., Zhang, J., Shen, C., Xia, Y.: CoTr: efficiently bridging CNN and transformer for 3D medical image segmentation. In: de Bruijne, M., et al. (eds.) MICCAI 2021. LNCS, vol. 12903, pp. 171–180. Springer, Cham (2021). https://doi.org/10.1007/978-3-030-87199-4_16
29. Zhang, Z., Liu, Q., Wang, Y.: Road extraction by deep residual U-Net. IEEE Geosci. Remote Sens. Lett. **15**(5), 749–753 (2018)
30. Zhou, Z., Rahman Siddiquee, M.M., Tajbakhsh, N., Liang, J.: UNet++: a nested U-Net architecture for medical image segmentation. In: Stoyanov, D., et al. (eds.) DLMIA/ML-CDS -2018. LNCS, vol. 11045, pp. 3–11. Springer, Cham (2018). https://doi.org/10.1007/978-3-030-00889-5_1

Opportunistic Hip Fracture Risk Prediction in Men from X-ray: Findings from the Osteoporosis in Men (MrOS) Study

Lars Schmarje[1]([envelope])[iD], Stefan Reinhold[1][iD], Timo Damm[2][iD], Eric Orwoll[3][iD], Claus-C. Glüer[2][iD], and Reinhard Koch[1][iD]

[1] MIP, Computer Science, Kiel University, Kiel, Germany
{las,sre,rk}@informatik.uni-kiel.de
[2] MOINCC, Kiel University, Kiel, Germany
{timo.damm,glueer}@rad.uni-kiel.de
[3] Oregon Health & Science University, Portland, USA
orwoll@ohsu.edu

Abstract. Osteoporosis is a common disease that increases fracture risk. Hip fractures, especially in elderly people, lead to increased morbidity, decreased quality of life and increased mortality. Being a silent disease before fracture, osteoporosis often remains undiagnosed and untreated. Areal bone mineral density (aBMD) assessed by dual-energy X-ray absorptiometry (DXA) is the gold-standard method for osteoporosis diagnosis and hence also for future fracture prediction (prognostic). However, the required special equipment is not broadly available everywhere, in particular not to patients in developing countries. We propose a deep learning classification model (FORM) that can directly predict hip fracture risk from either plain radiographs (X-ray) or 2D projection images of computed tomography (CT) data. Our method is fully automated and therefore well suited for opportunistic screening settings, identifying high risk patients in a broader population without additional screening. FORM was trained and evaluated on X-rays and CT projections from the Osteoporosis in Men (MrOS) study. 3108 X-rays (89 incident hip fractures) or 2150 CTs (80 incident hip fractures) with a 80/20 split (training/validation) were used. We show that FORM can correctly predict the 10-year hip fracture risk with a validation AUC of 81.44% ± 3.11%/81.04% ± 5.54% (mean ± STD) including additional information like age, BMI, fall history and health background across a 5-fold cross validation on the X-ray and CT cohort, respectively. Our approach significantly (p < 0.01) outperforms previous methods like Cox Proportional-Hazards Model and FRAX® with 70.19 ± 6.58 and 74.72 ± 7.21 respectively on the X-ray cohort. Our model outperform on both cohorts hip aBMD based predictions (validation AUC 82.67% ± 0.21% vs. 71.82% ± 0.50% and 78.41% ± 0.33 vs. 76.55% ± 0.89%). We are confident that FORM can contribute on improving osteoporosis diagnosis at an early stage.

Supplementary Information The online version contains supplementary material available at https://doi.org/10.1007/978-3-031-16919-9_10.

I. Rekik et al. (Eds.): PRIME 2022, LNCS 13564, pp. 103–114, 2022.
https://doi.org/10.1007/978-3-031-16919-9_10

Keywords: fracture risk prediction · osteoporosis · opportunistic screening

1   Introduction

Osteoporosis is a wide-spread systemic disease that leads to deterioration of bone mass and micro structure and subsequently to decreased bone strength inducing an increased fracture risk [23]. According to the United States Preventive Services Task Force, the lifetime risk of an osteoporotic fracture is about 50% in women and about 20%–25% in men [22,34]. While osteoporosis affects all bones, fractures of the spine and hip are the most frequent. Especially hip fractures lead to increased morbidity, decreased quality of life and increased mortality—20% of osteoporotic hip fractures lead to death within six month [7]. Being a silent disease before fracture, osteoporosis often remains undiagnosed and consequently untreated. Especially in men, only about 2% are diagnosed before fracture [22].

The gold-standard method for osteoporosis diagnosis is based on areal bone mineral density (aBMD) assessed by dual-energy X-ray absorptiometry (DXA). This modality is in general broadly available to patients in many countries worldwide - with some degree of uneven distribution among industrial nations. In developing countries in African and South America and the Middle East, the availability is poor [11,17]. More elaborate methods like volumetric bone mineral density (vBMD) assessed by quantitative computed tomography (QCT) or finite element modeling (FEM) of bone strength, either based on QCT or DXA, have shown to be superior to standard aBMD [2,20,29,35,39]. However, all these method either require special equipment, protocols or domain experts and the prognosis of osteoporotic fractures is an even more challenging and labor-intensive task.

In this paper, we focus on fracture prognosis in an opportunistic screening scenario: whenever radiographic imaging is available an automated method inspects the image for indicators of possible future fractures. Patients with high fracture risk could be advised to see a specialist to confirm the risk and possibly initiate preventive actions. Due to their outstanding capacity to learn task-relevant image features such methods - in particular convolutional neural networks (CNN) - have outperformed "classical" machine learning algorithms in many image analysis tasks [10,24–27,31]. We predict the risk of future fractures (prognostics), in contrast to detecting acute osteoporosis or incident fractures (diagnostics).

The goal is to develop a pipeline that can be used for opportunistic screening and hence beneficially leverage additional risk factors. For this purpose we propose a two-stage deep learning based classification method that is able to predict the 10-year fracture risk using only X-ray or CT scans and optionally case history as inputs. We train and evaluate our method on a dataset from the Osteoporotic Fractures in Men (MrOS[1]) study. We restrict our main evaluation to information (e.g. age, weight, height, etc.) that would be collectible in this setting; other information (e.g. aBMD) is only included for comparison.

---

[1] The Osteoporotic Fractures in Men (MrOS) Study: https://mrosonline.ucsf.edu.

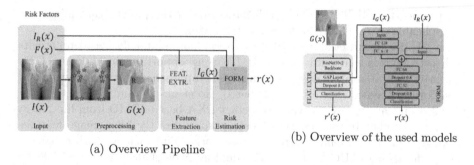

(a) Overview Pipeline

(b) Overview of the used models

Fig. 1. Illustration of proposed pipeline. (a) Inputs and pipeline stages: preprocessing, feature extraction and risk estimation. (b) Detailed view of models in (a) (yellow, green). Parameter of fully connected (FC) layers: number of hidden neurons. Further information can be found in Sect. 2. (Color figure online)

Our key contributions are: (1) a fully automated system that can be used in an prognostic opportunistic screening scenario, (2) val AUC results of 81.44% and 81.04% on the X-ray and CT cohort respectively. (3) we significantly outperform previous methods like Cox Proportional-Hazards Model and FRAX® in the opportunistic use case and achieve improved or competitive results for non-opportunistic settings, (4) beneficial integration of clinical risk factors with image based features into a deep learning pipeline.

1.1 Related Work

In the past numerous risk factors for osteoporotic fractures were identified. Among them are increased age, low body mass index (BMI), previous fragility fractures, smoking or alcohol intake. While aBMD alone has shown to be a not sufficiently sensitive predictor for screening applications [18], the combination with other risk factors (RF) is more promising. In [28] Schousboe et al. found that additional RF are better than a model using only aBMD and age for vertebrae fracture prediction. Elaborate statistical shape and density modeling based on volumetric QCT data has proven to be superior to DXA based aBMD models [3] for hip fracture prognosis. Hippisley-Cox et al. proposed the QFractureScores algorithm [13] to predict the 10-year fracture risk. FRAX® [18] is a fracture risk assessment tool that uses various RF with or without additional aBMD measurements to predict a 10-year fracture risk. The National Osteoporosis Foundation included FRAX® in its guidelines to recommend aBMD measurements or even treatment based on predicted fracture risk [36]. Su et al. [32] used classification and regression trees (CART) on common RF to predict fracture risk on the MrOS data and found a slight improvement over FRAX® based predictions. Treece et al. [33] used cortical bone mapping (CBM) to predict osteoporotic fractures in the MrOS study. They found that adding CBM to aBMD can improve fracture prognosis performance. Most of these methods do, however, require special protocols, modalities or in-depth interviews of the patient that might not be applicable to an opportunistic screening setting.

In [21], Pickhardt et al. were able to discriminate manually between patients with osteoporosis and with normal BMD using opportunistic abdomen CTs. Recently, several related deep learning based approaches for semi-automated osteoporosis diagnosis have been presented. Ho et al. [14] and Hsieh et al. [15] used a deep learning architecture to predict DXA based aBMD from hip X-ray. Other works like [16] or [38] detect osteoporosis directly from image features of X-ray using end-to-end classification networks. They achieve high classification performance (AUC > 0.9) which could even be slightly improved [38] by incorporating clinical risk factors (AUC > 0.92). However, this diagnosis task it not comparable to the prognosis task that we target in our work. For prognosis, Hsieh et al. [15] used their predicted aBMD as input to FRAX® to predict a 10-year fracture risk. However, since the performance of this combination is limited by the performance of DXA-based aBMD, they were unable to achieve any improvement over baseline FRAX® + (DXA-based) aBMD.

Recently, Damm et al. proposed a fully automatic deep learning method to predict hip fractures in women using X-rays from the Study of Osteoporotic Fractures (SOF[2]) [6]. They showed that deep learning based methods are able to improve the prognostic performance of classical aBMD based models while maintaining a high degree of automation. However, they did not investigate additional risk factors and other image modalities as input such as CT.

2   Method

We propose an automatic image processing pipeline for the prediction of **F**uture **O**steoporotic Fractures **R**isk in **M**en for Hips (FORM). The pipeline consists of a preprocessing, a feature extraction and a risk estimation stage for each patient x. An overview is given in Fig. 1a.

2.1   Preprocessing

The proposed method should be able to process 2D X-rays as well as 3D CT scans. To share both architecture and hyperparameters for both input modalities, we compute 2D projections from the 3D CT scans. This way, however, most of the 3D structural information from the CT scans is lost. To fully exploit the 3D information, a native 3D CNN could have been used, but this would have resulted in a much larger memory footprint and thus higher hardware requirements. Therefore, in this work, we have focused at first on confirming the usefulness of CT image data for predicting future fractures. In the following, the CT projections will be referred to simply as CT.

A Hough transform is used to detect the QCT calibration phantom that is present in all scans in order to remove it and the underlying table from the

---

[2] The Study of Osteoporotic Fractures (SOF:) https://sofonline.ucsf.edu.

image[3,4]. Since the phantom is always located beneath the patient, the scans can easily be cropped to exclude the phantom and the table. The cropped 3D scans are then projected onto the coronal plane and re-scaled by a constant value to achieve pixel value range of $[0, 1]$. We also investigated a re-scaling per patient to investigate the influence of the scanner HU calibration; results on these normalized CTs (CTN) are reported in the supplement.

CT projections and X-ray images $I(x)$ were split into two halves depicting the right and the left hip, respectively; images of the left hip were vertically flipped. A key point detection CNN inspired by [6] were used to detect 12 key points located around the femur. The key point detector was trained jointly on 1797 X-ray images and 208 CT projections (104 CT, 104 CTN) with manually annotated key point positions. The key point CNN classifies the image halves into three classes: *complete* (full proximal femur is visible), *incomplete* (proximal femur not completely visible) and *implant*. A selection of key points is used to crop the image to the proximal femur region (including the trochanter minor and the femoral head). This automatic selection of the region of interest leads to a more suitable input size for the neural networks without any loss of quality. These cropped images $G(x)$ are included in the dataset if the predicted class is *complete* with a confidence above 0.01 (X-ray) or 0.2 (CT).

The risk factors (RF) are additional information about the patient which might improve the hip fracture risk prediction. As we are not interested on the impact of a single risk factor, but rather whether the information is helpful in combination with image data, we grouped the RF for better referencing: *Base*, *Multiple*, *aBMD*, *FRAX®* and *TBS* [30]. The details are summarized in the supplementary. The *Base* group contains basic patient information like age and BMI. The *Multiple* group extends *base* and adds additional information from the case history and health background. This information might not be present in clinical routine but could be acquired from every patient via a questionaire (non-densitometric). The other groups consists of other well-known risk factors, also including densitometry. For densitometry, additional imaging and evaluation is required and thus is not suitable for opportunistic screening. We included these risk factors as a comparison. 52 patients were excluded from the dataset due to missing data for at least one risk factor.

2.2 Feature Extraction

We train a CNN as a Feature Extractor with output $r'(x)$ on the cropped femur images $G(x)$ and extract the predicted Global Average Pooling (GAP) Features of the network. These GAP features $I_G(x) \in \mathbb{R}^{2048}$ are used as input for the next pipeline stage. For the training of the CNN, a ground truth label $F_t(x)$ is needed indicating whether the patient x will fracture by time horizon t (e.g.

---

[3] Example image and key points only for illustrative purpose; image source https://radiopaedia.org/cases/normal-hip-x-rays.

[4] In the MrOS study, the phantoms are used to calibrate HU to BMD. In this work no BMD calibration is performed for a more realistic opportunistic screening setting.

10 years) or not. All patients with unknown fracture status, e.g., due to death before time horizon t, were excluded from the dataset. This renders all predicted risks conditional on the patient survival to time horizon t. This is acceptable for an opportunistic screening because we need to screen all patients regardless of whether or not they would survive to t [4] but might introduce a bias. FORM has a ResNet50v2 [12] backbone pretrained on ImageNet [19] with three additional layers depicted in Fig. 1b. Data was augmented with random flips, zooms and color changes; classes were weighted. Input image dimensions were 96×96 (CT) or 224×244 (X-ray) pixels. Training was performed for 50 epochs, a batch size of 36, learning rate of 10^{-4}, dropout $(0.5)^5$. A cross-entropy loss was used and input samples were weighted based on their class distribution. GAP features $G(x)$ were extracted after early stopping (see Subsect. 3.1 for details about the metrics).

2.3   Risk Estimation

For the risk estimation $r(x)$, we train a multi layer perceptron (MLP) to predict hip fractures up to the horizon t with the target $F_t(x)$. Its input can be varied: GAP-Features $I_G(x)$, RF $I_R(x)$ or both. Categorical data is one hot encoded and concatenated with normalized continuous data into the input vector $I_R(x)$. Using many RF together with the high-dimensional GAP features might make the model more prone to overfitting because individual datapoints become more distinct [1,9]. This is counteracted by a high dropout rate. To prevent imbalancing between $I_G(x)$ and $I_R(x)$ due to high dimensional differences (e.g. 2048 vs. 4) an MLP with 128 and $s \cdot k$ hidden nodes is used to reduce the dimension of the GAP features before concatenation. Here k is the dimension of $I_R(x)$ and s is a scaling hyperparameter set to 5. Hyperparameters are mostly shared in Feature Extraction and Risk Estimation and the differences are illustrated in Fig. 1b. An ablation study to inspect the impact of the hyperparameters is included in the supplementary material and discussed in Subsect. 3.3.

3   Evaluation

3.1   Datasets and Baseline Methods

For training and evaluation, we used the dataset from the Osteoporosis in Men (MrOS) study[6]. Patients were followed for more than 10 years. We used the first hip fracture that occurred after the baseline visit as our primary outcome. A detailed overview of the datasets statistics for the X-ray and the CT cohort in comparison to the complete study population can be found in Table 1. The number of included patients n is decreased by about one third of the overall number of patients with available image data due to censoring and excluded image

---

[5] Implemented in Tensorflow 2.4, source code will be release on publication, experiments executed on Nvidia RTX 3090, inference < 1 s per image.

[6] https://mrosonline.ucsf.edu, Update august 2021.

Table 1. Statistics for three different cohorts (all, CT or X-Ray data available). For each cohort we give the statistics for the complete cohort and with respect to the hip fracture horizon with (w) and without (w/o) fracture (fx). n represents the number of samples. Age is given as relative percentage for a specific range from n. Training/validation refer to the number of used images in the respective sets in the first fold. - means that no data was used for training or validation. All other risk factors are given as mean (STD in brackets).

		Cohort All			Cohort CT					Cohort X-Ray		
		$t = 10$ year			$t = 10$ year		$t = 5$ year			$t = 10$ year		
		all	w/o fx	w fx	all	w/o fx	w fx	w/o fx	w fx	all	w/o fx	w fx
n		5994	4004	185	3165	2150	80	2198	32	3895	3108	89
	64-69	29.51	36.69	10.27	30.74	37.86	16.25	37.44	12.50	32.99	37.32	15.73
Age [%]	70-74	28.50	31.87	16.22	28.44	32.00	15.00	31.71	9.38	30.40	31.66	19.10
	75-79	24.11	21.98	33.51	23.70	21.44	37.50	21.84	34.38	23.90	22.30	39.33
	80+	17.88	9.47	40.00	17.12	8.70	31.25	9.01	43.75	12.71	8.72	25.84
Height [m]		1.74	1.75	1.73	1.74	1.75	1.74	1.75	1.72	1.74	1.74	1.74
		(0.07)	(0.07)	(0.06)	(0.07)	(0.07)	(0.06)	(0.07)	(0.06)	(0.07)	(0.07)	(0.06)
BMI $[\frac{kg}{m^2}]$		25.90	26.00	25.11	25.80	25.89	24.77	25.86	24.68	25.86	25.90	24.86
		(3.65)	(3.54)	(3.63)	(3.60)	(3.48)	(3.38)	(3.49)	(3.02)	(3.57)	(3.48)	(3.65)
Femoral aBMD		0.78	0.79	0.66	0.78	0.79	0.65	0.79	0.62	0.79	0.79	0.68
$[\frac{g}{cm^2}]$		(0.13)	(0.13)	(0.11)	(0.13)	(0.13)	(0.08)	(0.13)	(0.08)	(0.13)	(0.12)	(0.10)
Spine aBMD		1.07	1.07	1.01	1.07	1.06	1.00	1.06	0.98	1.07	1.07	1.00
$[\frac{g}{cm^2}]$		(0.19)	(0.18)	(0.19)	(0.19)	(0.18)	(0.16)	(0.18)	(0.19)	(0.18)	(0.18)	(0.20)
Avg. TBS		1.23	1.23	1.19	1.23	1.24	1.20	1.24	1.17	1.24	1.24	1.19
		(0.13)	(0.13)	(0.13)	(0.13)	(0.12)	(0.12)	(0.12)	(0.13)	(0.12)	(0.12)	(0.12)
FRAX* [%]		4.14	3.14	7.04	4.01	3.04	6.29	3.07	8.53	3.54	3.07	5.76
		(4.39)	(3.07)	(5.67)	(4.28)	(2.93)	(5.85)	(2.94)	(7.97)	(3.56)	(2.89)	(4.87)
FRAX* (w. aBMD)		4.45	3.38	10.86	4.33	3.35	10.47	3.45	14.38	3.85	3.34	9.41
[%]		(5.54)	(4.04)	(9.09)	(5.41)	(3.95)	(8.92)	(4.12)	(9.41)	(4.74)	(3.95)	(8.56)
Training		-	-	-	-	3403	128	3478	53	-	4353	107
Validation		-	-	-	-	790	27	810	7	-	1086	35

halves (e.g. due to implants). During a 5/10 year follow-up 1.45% and 3% of the men suffered a hip fracture, respectively. This low number of cases limits the generalizability but it is possible to identify trends which repeat across different modalities, horizons and settings. Therefore, we use the same training validation split based on the patient IDs across all experiments for the respective cohorts. We used area under the receiver-operator curve (AUC) as the main metric. A 5-fold cross-validation was used to ascertain the validity of the comparison with the established baselines; across folds validation means and standard deviations (STD) are reported. To ensure reproducibility training was repeated 10 times for deep learning models. In the ablation studies, we analyzed only one fold across 10 repetitions and report means with their standard errors (SE). A two-sided Welch-Test [37] was used to compare the calculated means.

As baselines a Cox Proportional-Hazards Model (Cox) [5] and FRAX® was used. For the Cox model the same input as to our model FORM was used. However, the low variance of the high dimensional GAP features lead to a numerical degeneration of the Cox model. This was circumvented by performing a dimensionality reduction using Principal Component Analysis (PCA) [8] of the GAP feature space. The Cox model was fitted on the training data and used for prediction on the validation data. Best performing number of PCA components are reported based on the validation set.

Table 2. Cross-validation results (mean val. AUC ± STD) – columns: different methods/inputs; rows: cohort. Bold: results within a one percent margin of the best for each cohort.

Cohort	FORM			Cox			FRAX°
	GAP	GAP + Base	GAP + Multiple	GAP	GAP + Base	GAP + Multiple	
X-Ray	**81.57 ± 3.13**	**81.09 ± 3.18**	**81.44 ± 3.11**	61.14 ± 16.80	70.26 ± 5.71	70.19 ± 6.58	74.72 ± 7.21
CT	77.53 ± 5.81	**80.66 ± 3.75**	**81.04 ± 5.54**	67.56 ± 23.97	73.69 ± 9.22	75.35 ± 9.11	74.74 ± 5.70

Table 3. Comparison fracture risk prediction – columns: different inputs which were used to train FORM; rows: different cohorts. All scores are given as mean val AUC ± SE. Significant differences between the first and the other columns are marked italic (p < 0.05) or bold (p < 0.01). † input not used for FORM

Cohort	GAP + Multiple	Base	Multiple	GAP	GAP + Base	FRAX° †
X-Ray	78.41 ± 0.33	66.38 ± 1.76	69.67 ± 0.99	*77.24 ± 0.30*	77.81 ± 0.38	77.43
CT	82.67 ± 0.21	**60.89 ± 0.73**	**67.03 ± 0.93**	82.58 ± 0.21	82.48 ± 0.24	75.94

(a) Non-densitometric Settings

Cohort	GAP + Multiple	aBMD + Base	FRAX° + aBMD + Base	TBS + Base	FRAX° + aBMD†
X-Ray	78.41 ± 0.33	**76.55 ± 0.89**	**81.50 ± 0.83**	**72.66 ± 1.34**	80.92
CT	82.67 ± 0.21	**71.82 ± 0.50**	**81.08 ± 0.34**	**71.56 ± 0.39**	79.19

(b) Densitometric Settings

3.2 Results

The proposed method (FORM), a Cox Proportional-Hazards Model (Cox) and FRAX° are compared using a five-fold cross-validation analysis in Table 2. It can be seen, that the proposed method outperforms Cox and FRAX° on both cohorts by around 6%. In general, using more risk factors in the GAP feature input improves the prediction; this benefit is slightly higher on the CT cohort. Especially for Cox, a high variance without risk factors can be observed which can be credited to one or two folds with significant lower performance (e.g. around 35% on one fold for the X-ray Cohort).

On one fold the power to predict hip fractures were analyzed further by adding comparisons without GAP features and evaluations including densitometric inputs variables in Table 3. Across both cohorts, a significant improvement of around 20% to only using the risk factors group Base or Multiple can be seen. Moreover, a significant improvement of up to one percent is achieved when adding information about risk factors on X-ray and the vanilla FRAX° is worse for both cohorts. Overall the image-based result are all similar and within a range of around three percent of 80%. For the densitometric settings, only the usage of Base risk factors is reported, because further information did not improve the results. In the comparison of the best non-densitometric model, with densitometric settings FORM still outperform most risk factors or the vanilla FRAX° + aBMD predictor. Only X-ray based imaging is up to three percent worse than FRAX° based predictions. We see an improvement of using the FRAX° + Base as input to FORM in comparison to the vanilla FRAX° predictor. Further results and ablations are in the supplementary.

3.3   Discussion

We conclude three major results: (1) FORM outperforms Cox and FRAX® on two image cohorts and performs similarly or better even if we include densitometric inputs as comparison, (2) only image information can be used for fracture risk prediction but additional risk factors can help the risk estimation and (3) FORM can leverage the combined information of image information and risk factors better than Cox. Across all experiments FORM outperforms the other non-densitometric models. Only the densitometric FRAX® predictor (including aBMD) performs better on the X-ray cohort than FORM.

However, our models do not require additional imaging with DXA. Future research could highlight important image regions for the risk estimation or the importance of additional risk factors which could improve the interpretability and therefore the acceptance of the system in clinical routine. For Cox and FORM in Table 2, it can be seen that a fracture risk estimation only based on image information is possible and even outperforms predictions only based on risk factors in Table 3. Using additional risk factors as input can improve the results significantly by up to four percent. This shows that risk factors are a valid source for additional information but also that a majority of the information is already encoded in a patient's X-ray or CT. The Cox model performs in the best case similar or worse than FRAX® but is outperformed by FORM. While FRAX® might use other input variables, the Cox model is trained with the same inputs as FORM. We conclude that our model can learn from the high dimensional data better than Cox due to two reason: The Cox model required preprocessed inputs via PCA to prevent degeneration. The overfitting prevents adding more than one or two PCA components as input. In Subsect. 2.2, we explained that patients were excluded due to early death. The censored patients cannot be directly evaluated, but their subgroup which survived for at least the first 5 years without a fracture. The number of false positive predicted patients across 20 repetitions are $3.63\% \pm 0.51\%$ SE and $5.01\% \pm 0.80\%$ SE for the validation and censored subset, respectively. We conclude that our model is performing at least plausible on this subset.

3.4   Limitations and Future Work

This study is based solely on the MrOS dataset, which consists only of men and contains an expected low number of incident (future) fractures. The identified trends are supported across different cohorts and settings but have to be confirmed on other studies. This study can only analyze the benefits of image data for opportunistic screening in a proof-of-concept fashion, since the strict imaging protocols were imposed for the study. A long term study in clinical routine is required to evaluate the practicability and questions about sensitivity/specificity calibration.

3.5 Conclusion

We have shown that X-ray and CT data can be automatically analyzed and processed by our method FORM for opportunistic hip fracture prognosis. We achieved a mean validation AUC of greater than 80% for 10-year hip fracture risk in a five-fold cross-validation in both cohorts based on radiographic and CT data. This is significantly better than previous methods like Cox or FRAX® on the same or comparable input. Even in most cases, with additional densitometric RF, our method is signficantly better. Overall, we are confident that our method FORM and image input in general are promising candidates for improving the identification of men at high risk of future osteoporotic hip fractures.

Acknowledgements. We acknowledge funding of Lars Schmarje, Stefan Reinhold, Timo Damm and Claus C. Glüer by the ARTEMIS project (grant no. 01EC1908E) funded by the Federal Ministry of Education and Research (BMBF), Germany.

References

1. Bishop, C.M.: Neural Networks for Pattern Recognition. Oxford University Press, Inc., Oxford (1996)
2. Black, D.M., et al.: Proximal femoral structure and the prediction of hip fracture in men: a large prospective study using QCT. J. Bone Mineral Res. **23**(8), 1326–1333 (2008)
3. Bredbenner, T.L., Mason, R.L., Havill, L.M., Orwoll, E.S., Nicolella, D.P., Osteoporotic Fractures in Men (MrOS) Study: Fracture risk predictions based on statistical shape and density modeling of the proximal femur. J. Bone Mineral Res. **29**(9), 2090–2100 (2014)
4. Camacho, P.M., et al.: American Association of Clinical Endocrinologists/American College of Endocrinology clinical practice guidelines for the diagnosis and treatment of postmenopausal osteoporosis-2020 update. Endocr. Pract. **26**, 1–46 (2020)
5. Cox, D.R.: Regression models and life-tables. J. R. Stat. Soc. Ser. B (Methodol.) **34**(2), 187–202 (1972)
6. Damm, T., et al.: Artificial intelligence-driven hip fracture prediction based on pelvic radiographs exceeds performance of DXA: the "Study of Osteoporotic Fractures" (SOF). J. Bone Mineral Res. **37**, 193 (2021)
7. Ebeling, P.R.: Osteoporosis in men: why change needs to happen. World Osteoporosis Day Thematic Report International Osteoporosis Foundation, Nyon (2014)
8. Pearson, K.: LIII. On lines and planes of closest fit to systems of points in space. Lond. Edinb. Dublin Philos. Mag. J. Sci. **2**(11), 559–572 (1901)
9. Goodfellow, I., Bengio, Y., Courville, A.: Deep Learning. MIT Press, Cambridge (2016)
10. Grossmann, V., Schmarje, L., Koch, R.: Beyond hard labels: investigating data label distributions. arXiv preprint arXiv:2207.06224 (2022)
11. Hamidi, Z.: What's BMD and What We Do in a BMD Centre?, pp. 225–246 (2012)
12. He, K., Zhang, X., Ren, S., Sun, J.: Deep residual learning for image recognition. In: IEEE Conference on Computer Vision and Pattern Recognition (CVPR), pp. 770–778 (2015)

13. Hippisley-Cox, J., Coupland, C.: Predicting risk of osteoporotic fracture in men and women in England and Wales: prospective derivation and validation of QFractureScores. BMJ **339**, b4229 (2009)
14. Ho, C.-S., et al.: Application of deep learning neural network in predicting bone mineral density from plain X-ray radiography. Arch. Osteoporos. **16**(1), 1–12 (2021). https://doi.org/10.1007/s11657-021-00985-8
15. Hsieh, C.I., et al.: Automated bone mineral density prediction and fracture risk assessment using plain radiographs via deep learning. Nat. Commun. **12**(1), 1–9 (2021)
16. Jang, R., Choi, J.H., Kim, N., Chang, J.S., Yoon, P.W., Kim, C.H.: Prediction of osteoporosis from simple hip radiography using deep learning algorithm. Sci. Rep. **11**(1), 1–9 (2021)
17. Johnell, O., Kanis, J.A.: An estimate of the worldwide prevalence and disability associated with osteoporotic fractures. Osteoporos. Int. **17**(12), 1726–1733 (2006)
18. Kanis, J.A., Johnell, O., Odén, A., Johansson, H., McCloskey, E.: FRAX^{TM} and the assessment of fracture probability in men and women from the UK. Osteoporos. Int. **19**(4), 385–397 (2008)
19. Krizhevsky, A., Sutskever, I., Hinton, G.E.: ImageNet classification with deep convolutional neural networks. In: Advances in Neural Information Processing Systems, vol. 60, pp. 1097–1105. Association for Computing Machinery (2012)
20. Langsetmo, L., et al.: Volumetric bone mineral density and failure load of distal limbs predict incident clinical fracture independent of FRAX and clinical risk factors among older men. J. Bone Mineral Res. **33**(7), 1302–1311 (2018)
21. Pickhardt, P.J., Pooler, B.D., Lauder, T., del Rio, A.M., Bruce, R.J., Binkley, N.: Opportunistic screening for osteoporosis using abdominal computed tomography scans obtained for other indications. Ann. Intern. Med. **158**(8), 588–595 (2013)
22. Prasad, D., Nguyen, M.H.: Chronic hepatitis, osteoporosis, and men: underrecognised and underdiagnosed. Lancet Diabetes Endocrinol. **9**(3), 141 (2021)
23. Salari, N., et al.: The global prevalence of osteoporosis in the world: a comprehensive systematic review and meta-analysis. J. Orthop. Surg. Res. **16**(1), 1–20 (2021)
24. Santarossa, M., et al.: MedRegNet: unsupervised multimodal retinal-image registration with GANs and ranking loss. In: Medical Imaging 2022: Image Processing, vol. 12032, pp. 321–333. SPIE (2022)
25. Schmarje, L., Brünger, J., Santarossa, M., Schröder, S.M., Kiko, R., Koch, R.: Fuzzy overclustering: semi-supervised classification of fuzzy labels with overclustering and inverse cross-entropy. Sensors **21**(19), 6661 (2021)
26. Schmarje, L., et al.: Is one annotation enough? A data-centric image classification benchmark for noisy and ambiguous label estimation. arXiv preprint arXiv:2207.06214 (2022)
27. Schmarje, L., et al.: A data-centric approach for improving ambiguous labels with combined semi-supervised classification and clustering. arXiv preprint arXiv:2106.16209 (2022)
28. Schousboe, J.T., et al.: Prediction models of prevalent radiographic vertebral fractures among older men. J. Clin. Densitom. **17**(4), 449–457 (2014)
29. Schousboe, J.T., et al.: Prediction of incident major osteoporotic and hip fractures by trabecular bone score (TBS) and prevalent radiographic vertebral fracture in older men. J. Bone Mineral Res. **31**(3), 690–697 (2016)
30. Schousboe, J.T., et al.: Predictors of change of trabecular bone score (TBS) in older men: results from the Osteoporotic Fractures in Men (MrOS) Study. Osteoporos. Int. **29**(1), 49–59 (2017). https://doi.org/10.1007/s00198-017-4273-z

31. Sohn, K., et al.: FixMatch: simplifying semi-supervised learning with consistency and confidence. In: Advances in Neural Information Processing Systems 33 Preproceedings (NeurIPS 2020) (2020)

32. Su, Y., Kwok, T.C.Y., Cummings, S.R., Yip, B.H.K., Cawthon, P.M.: Can classification and regression tree analysis help identify clinically meaningful risk groups for hip fracture prediction in older American men (the MrOS cohort study)? JBMR Plus **3**(10), e10207 (2019)

33. Treece, G.M., Osteoporotic Fractures in Men (MrOS) Study, et al.: Predicting hip fracture type with cortical bone mapping (CBM) in the osteoporotic fractures in men (MrOS) study. J. Bone Mineral Res. **30**(11), 2067–2077 (2015)

34. US Preventive Services Task Force: Screening for osteoporosis: US preventive services task force recommendation statement. Ann. Intern. Med. **154**(5), 356–364 (2011)

35. Wang, X., et al.: Prediction of new clinical vertebral fractures in elderly men using finite element analysis of CT scans. J. Bone Mineral Res. **27**(4), 808–816 (2012)

36. Watts, N.B.: The fracture risk assessment tool (FRAX®): applications in clinical practice. J. Women's Health **20**(4), 525–531 (2011)

37. Welch, B.L.: The generalization of 'student's' problem with several different population variances are involved. Biometrika **34**(1–2), 28–35 (1947)

38. Yamamoto, N., et al.: Deep learning for osteoporosis classification using hip radiographs and patient clinical covariates. Biomolecules **10**(11), 1534 (2020)

39. Yang, L., Parimi, N., Orwoll, E.S., Black, D.M., Schousboe, J.T., Eastell, R.: Association of incident hip fracture with the estimated femoral strength by finite element analysis of DXA scans in the Osteoporotic Fractures in Men (MrOS) study. Osteoporos. Int. **29**(3), 643–651 (2017). https://doi.org/10.1007/s00198-017-4319-2

Weakly-Supervised TILs Segmentation Based on Point Annotations Using Transfer Learning with Point Detector and Projected-Boundary Regressor

Siwoo Nam[1], Myeongkyun Knag[1], Dongkyu Won[1], Philip Chikontwe[1], Byeong-Joo Noh[2,4], Heounjeong Go[3,4], and Sang Hyun Park[1(✉)]

[1] Daegu Gyeongbuk Institute of Science and Technology (DGIST), Daegu, Korea
{siwoonam,mkkang,shpark13135}@dgist.ac.kr
[2] Department of Pathology, Gangneung Asan Hospital, Gangneung, Korea
[3] Department of Pathology, Asan Medical Center, Seoul, Korea
[4] Department of Pathology, College of Medicine, University of Ulsan, Ulsan, Korea

Abstract. In Whole Slide Image (WSI) analysis, detecting nuclei sub-types such as Tumor Infiltrating Lymphocytes (TILs) which are a primary bio-marker for cancer diagnosis, is an important yet challenging task. Though several conventional methods have been proposed and applied to target user's nuclei sub-types (*e.g.*, TILs), they often fail to detect subtle differences between instances due to similar morphology across sub-types. To address this, we propose a novel decoupled segmentation architecture that leverages point annotations in a weakly-supervised manner to adapt to the nuclei sub-type. Our design consists of an encoder for feature extraction, a boundary regressor that learns prior knowledge from nuclei boundary masks, and a point detector that predicts the center positions of nuclei, respectively. Moreover, employing a frozen pre-trained nuclei segmenter facilitates easier adaptation to TILs segmentation via fine-tuning, while learning a decoupled point detector. To demonstrate the effectiveness of our approach, we evaluated on an in-house Melanoma TIL dataset, and report significant improvements over a state-of-the-art weakly-supervised TILs segmentation method, including conventional approaches based on pseudo-label construction.

Keywords: Point annotation · TILs segmentation · Transfer learning · Weakly-supervised learning

1 Introduction

In digital pathology, the analysis of whole slide images (WSIs) is crucial for cancer diagnosis and immune response prognoses. Prior to computer-aided WSI, conventional analysis involved manually counting the number of nuclei, and measuring the density of abnormal nuclei such as Tumor Infiltrating Lymphocytes

---

S. Nam and M. Knag—Equal contribution.

© The Author(s), under exclusive license to Springer Nature Switzerland AG 2022
I. Rekik et al. (Eds.): PRIME 2022, LNCS 13564, pp. 115–125, 2022.
https://doi.org/10.1007/978-3-031-16919-9_11

(TILs) for diagnosis [1]. However, due to the extremely large high resolution nature of WSIs, as well as the presence of diverse types of nuclei, pathologists find analysis laborious and tedious. Thus, many experts prefer employing automated tools yet these require the curation of precise annotations per sub-type, which is equally time consuming.

Following the advances in deep learning, several deep-learning based methods [5,10,16] have been proposed for nuclei segmentation. For instance, Kumar *et al.* [10] separates adjacent nuclei by training a segmentation model with additional boundary labels. Graham *et al.* [5] jointly trained three classification modules to handle multiple types of nuclei in WSIs. Yao *et al.* [16] performs a multi-class nuclei segmentation using center positions and corresponding class-agnostic masks through a keypoint detector and a dynamic instance segmentation, respectively. Though promising, these works are fully-supervised and require accurate pixel-level labels for training. Thus, recent works tend towards weakly-supervised approaches where less accurate/weaker annotations are cheaper to collect.

In particular, several point-based weakly-supervised learning methods have been proposed [13,15,17] to ease human annotation efforts. These methods use point annotations (*e.g.*, center of nuclei) to perform mask delineation, and show comparable performance to methods that use more complete annotations. For example, Qu *et al.* [13] generated pseudo-labels using Voronoi diagrams and k-means clustering algorithm, and then trained a segmentation model using a constructed pseudo-labels. Tian *et al.* [15] proposed a two-strategy processes for coarse-to-fine segmentation using point distance maps, Voronoi edge maps, and edge maps to focus more on the contour of nuclei. Yoo *et al.* [17] proposed an auxiliary network with an attention module that predicts edges and blobs from point annotations. However, these methods tend to segment for all nuclei present in WSI without considering the type of instances and predict touching and overlapped nuclei as one instance due to uncertainty in the boundary information.

In this paper, we propose a novel point-based weakly-supervised TILs segmentation model using a transfer learning strategy that distinguishing similar appearance nuclei (*e.g.*, tumor cells, lymphocytes) more effectively. We decouple the segmentation task into point detection and boundary regression *i.e.*, center position- and nuclei boundary vector-predictions. We first train our segmentation model in a fully supervised manner using pixel-level supervision to acquire prior knowledge of nuclei. Later, we fine-tune the point detector in order to adapt a target instance from nuclei to TILs using point annotations alone, while exploiting a pre-trained boundary regressor on nuclei. Our final segmentation results can be obtained by a contour-filling algorithm using predicted center points and boundary-projected vectors. The main contributions of this work are summarized as follows:

- We propose a point-based weakly-supervised learning method for TILs segmentation. To the best of our knowledge, this is the first attempt to segment TILs in H&E stained WSI using weak supervision.

- We decouple the segmentation task into a point detection and a boundary regression. This approach facilitates to adapt pre-trained nuclei segmentation to TILs easier.
- We evaluated our method on an in-house dataset with TIL point annotations, and outperformed a state-of-the-art weakly-supervised nuclei segmentation method and two traditional pseudo-label construction approaches.

2   Related Works

2.1   Nuclei Segmentation

In literature, the majority of nuclei segmentation methods are fully-supervised and use expert curated masks to train deep models [5,10,16]. Kumar *et al.* [10] proposed to divide masks into three classes: inside, boundary, and background, enabling accurate distinction of over-lapped or touched nuclei by predicting the boundary. The foreground classes (*i.e.*, inside and boundary) perform the nuclei instance segmentation through using the boundary-map to separate the inside-map. Graham *et al.* [5] designed a network that jointly segments and classifies nuclei types using multiple branches. Each branch predicts a nuclei pixel, horizontal and vertical map, nuclei types, respectively. The nuclei instance segmentation is performed using a constructed boundary map that is post-processed by combining the horizontal and vertical maps. Yao *et al.* [16] considered nuclei instance segmentation as a keypoint detection task *i.e.*, a novel network design with three branches that predicts keypoint heatmaps per class, kernels, and feature maps, respectively. From the predicted heatmaps, the center peak points of nuclei are obtained via the normalized Gaussian kernel; with predicted kernels and features later are used in a dynamic convolution operation for instance segmentation. However, several nuclei that have various shapes and types exist in the extremely high-resolution WSIs, following labor-expensive and time-consuming annotation costs are required for WSIs analysis.

2.2   Weakly-Supervised Segmentation

To reduce the time-consuming annotation process in WSIs, weakly-supervision approaches have been introduced. Among the existing types of weakly-supervision (*e.g.*, bounding box [7], scribble [11], and point annotation [13]), A point annotation is being considered as an easy and effective annotation for WSIs, and can expanded to various informative cues to detect nuclei in WSIs [13,15,17]. Qu *et al.* [13] suggested two types of coarse labels from point annotations that provide the approximated foreground and background information using Voronoi diagram and k-means clustering algorithm. These coarse labels were used to optimize loss functions alongside the main nuclei segmentation model. Tian *et al.* [15] performs nuclei segmentation with a coarse-to-fine strategy. In coarse strategy, three maps *i.e.*, point distance maps, Voronoi maps, and self-predicted maps are used to train the segmentation model in a weakly and

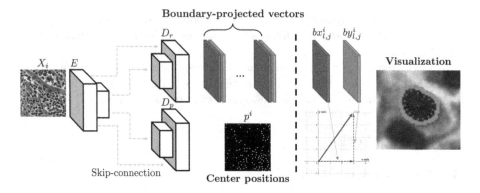

Fig. 1. Diagram of the proposed method.

self-supervised manners. In fine strategy, edge maps of self-predicted maps using Sobel operator are used to further improve the prediction of the nucleus contour. Yoo *et al.* [17] proposed an auxiliary network combining an edge network with an attention module to find edges and blobs of nuclei using point annotations only. From the input image, the edge network and attention module predict the sparse edges and contour maps that visualize coarse structures of nuclei, respectively. Despite the success in detecting nuclei, none of the prior methods have explored targeting TILs, even though TILs are the most prominent factor for cancer diagnosis in WSIs. To the best of our knowledge, our method is the first to address TILs segmentation using weak supervision.

3   Method

Although various weakly-supervised nuclei segmentation approaches have been proposed, training TILs with weak-supervision is challenging since they assume all nuclei in the image as the same instance and unable to adapt to other types of nuclei with only point annotations. To this end, we propose a novel decoupled segmentation architecture that learns and transfers to targeted nuclei by leveraging the prior knowledge of common nuclei.

Our model consists of three modules: feature extractor E, point detector D_p, and a boundary regressor D_r where each module outputs intermediate features, center positions, and boundary-projected vectors of TILs (or nuclei), respectively. Given a nuclei segmentation dataset with a full pixel-level annotations, we first pre-train the model to obtain representative features for common nuclei. In the subsequent stage, we fix E and D_r, and only fine-tune D_p to identify TILs in an image using point annotations (*i.e.*, center positions). Consequently, an accurate segmentation model for new types of nuclei (*e.g.*, TILs) can be obtained. The overall framework is shown in Fig. 1 and 2.

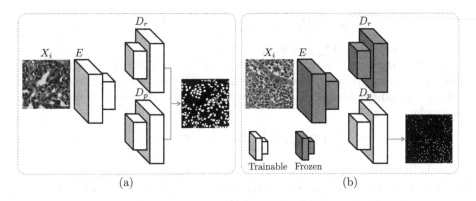

Fig. 2. Overview of pre-training and fine-tuning stages for TIL segmentation. (a) pre-training stage using segmentation masks, and (b) fine-tuning stage using point annotations only.

3.1 Center Positions and Boundary-Projected Vectors

To learn prior knowledge of nuclei, our model uses a multi-organ histopathology dataset $\mathcal{D}_{nuclei} = \{X^1_{nuclei}, \cdots, X^m_{nuclei}\}$ with a corresponding segmentation labels (a full pixel annotation) $mask^i$ (*e.g.*, MoNuSeg [9]). Also, we employ TIL histopathology images denoted $\mathcal{D}_{til} = \{X^1_{til}, \cdots, X^n_{til}\}$ with k TIL center positions $\{(cx^i_1, cy^i_1), \cdots, (cx^i_k, cy^i_k)\}$ corresponding to each image X^i_{til}. In particular, we compose $mask^i$ as a combination of center positions and boundary-projected vectors *i.e.*, a single instance is a combination of (cx^i_l, cy^i_l) and $\{(bx^i_{l,1}, by^i_{l,1}), \cdots, (bx^i_{l,j}, by^i_{l,j})\}$, where $(bx^i_{l,j}, by^i_{l,j})$ denotes a boundary vector. The center position indicates the central location of a nucleus, and each element is represented with boundary-projected vectors ($j = 18$) from the center position to the nucleus boundary at every $20°$ angle (*e.g.*, 20, 40, $\cdots$, $360°$), as shown in Fig. 1. The combination of center positions with corresponding boundary-projected vectors can be decoded into a segmentation mask using a contour-filling algorithm.

3.2 Network Training

We first input X^i_{nuclei} (or X^i_{til}) to E, and feed the output features to D_r and D_p to predict the center positions and boundary-projected vectors of nuclei (or TILs). In particular, D_p outputs the probabilities of nuclei centers, and the output of D_r indicates the x and y coordinates of boundary-projected vectors corresponding to a center position in D_p. For D_p training, center positions are converted to a point map p^i as illustrated in Fig. 1. We used dice and cross-entropy losses for D_p training.

$$\mathcal{L}_{dice}(E, D_p) = \frac{2D_p(E(X^i))p^i}{2(D_p(E(X^i))p^i) + D_p(E(X^i))(1 - p^i) + (1 - D_p(E(X^i)))p^i},$$

$$(1)$$

$$\mathcal{L}_{ce}(E, D_p) = -\sum p^i \log(D_p(E(X^i))), \tag{2}$$

where X^i denotes the X^i_{nuclei} (or X^i_{til}).

For boundary regression, the ground-truth center position is employed to index D_r during training; also, the ground-truth boundary-projected vectors and corresponding outputs of D_r are used in the loss objective. We employ the L1 loss for this task:

$$\mathcal{L}_{reg}(E, D_r) = \sum ||b^i - D_r(E(X^i))_I||, \tag{3}$$

b^i is the flattened vector (dim $= 36$) of $\{(bx^i_{l,1}, by^i_{l,1}), \cdots, (bx^i_{l,j}, by^i_{l,j})\}$ and I denotes an index where the corresponding center position is located. Finally, the overall loss function is defined as:

$$\mathcal{L}_{total} = \mathcal{L}_{reg}(E, D_r) + \mathcal{L}_{ce}(E, D_p) + \mathcal{L}_{dice}(E, D_p). \tag{4}$$

In the inference stage, the output of D_p is post-processed to obtain center positions by thresholding D_p's probability map. The final segmentation results can be decoded by using a contour-filling algorithm with corresponding boundary-projected vectors from D_r.

3.3   TILs Adaptation

Since our method consists of two separate decoders *i.e.*, D_r and D_p for each task, we can easily update our modules (*e.g.*, detection or mask prediction) toward the target task. Towards this goal, we adapt a pre-trained segmentation model with common nuclei for TILs segmentation by fine-tuning with $\mathcal{L}_{ce}(E, D_p) + \mathcal{L}_{dice}(E, D_p)$ using point annotations whilst the parameters in E and D_r are frozen as shown in Fig. 2. Consequently, we can obtain precise mask predictions by transferring the boundary-projected vectors trained by common nuclei (from fixed E and D_r) with accurate TILs identification trained from TILs (using updated D_p) for TILs segmentation.

4   Experiments

4.1   Datasets

To evaluated our approach on different nuclei types, we constructed an in-house H&E stained WSI **Melanoma** dataset as shown in Fig. 3(a). An expert pathologist annotated center positions of TILs using the automated slide analysis platform [4]. During pre-processing, we cropped 5 WSIs scanned at x40 magnification into 512×512 patches, obtaining a total of 200 patches. 120 patches were used for training, the remaining 40 and 60 patches are used for validation and test, respectively. Since segmentation masks are not provided for evaluation, we constructed the ground-truth segmentation mask of TILs by assigning point annotations to the closest mask prediction using state-of-the-art nuclei segmentation method [12], as shown in Fig. 3.

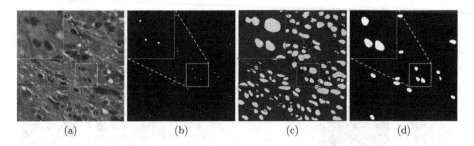

Fig. 3. TILs ground-truth construction. (a) input image, (b) center positions (point annotations), (c) Luna *et al.* [12] nuclei segmentation results, and (d) constructed TIL segmentation masks.

In the pre-training stage, we used a public multi-organ histopathology dataset *i.e.*, **MoNuSeg** [9]. This dataset has a 30 images with seven different organs, each image having dimensions 1000 × 1000. 16 images (breast: 4, liver: 4, kidney: 4, and prostate: 4) for training, and 14 images (breast: 2, liver: 2, kidney: 2, prostate: 2, bladder: 2, brain: 2, and stomach: 2) in testing splits, respectively. The images were cropped into patches of size 512 × 512 at stride 162 pixels, obtaining 396 patches in total.

4.2   Experimental Settings

Our method is based on a U-Net [14] architecture with two decoders. For training, Adam optimizer [8] with batch size 8 is used. The model is trained for 300 epochs using a Plateau learning rate scheduler with patience value of 30 and a decrease-factor value of 0.2. The initial learning-rate is set to 0.0003, and we set the minimum learning-rate threshold to 0.000001. For augmentation, we applied random affine translation, random flipping, random gamma contrast, and elastic transformation.

To demonstrate the usefulness of the proposed method, a state-of-the-art point based weakly-supervised nuclei segmentation method [13] and two marker based pseudo label construction approaches (*i.e.*, Watershed [3], Flood fill [6]) were compared to our method. For Qu *et al.* [13]'s method training, we followed the same network architecture and training settings described in the original paper. To implement the traditional pseudo-label construction approaches, we used OpenCV libraries [2] to create segmentation masks from TIL center positions and trained them with the U-Net model. The rest of the training setting is identical to our method. For the evaluation metric, the dice coefficient score (DSC) was used.

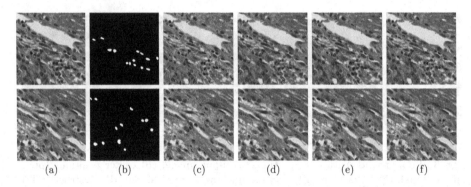

| (a) | (b) | (c) | (d) | (e) | (f) |

Fig. 4. Qualitative results of the proposed method and competitors. (a) input images, (b) ground-truth masks, (c) Qu *et al.* [13], (d) Watershed + U-Net, (e) Flood fill + U-Net, and (f) Ours.

Table 1. Test results (DSC) on Melanoma dataset.

Method	DSC
Qu *et al.* [13]	18.57
Watershed + UNet	52.67
Flood fill + UNet	52.28
Proposed method	**63.80**

5   Results

Table 1 shows the overall performance of the evaluated methods. Our method outperformed the state-of-the-art point based weakly-supervised method [13] and traditional label construction approaches, *i.e.*, Watershed [3] and Flood fill [6] algorithms with significant margins. In addition, segmentation results in Fig. 4 show that our method (Fig. 4(f)) could delineated masks precisely and can distinguish TILs from nuclei more accurately than the compared methods (in Fig. 4(c), (d), (e)).

Moreover, Fig. 4(c) shows that the previous state-of-the-art weakly segmentation methods for nuclei segmentation could not distinguish TILs from non-TIL nuclei correctly in most cases. The pseudo labels generated by Qu *et al.* [13] using k-means clustering failed to exclude non-TIL instances, instead captured most nuclei in the image and considered them as TILs. As shown in Fig. 5, we illustrate how the quality of the pseudo label depends on the different clipped value *i.e.*, none of choosen values could were optimal to generate accurate TIL segmentation masks. For instance, all non-TIL nuclei or tissues are included in the pseudo mask when using low clip values. Even if high clip values were used (Fig. 5(e)), the boundary information of the nucleus was not considered as all TILs were over-segmentated. Therefore, the performance of segmentation model was low since the pseudo label is extremely poor.

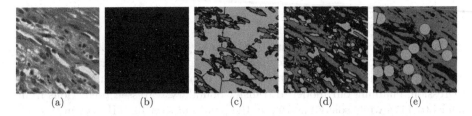

Fig. 5. Pseudo segmentation masks obtained using Qu *et al.* [13] by varying clip values. Green color indicates pseudo TIL masks, red and black color indicates background and ignored regions, respectively. In general, all the generated masks were low quality, and are sensitive to the chosen clip value. (a) an input image, (b) center positions, (c) a pseudo segmentation mask using clip value 20, (d) a pseudo mask using clip value 35, and (e) using clip value 50. (Color figure online)

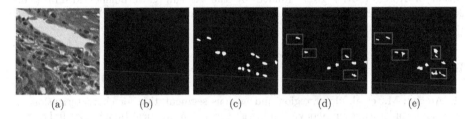

Fig. 6. Pseudo segmentation masks of Watershed and Flood fill algorithms. The boundary of the constructed TIL's masks are not clear. (a) an input image, (b) center positions, (c) a ground-truth mask, and (d) a pseudo mask of Watershed, and (e) a pseudo mask of Flood fill.

On the other hand, the pseudo segmentation masks using Watershed [3] and Flood fill [6] algorithms are shown in Fig. 6. These masks are relatively similar to the ground-truth TIL mask. However, the generated mask does not find the proper boundaries of TILs or misses some TILs that have a point annotation. Due to the uneven pixel values of the cytoplasm and the nucleus, as well as unclear boundaries of TILs, it is difficult to generate an accurate mask using traditional algorithms.

Unlike prior methods, our method is able to distinguish TILs correctly and segments the boundary of instances more accurately. Since all nuclei of H&E stained pathology images have similar shapes and boundaries, knowledge of nucleus' contour can be transferred to TILs appropriately. Our novel decoupled segmentation model could successfully detect TILs by solely fine-tuning the separated D_p parameters while ignoring the non-TIL instances. Thus, we believe transfer learning strategy with a decoupled architecture is a valid choice for TILs segmentation.

6   Conclusion

In this paper, we proposed a point based weakly-supervised TILs segmentation model using a novel decoupled segmentation approach with a transfer learning strategy. We separate the segmentation task into point detection and boundary regression, enabling our model to transfer boundary regressed predictions from nuclei to TILs while solely fine-tuning the point detector for TILs segmentation. We compared our method against a state-of-the-art nuclei segmentation model and two traditional pseudo label construction algorithms. Our method outperformed all competitors and showed improved segmentation results with precise predictions and accurate TILs delineation.

Acknowledgment. This work was supported by the National Research Foundation of Korea (NRF) grant funded by the Korean Government (MSIT) (No. 2019R1C1C1008727), and Smart Health Care Program funded by the Korean National Police Agency (220222M01).

References

1. Amgad, M., et al.: Joint region and nucleus segmentation for characterization of tumor infiltrating lymphocytes in breast cancer. In: Medical Imaging 2019: Digital Pathology, vol. 10956, p. 109560M. International Society for Optics and Photonics (2019)
2. Bradski, G.: The OpenCV Library. Dr. Dobb's Journal of Software Tools (2000)
3. Deng, Y., Manjunath, B.S., Shin, H.: Color image segmentation. In: Proceedings of the 1999 IEEE Computer Society Conference on Computer Vision and Pattern Recognition (Cat. No. PR00149), vol. 2, pp. 446–451. IEEE (1999)
4. Gardeux, V., David, F.P., Shajkofci, A., Schwalie, P.C., Deplancke, B.: ASAP: a web-based platform for the analysis and interactive visualization of single-cell RNA-seq data. Bioinformatics **33**(19), 3123–3125 (2017)
5. Graham, S., et al.: Hover-Net: simultaneous segmentation and classification of nuclei in multi-tissue histology images. Med. Image Anal. **58**, 101563 (2019)
6. Heckbert, P.S.: A seed fill algorithm. Graph. Gems **275**, 721–722 (1990)
7. Khoreva, A., Benenson, R., Hosang, J., Hein, M., Schiele, B.: Simple does it: weakly supervised instance and semantic segmentation. In: Proceedings of the IEEE Conference on Computer Vision and Pattern Recognition, pp. 876–885 (2017)
8. Kingma, D.P., Ba, J.: Adam: a method for stochastic optimization. arXiv preprint arXiv:1412.6980 (2014)
9. Kumar, N., et al.: A multi-organ nucleus segmentation challenge. IEEE Trans. Med. Imaging **39**(5), 1380–1391 (2019)
10. Kumar, N., Verma, R., Sharma, S., Bhargava, S., Vahadane, A., Sethi, A.: A dataset and a technique for generalized nuclear segmentation for computational pathology. IEEE Trans. Med. Imaging **36**(7), 1550–1560 (2017)
11. Lin, D., Dai, J., Jia, J., He, K., Sun, J.: Scribblesup: scribble-supervised convolutional networks for semantic segmentation. In: Proceedings of the IEEE Conference on Computer Vision and Pattern Recognition, pp. 3159–3167 (2016)

12. Luna, M., Kwon, M., Park, S.H.: Precise separation of adjacent nuclei using a Siamese neural network. In: Shen, D., et al. (eds.) MICCAI 2019. LNCS, vol. 11764, pp. 577–585. Springer, Cham (2019). https://doi.org/10.1007/978-3-030-32239-7_64

13. Qu, H., et al.: Weakly supervised deep nuclei segmentation using points annotation in histopathology images. In: International Conference on Medical Imaging with Deep Learning, pp. 390–400. PMLR (2019)

14. Ronneberger, O., Fischer, P., Brox, T.: U-Net: convolutional networks for biomedical image segmentation. In: Navab, N., Hornegger, J., Wells, W.M., Frangi, A.F. (eds.) MICCAI 2015. LNCS, vol. 9351, pp. 234–241. Springer, Cham (2015). https://doi.org/10.1007/978-3-319-24574-4_28

15. Tian, K., et al.: Weakly-supervised nucleus segmentation based on point annotations: a coarse-to-fine self-stimulated learning strategy. In: Martel, A.L., et al. (eds.) MICCAI 2020. LNCS, vol. 12265, pp. 299–308. Springer, Cham (2020). https://doi.org/10.1007/978-3-030-59722-1_29

16. Yao, K., Huang, K., Sun, J., Hussain, A., Jude, C.: PointNu-Net: simultaneous multi-tissue histology nuclei segmentation and classification in the clinical wild. arXiv preprint arXiv:2111.01557 (2021)

17. Yoo, I., Yoo, D., Paeng, K.: PseudoEdgeNet: nuclei segmentation only with point annotations. In: Shen, D., et al. (eds.) MICCAI 2019. LNCS, vol. 11764, pp. 731–739. Springer, Cham (2019). https://doi.org/10.1007/978-3-030-32239-7_81

Discriminative Deep Neural Network for Predicting Knee OsteoArthritis in Early Stage

Yassine Nasser[1]([✉]) [iD], Mohammed El Hassouni[1] [iD], and Rachid Jennane[2] [iD]

[1] FLSH, Mohammed V University in Rabat, Rabat, Morocco
{yassine_nasser,Mohamed.Elhassouni}@um5.ac.ma
[2] Institut Denis Poisson, University of Orleans, 45100 Orleans, France
Rachid.Jennane@univ-orleans.fr

Abstract. Knee osteoarthritis (OA) is a degenerative joint disease that causes physical disability worldwide and has a significant impact on public health. The diagnosis of OA is often made from X-ray images, however, this diagnosis suffers from subjectivity as it is achieved visually by evaluating symptoms according to the radiologist experience/expertise. In this article, we introduce a new deep convolutional neural network based on the standard DenseNet model to automatically score early knee OA from X-ray images. Our method consists of two main ideas: improving network texture analysis to better identify early signs of OA, and combining prediction loss with a novel discriminative loss to address the problem of the high similarity shown between knee joint radiographs of OA and non-OA subjects. Comprehensive experimental results over two large public databases demonstrate the potential of the proposed network.

Keywords: Convolutional Neural Network · Discriminative loss · Knee osteoarthritis · Plain radiography

1 Introduction

Osteoarthritis (OA) is a degenerative joint disease caused by the breakdown of the cartilage located at the end of the bone. Generally, OA is characterized by stiffness, swelling, pain and a grating sensation on movement which lead to a decrease in quality of life. Knee OA is the most common type of osteoarthritis. Due to their safety, availability and accessibility, the standard imaging modality for knee OA diagnosis is radiography (X-ray). The major hallmarks features of knee OA such as joint space narrowing, osteophytes formation, and subchondral bone changes could be visualized using X-ray images. Based on these pathological features, The Kellgren and Lawrence (KL) grading system [1] splits knee OA severity into five grades from grade 0 to grade 4. Grade 0 indicates the definite absence of OA and grade 2 early presence of OA. However, X-ray image patterns at early stage of knee OA present differentiation challenges and often result in

I. Rekik et al. (Eds.): PRIME 2022, LNCS 13564, pp. 126–136, 2022.
https://doi.org/10.1007/978-3-031-16919-9_12

high inter-reader variability across radiologists. Hence, the KL grading system is semi-quantitative, which introduces subjectivity/ambiguity into decision making and makes knee OA diagnosis more challenging.

Recently, a significant body of literature has been proposed on the application of deep learning networks to X-ray images for knee OA detection and prediction. In [2,3], Anthony et al. applied deep Convolutional Neural Networks (CNN) to automatically detect knee joint regions and classify the different stages of knee OA severity. In [4], Tiulpin et al. proposed an approach based on Deep Siamese CNN, which reduces the number of learnable parameters compared to standard CNNs. In their paper, the authors use an independent test set for evaluating its obtained results. In [5], Chen et al. applied a custom YOLOv2 model to detect the knee joint and fine-tuned a CNN model with a novel ordinal loss to classify knee OA severity.

All aforementioned deep learning based studies used Convolutional Neural Networks. However, classical CNNs rely mainly on the global shape information extracted from the last layers and ignore the texture information that characterizes bone architecture changes due to OA.

In [6], Nasser et al. introduced a Discriminative Regularized Auto-Encoder (DRAE) for early knee OA prediction using X-ray images. The proposed DRAE was based on Auto-Encoders (AE) with a combination between the standard AE training criterion and a novel discriminative loss. The mean goal was to maximize the class separability and learn the most useful discriminative features into the classifier. The limitation of this study that it was focused only on texture changes and neglected the overall deformation of the knee shape.

In this study, we propose to use a deep CNN model to predict knee OA in early stage from plain radiographs. Inspired by previous research in texture CNN [10,11], and the recently proposed discriminative regularization [6], we propose a new network to consider both shape and texture changes and maximize the class separability between OA and non-OA subjects.

The remainder of this paper is organized as follows. We report in Sect. 2 a detailed description of the proposed method. Section 3 presents the experimental settings. The results of a comparative evaluation with effective alternative solutions are discussed in Sect. 4. Finally, we give some concluding remarks and perspectives in Sect. 5.

2   Proposed Method

2.1   Overview

Conventional CNN architectures usually lead to extract complex correlations in upper layers corresponding to shape information and neglecting fine properties that contain the texture information [10,11]. However, knee osteoarthritis diagnosis depends on shape and texture properties across the entire distal knee joint. Thus, it is important to consider both features to create the training model. Nevertheless, early diagnosis of OA remains a challenging task, due to the high degree of similarity between non-OA and OA cases. Moreover, several studies

[7–9] have shown that in case of strong inter-class similarities or strong intra-class variations, and using only softmax loss, features learned with conventional CNNs of the same class are often scattered, and those learned from different classes overlap. Therefore, the discriminative aspect of the OA diagnostic model should also be improved.

To address these issue, we propose a new method based on the standard DenseNet [12]. The method combines texture information extracted from the mid-level layers with deep features in the top layer to better identify early signs of OA from inputs images (see Fig. 2). Moreover, we propose to add a novel discriminative loss function to the standard softmax in order to maximize the distance between non-OA and OA subjects.

2.2 DenseNet Learning Model

Our proposed network is derived from the classical DenseNet architecture [12], which is a densely connected convolutional network pre-trained on ImageNet [14]. In this section, a brief review of its architecture is given.

Let x_l be the output of the lth layer. In conventional CNNs, x_l is computed by applying a nonlinear transformation H_l to previous layer's output x_{l-1}:

$$x_l = H_l(x_{l-1}) \tag{1}$$

During consecutive convolutions, activation function and pooling operation, the network obtains robust semantic features in the top layers. However, fine image details related texture tend to disappear in the top layers of the network.

Inspired by the main idea of the ResNet learning model [13], which introduces a residual block that sums the identity mapping of the input to the output of a layer, and in order to improve the information flow between layers, DenseNet proposes a direct connection from any layer to all subsequent layers. Consequently, the lth layer receives the feature maps from all preceding layers as inputs. Thus, it is possible to define the output of the lth layer as:

$$x_l = H_l([x_0, x_1, ..., x_{l-1}]) \tag{2}$$

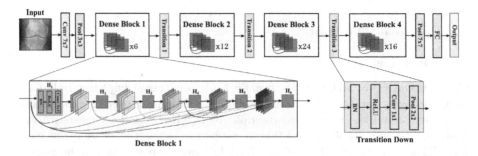

Fig. 1. Architecture of the DenseNet-121 learning model.

where [...] represents the concatenation operation, $H_l(.)$ is a composite function of the following consecutive operations: Batch Normalization (BN), Rectified Linear Units (ReLU), and a 3×3 Convolution (Conv). We denote such composite function as one layer.

DenseNet-121 used in our experiments consists of four dense blocks, each of which has 6, 12, 24 and 16 layers. In order to reduce the number of feature-maps, DenseNet introduces a transition down block between each two contiguous dense blocks. A transition down layer consists of a batch of normalization followed by a ReLU function, and a 1×1 convolutional layer followed by a 2×2 max-pooling layer. Figure 1 provides an illustrative overview of the architecture of DenseNet and the composition of each block.

2.3   Proposed Discriminative Shape-Texture DenseNet

In order to tackle the high similarity between OA and non-OA knee X-ray images at the early stages and to better detect the early signs of OA, we force the proposed network to : (i) learn a deep discriminative representation and (ii) consider both texture and shape information at the different layers of the model.

Learning a Deep Discriminative Representation. To learn deep discriminative features, a penalty term is imposed on the mid-level representations of the DenseNet (see Fig. 2). Apart from minimizing the standard classification loss, the objective is to improve the discriminative power of the network by forcing the representations of the different classes to be mapped faraway from each other. More specifically, we incorporate an additional discriminative term to the original classification cost function. The new objective function, $\mathcal{L}_T$ consists of two terms including the softmax cross-entropy loss and the discriminative penalty one:

$$\mathcal{L}_T = \mathcal{L}_C + \lambda \mathcal{L}_D \tag{3}$$

where λ is a trade-off parameter which controls the relative contribution of these two terms.

$\mathcal{L}_C$ is the softmax cross-entropy loss, which is the traditional cost function of the DenseNet model. It aims at minimizing the classification error for each

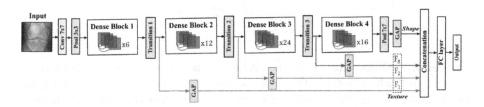

Fig. 2. Overview of the proposed method. Combination of texture and shape information to improve the prediction of OA in early stage. F_l is the global average pooling of the output of the lth transition layer.

given training sample. Over a batch X of multiple samples of size N, the binary CE loss is defined as:

$$J_{Cls} = -\frac{1}{N} \sum_{i=1}^{N} y_i \log(\hat{y}_i) + (1 - y_i) \log(1 - \hat{y}_i) \tag{4}$$

$\mathcal{L}_D$ represents the discriminative loss used to enforce the discriminative ability of the proposed model. $\mathcal{L}_D$ attempts to bring "similar" inputs close to each other and "dissimilar" inputs apart. To compute $\mathcal{L}_D$, we first feed the set of training samples X to the network and compute the outputs (feature maps) in each layer for each training sample, $x_i \in X$. Then, we compute $F_l(x_i)$, the Global Average Pooling (GAP) of the output feature maps of each transition layer l. Finally, the total discriminative loss $\mathcal{L}_D$ is defined as follows:

$$\mathcal{L}_D = \sum_{l=1}^{L} E_l \tag{5}$$

where E_l is the discriminative loss at a transition layer l. In the current study, we test two loss functions, the online Triplet Hard and SemiHard losses [21] and the Ω_{disc} one used in [6].

The Triplet loss [21], aims to ensure that the image x_i^a (anchor) is closer to all images x_i^p (positive) belonging to the same class, and is as far as possible from the images x_i^n (negative) belonging to an other class. Hence, when using a triple loss, E_L can be defined as

$$E_l = \sum_{i=1}^{N} \max(d(F_l(x_i^a), F_l(x_i^p)) - d(F_l(x_i^a), F_l(x_i^n)) + \epsilon) \tag{6}$$

where d is a distance metric, ϵ is a margin that is enforced between positive and negative pairs.

The Ω_{disc} loss [6], attempts to encourage classes separability, at each transition layer l, by maximizing the distance between the means μ_l^p and μ_l^n of the learned feature sets $(F_l(x_i^p)$ and $F_l(x_i^n))$ of each class and minimizing their variances v_l^p and v_l^n. The discriminative loss E_l which will be minimized in the use case of Ω_{disc} is defined then

$$E_l = \frac{v_l^p + v_l^n}{|\mu_l^p - \mu_l^n|^2} \tag{7}$$

Combining Shape and Texture. As mentioned above, several studies have shown that the first layers of CNNs are designed to learn low-level features, such as edges and curves which characterize the texture information, while the deeper layers are learned to capture more complex and high-level patterns, such as the overall shape information [17,18]. Moreover, CNN layers are highly related to filter banks methods widely used in texture analysis, with the key advantages that the CNN filters learn directly from the data rather than from handcrafted features. CNNs have also an architecture of learning which increases the abstraction level of the representation with depth [10,11,19].

Based on these studies and especially on the main idea of the texture and shape CNN (T-CNN) learning model [10], we propose a simple and efficient modification to the DenseNet architecture to improve its ability to consider both texture and shape.

Figure 2 illustrates the proposed architecture for combining texture information of the mid-level layers with the shape information of the top layer. First, using a specific concatenation layer, we fuse into a single vector the selected $\{F_l | l = 1, .., L\}$ which contain meaningful information about texture with the features of the last network layer that represent shape information. Then, we feed this vector to the final classification layer (i.e. the Fully Connected (FC) layer). Consequently, the network can learn texture information as well as the overall shape from the input image. This combination of features at different hierarchical layers enables to describe the input image at different scales.

3   Experimental Setup

3.1   Data Description

Knee X-ray images used to train and evaluate the proposed model were obtained from two public datasets: The Multicenter Osteoarthritis Study (MOST) [16] and the OsteoArthritis Initiative (OAI) [15]. The entire MOST database (3026 subjects) is used for the training, and the OAI baseline database (4796 subjects) is used for validation and test. The model was trained with regions of interest (ROI) corresponding to the distal area of the knee extracted from right knees and horizontally flipped left ones. Each ROI was associated with its KL grade. The objective of this study is to distinguish between the definite absence (KL-G0) and the definite presence of OA (KL-G2), which is the most important and challenging task, due to the high degree of similarity between their corresponding X-ray images, as shown in Fig. 3. KL-G1, is a doubtful one and was not considered in the current study. Table 1 summarizes the number of training, validation and testing samples.

3.2   Implementation Details

Our experiments were conducted using Python with the framework Tensorflow on Nvidia GeForce GTX 1050 Ti with 4 GB memory. The proposed approach was evaluated quantitatively using four metrics: Accuracy (Acc); Precision (Pr); Recall (Re) and F1-score (F1).

Dataset Preparation. As shown in Table 1, data are imbalanced. To overcome this issue during the training stage, data were balanced using the oversampling technique. To do so, different random linear transformations were applied to

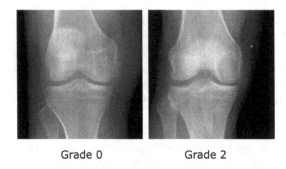

Grade 0   Grade 2

Fig. 3. Knee joint X-ray samples showing the high similarity between KL grades 0 and 2.

Table 1. Dataset description and distribution

Group	Dataset	KL-0	KL-2
Train	MOST	6008	3045
Validation	OAI	1116	806
Test	OAI	2313	1545

the samples, including: (i) random rotations using a random angle varying from -15^0 to 15^0, (ii) color jittering with random contrast and random brightness with a factor of 0.3, and (iii) a gamma correction.

Training Phase. As mentioned previously, DenseNet [12] pre-trained on ImageNet [14] was retained as our basic network structure (section II). The input size of the ROIs is 224 × 224, which is the standard size used in the literature. The proposed model was trained and optimized end-to-end using Adam optimizer with an initial learning rate of 0.0001. Hyper-parameters (λ, batch size, size of the fully connected layer, ration of dropout) were tuned using grid search on the validation set.

4   Experimental Results

In this section, the performance of our proposed method is evaluated for early knee OA detection. Firstly, two discriminative loss functions are tested. Then, the proposed network is compared to the deep learning pre-trained models, including the standard DenseNet [12], ResNet [13] as well as to Inception-V3 [20]. Finally, a visualisation analysis using t-SNE scatter plots is performed.

We test Triplet Hard and SemiHard losses with three distance metrics: l2-norm, squared l2-norm and the cosine similarity distance. We test also the discriminative loss Ω_{disc} proposed in [6]. The results are reported in Table 2. As can be seen, the best overall classification performance is obtained using the Ω_{disc}

discriminative loss with an accuracy rate of 87.69%. In term of the F1-score, the highest value (87.06%) is also reached using the Ω_{disc} discriminative loss, which corresponds to a precision rate of 87.48% and recall rate of 86.72%. We notice that Triplet SemiHard loss with l2-norm distance achieves competitive performance with Ω_{disc} loss. These results show that Ω_{disc} discriminative loss, leads generally to better performance compared to other tested losses. Hence, it is retained for the following experiments.

Table 2. Classification Performance of the proposed method using different discriminative loss functions

Discriminative loss	Distance metric	Acc (%)	Pr (%)	Re (%)	F1 (%)
Triplet hard	l2-norm	86.21	85.51	86.31	85.82
	squared l2-norm	86.50	85.94	85.93	85.94
	cosine similarity	86.39	85.76	86.02	85.88
Triplet SemiHard	l2-norm	87.48	**87.88**	85.94	86.66
	squared l2-norm	86.91	86.74	85.82	86.21
	cosine similarity	85.82	85.16	85.49	85.31
Ω_{disc} used in [6]	x	**87.69**	87.48	**86.72**	**87.06**

The proposed method is compared to some deep learning pre-trained networks, that are the standard DenseNet [12], ResNet [13] as well as Inception-V3 [20]. Results are reported in Table 3. As can be seen, the proposed method achieved the highest prediction performance compared to the other networks. In terms of accuracy, our proposed method obtains a score of 87.69% compared to 85.07%, 86.49% and 84.03% achieved by ResNet-101, DenseNet-169 and Inception-V3, respectively. The highest F1-score (87.06%) is obtained also by our proposed model. Even though DenseNet-169 achieved a high precision compared to other networks, it still has a low recall (75.08%). Therefore, with the exception of the precision values of DenseNet-169, our approach outperforms all other networks for all four metrics. In particular, a significant improvement in terms of F1-score is observed, as our model increases results by 5.14% from the 81.92% achieved by the standard DenseNet to 87.06% for the proposed method.

In addition to the quantitative evaluation, we check whether our model is able to increase the segregation of classes. To this end, we display the 2D scatter plots using t-distributed Stochastic Neighbor Embedding (t-SNE) [22] on each features levels $\{F_1, F_2, F_3\}$. Results are illustrated in Fig. 4. The first column shows the feature vector F_1 extracted from the first transition layer. As can be seen, the two classes significantly overlap. This may be due to common textual features shared between classes, such as edges and contours that form the overall joint shape. The second column shows the learned feature vectors F_2 obtained from the second transition layer. In this case, the network improves the separation between the two classes but not enough. The last column shows the learned

Table 3. Comparison of the proposed method to the deep learning pre-trained networks

Methods		Acc (%)	Pr (%)	Re (%)	F1 (%)
ResNet	ResNet-50	83.23	88.41	74.49	80.85
	ResNet-101	85.07	83.56	80.04	81.76
	ResNet-152	84.86	75.99	84.64	80.08
DenseNet	DenseNet-121	85.66	82.76	81.10	81.92
	DenseNet-169	86.49	**89.50**	75.08	81.66
	DenseNet-201	84.76	86.22	73.72	79.48
Inception	Inception-V3	84.03	83.39	75.08	79.02
Proposed method		**87.69**	87.48	**86.72**	**87.06**

features vector F_3 obtained from the third transition layer. Results show that by going deeper, our proposed model learned two discriminant representations. Thus, it leads to a better classes discrimination and thus a good prediction of knee OA at an early stage.

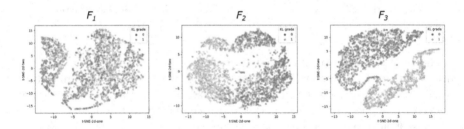

Fig. 4. Obtained t-SNE scatter plots for each feature levels using our proposed network.

5   Conclusion

In this paper, we proposed a novel deep learning method based on CNNs architecture with two distinct ideas: (i) combining the learned shape and texture features, (ii) enhancing the discriminative power to improve the challenging classification task, where a high similarity exists between early knee OA cases and healthy subjects. We tested the performance of our method using two discriminative losses with several distance metrics. The experimental results show that the proposed method surpasses the most influential deep learning pre-trained networks. The results are promising and a further extension in a context of multi-classification with more KL grades and other loss functions will be considered in a future work.

References

1. Kellgren, J.H., Lawrence, J.: Radiological assessment of osteo-arthrosis. Ann. Rheum. Dis. **16**(4), 494 (1957)
2. Antony, J., McGuinness, K., O'Connor, N.E., Moran, K.: Quantifying radiographic knee osteoarthritis severity using deep convolutional neural networks. In: 2016 23rd International Conference on Pattern Recognition (ICPR), pp. 1195–1200. IEEE (2016)
3. Antony, J., McGuinness, K., Moran, K., O'Connor, N.E.: Automatic detection of knee joints and quantification of knee osteoarthritis severity using convolutional neural networks. In: Perner, P. (ed.) MLDM 2017. LNCS (LNAI), vol. 10358, pp. 376–390. Springer, Cham (2017). https://doi.org/10.1007/978-3-319-62416-7_27
4. Tiulpin, A., Thevenot, J., Rahtu, E., Lehenkari, P., Saarakkala, S.: Automatic knee osteoarthritis diagnosis from plain radiographs: a deep learning-based (2018)
5. Chen, P., Gao, L., Shi, X., Allen, K., Yang, L.: Fully automatic knee osteoarthritis severity grading using deep neural networks with a novel ordinal loss. Comput. Med. Imaging Graph. **75**, 84–92 (2019)
6. Nasser, Y., Jennane, R., Chetouani, A., Lespessailles, E., El Hassouni, M.: Discriminative regularized auto-encoder for early detection of knee osteoarthritis: data from the osteoarthritis initiative. IEEE Trans. Med. Imaging **39**(9), 2976–2984 (2020)
7. Wen, Y., Zhang, K., Li, Z., Qiao, Yu.: A discriminative feature learning approach for deep face recognition. In: Leibe, B., Matas, J., Sebe, N., Welling, M. (eds.) ECCV 2016. LNCS, vol. 9911, pp. 499–515. Springer, Cham (2016). https://doi.org/10.1007/978-3-319-46478-7_31
8. Cai, J., Meng, Z., Khan, A.S., Li, Z., O'Reilly, J., Tong, Y.: Island loss for learning discriminative features in facial expression recognition. In: 2018 13th IEEE International Conference on Automatic Face & Gesture Recognition (FG 2018), pp. 302–309. IEEE (2018)
9. Cheng, G., Yang, C., Yao, X., Guo, L., Han, J.: When deep learning meets metric learning: Remote sensing image scene classification via learning discriminative CNNs. IEEE Trans. Geosci. Remote Sens. **56**(5), 2811–2821 (2018)
10. Cimpoi, M., Maji, S., Vedaldi, A.: Deep filter banks for texture recognition and segmentation. In: Proceedings of the IEEE Conference on Computer Vision and Pattern Recognition, pp. 3828–3836 (2015)
11. Andrearczyk, V., Whelan, P.F.: Using filter banks in convolutional neural networks for texture classification. Pattern Recogn. Lett. **84**, 63–69 (2016)
12. Huang, G., Liu, Z., van Der Maaten, L., Weinberger, K.Q.: Densely connected convolutional networks. In: Proceedings of the IEEE Conference on Computer Vision and Pattern Recognition, pp. 4700–4708 (2017)
13. He, K., Zhang, X., Ren, S., Sun, J.: Deep residual learning for image recognition. In: Proceedings of the IEEE Conference on Computer Vision and Pattern Recognition, pp. 770–778 (2016)
14. Russakovsky, O., et al.: Imagenet large scale visual recognition challenge. Int. J. Comput. Vision **115**(3), 211–252 (2015). https://doi.org/10.1007/s11263-015-0816-y
15. The Osteoarthritis Initiative (2020). https://nda.nih.gov/oai/
16. Multicenter Osteoarthritis Study (MOST) Public Data Sharing (2020). https://most.ucsf.edu/

17. Zeiler, M.D., Fergus, R.: Visualizing and understanding convolutional networks. In: Fleet, D., Pajdla, T., Schiele, B., Tuytelaars, T. (eds.) ECCV 2014. LNCS, vol. 8689, pp. 818–833. Springer, Cham (2014). https://doi.org/10.1007/978-3-319-10590-1_53

18. Springenberg, J.T., Dosovitskiy, A., Brox, T., Riedmiller, M.: Striving for simplicity: the all convolutional net. arXiv preprint arXiv:1412.6806 (2014)

19. Liu, L., Chen, J., Fieguth, P., Zhao, G., Chellappa, R., Pietikäinen, M.: From BoW to CNN: two decades of texture representation for texture classification. Int. J. Comput. Vision **127**(1), 74–109 (2019). https://doi.org/10.1007/s11263-018-1125-z

20. Szegedy, C., Vanhoucke, V., Ioffe, S., Shlens, J., Wojna, Z.: Rethinking the inception architecture for computer vision. In: Proceedings of the IEEE Conference on Computer Vision and Pattern Recognition, pp. 2818–2826 (2016)

21. Schroff, F., Kalenichenko, D., Philbin, J.: Facenet: a unified embedding for face recognition and clustering. In: Proceedings of the IEEE Conference on Computer Vision and Pattern Recognition, pp. 815–823 (2015)

22. van der Maaten, L., Hinton, G.: Visualizing data using t-SNE. J. Mach. Learn. Res. **9**, 2579–2605 (2008)

Long-Term Cognitive Outcome Prediction in Stroke Patients Using Multi-task Learning on Imaging and Tabular Data

Moritz Binzer[1](✉), Kerstin Hammernik[1,2], Daniel Rueckert[1,2], and Veronika A. Zimmer[1]

[1] Faculty of Informatics, Technical University of Munich, Munich, Germany
Moritz.binzer@gmail.com, veronika.zimmer@tum.de
[2] Department of Computing, Imperial College London, London, UK

Abstract. While the number of stroke patients is increasing worldwide and every fifth stroke survivor is developing long-term cognitive impairment, its prediction becomes more and more important. In this work, we address the challenge of predicting any long-term cognitive impairment after a stroke using deep learning. We explore multi-task learning that combines the cognitive classification with the segmentation of brain lesions such as infarct and white matter hyperintensities or the reconstruction of the brain. Our approach is further expanded to include clinical non-imaging data to the input imaging information. The multi-task model using an autoencoder for reconstruction achieved the highest performance in classifying post-stroke cognitive impairment when only imaging data is used. The performance can be further improved by incorporating clinical information using a previously proposed dynamic affine feature map transformation. We developed and tested our approach on an in-house acquired dataset of magnetic resonance images specifically used to visualize stroke damage right after stroke occurrence. The patients were followed-up after one year to assess their cognitive status. The multi-task model trained on infarct segmentation on diffusion tensor images and enriched with clinical non-imaging information achieved the best overall performance with a balanced accuracy score of 70.3% and an area-under-the-curve of 0.791.

Keywords: Post-stroke cognitive impairment · Multi-task learning · Deep learning · Stroke · Dementia · UNet · Autoencoder

1 Introduction

Up to one third of all people with a history of stroke are at risk of developing Post-Stroke Cognitive Impairment (PSCI) [1]. A reliable prediction whether the patients will suffer from long-term PSCI or recover to their old cognitive health is a missing piece in the medical treatment of stroke survivors. Currently, the lack of reliable predictive markers and the high variance of stroke characteristics challenge an early prediction of PSCI. Additionally, every brain has its own

I. Rekik et al. (Eds.): PRIME 2022, LNCS 13564, pp. 137–148, 2022.
https://doi.org/10.1007/978-3-031-16919-9_13

unique and flexible structure which challenges doctors to infer the long-term cognitive prognosis from damaged tissue.

The stroke might lead to damaged tissue in the brain with short- and long-term consequences for the patient. Infarct and White Matter Hyperintensities (WMH) are two types of lesions which occur due to a stroke. Both lesions can be visualized using Magnetic Resonance Imaging (MRI). An infarct is an area, which suffered a tissue death after an inadequate blood supply. Through the reduced blood flow, the infarct lesion is visible in Diffusion Tensor Images (DTI). WMH lesions are well visible as hyperintense structures in FLAIR images and are a direct sign for a white matter injury. Patients with WMH and infarct areas carry the worst prognosis of long-term survival, self-rated health and are strongly limited in their activities of daily living [2].

Previous work on the prediction of PSCI focused on the identification of imaging and non-imaging biomarkers. Research conducted by Zietemann et al. suggests a predictive importance of the Montreal Cognitive Assessment (MoCA) score regarding the prediction of long-term cognitive impairment [3]. The MoCA score consists out of 30 questions, which evaluate the cognitive status of the patient. In addition, markers of the small vessel disease such as lacunes, WMH, cerebral microbleeds and enlarged perivascular spaces were associated with a long-term cognitive and functional impairment [4].

Possible risk factors for PSCI were examined in [5]. Patient characteristics such as age as well as stroke characteristics like severity have shown an impact on the patients risk of developing PSCI. In addition, radiological data such as white matter changes can be considered as risk factor as well. However, the occurrence of white matter changes are coupled with the presence of cerebral atrophy and lacunar infarcts.

The expressiveness of computed tomography (CT) and MRI (T_1, T_2, FLAIR, and DWI) imaging data for PSCI prediction was demonstrated in [6] by showing the importance of spatial location of the infarct for the prediction. Their analyses of the stroke locations suggested that the left frontotemporal lobes, right parietal lobe, and left thalamus are the strongest predictors for PSCI [6]. Such works emphasize the importance of both imaging and non-imaging information for the prediction of PSCI.

In this work, we will explore deep learning (DL) techniques for the prediction of PSCI using MR images acquired directly after the stroke diagnosis. DL methods have shown remarkable success in image classification and prediction tasks. Such methods learn to extract features, which are most predictive for a given task. This is especially useful when it comes to complex prediction tasks such as PSCI prediction.

Multi-task learning is a learning paradigm in DL which aims at learning multiple related tasks simultaneously to leverage knowledge of each task for better performances. This can be used for example to cope with the lack of large annotated datasets [7,8]. There are two main approaches for multi-task learning: (i) hard parameter sharing, where the majority of network weights are shared among all task, and (ii) soft parameter sharing, where each task is learned by a separate network and the distance between network weights is minimized across tasks [9]. The former approach can be for example realized through a shared encoder. In a medical context such networks were successfully applied for detection and classification of breast tumors [10], placenta segmentation and location classification [8] and many more.

Contributions. The use of DL to predict long-term PSCI is very limited [11]. We compare for the first time different single- and multi-task DL approaches and the effectiveness of several surrogate tasks for the prediction of PSCI. The assumption is that additional tasks, such as segmentation of relevant structures, can improve the image feature extraction ability and enable the model to build a more meaningful latent space for the downstream task of PSCI prediction. We explore the use of different modalities for the prediction (FLAIR and DTI), and we evaluate different approaches to combine imaging and non-imaging data for PSCI prediction in the DL models.

2 Methodology

We explore the effect of multi-task learning with convolutional neural networks (CNNs) on the prediction of long-term PSCI. Additionally, we compare CNN models trained solely on imaging data with models incorporating non-imaging (tabular) information into the DL models. The models can be divided into single-task models, multi-task models and models which integrate non-imaging data into their training. An overview of all network architectures that were investigated are visualized in Fig. 1 and are described in detail below. As relevant tasks, we chose the classification of PSCI (diagnosed 12 months after the stroke) as the downstream task, and the segmentation of relevant structures and the reconstruction of the image as two surrogate tasks.

2.1 Single-Task Networks

The single-task models represent our baseline models. We conducted single-task experiments regarding classification, segmentation and image reconstruction.

Image Classification. A CNN encoder is used to extract the underlying features of the 3D image. This encoder (EncNet) consists of four residual blocks which are composed of a convolutional layer with batch normalization and ReLU activation. The encoder down-samples the whole 3D image to its latent feature space with the dimensions (256, 8, 8, 8) of channel dimension, height, width and depth. A subsequent linear block with batch normalization and Sigmoid activation outputs the classification result. An attention mechanism [12] is incorporated in the third layer of the encoder to improve the interpretation and performance of the model. To cope with imbalanced datasets, we use a weighted binary cross entropy as loss function for the classification task. We denote such loss function for optimizing the classification task between the reference label $C \in \{0,1\}$ and the predicted label $\widetilde{C} \in \{0,1\}$ as $L_{Class}(\widetilde{C}, C)$.

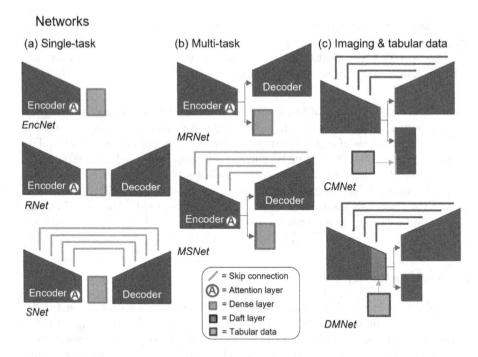

Fig. 1. Convolutional neural network architectures investigated in this work divided by tasks and input data. (a) single task networks for classification (EncNet), reconstruction (RNet) and segmentation (SNet); (b) multi-task networks for classification and reconstruction (MRNet) and classification and segmentation (MSNet); (c) multi-task networks for classification and segmentation combining both imaging and tabular data using two different methods: concatenation in latent space (CMNet) and DAFT [15] (DMet). The grey boxes in (c) represent the MSNet architecture and visualize which input was enriched with tabular data. (Color figure online)

Image Segmentation. We used a modified UNet architecture to segment the infarct or WMH areas based on manual labeled reference segmentation, denoted as SNet. The original UNet has an encoder-decoder structure with convolutional layers and symmetric skip connections from the encoder to the decoder [13]. Our network uses residual blocks with strided convolution, batch normalization and ReLU activation. The encoder and decoder consists of four layers each, which are symmetrically connected via skip connections. During the training we use the sum of the binary cross-entropy loss and Dice loss between the predicted segmentation mask $\widetilde{S} \in \mathbb{R}^{l \times h \times w}$ and the manual reference segmentation $S \in \mathbb{R}^{l \times h \times w}$ as loss function for the optimization, where l, h, w denote the length, height and width of the 3D image. We denote this loss function as $L_{Seg}(\widetilde{S}, S)$.

Image Reconstruction. For the reconstruction of the image we adapt an Autoencoder (AE) network from [14], which we denote as RNet. Similar to the SNet, we use an encoder-decoder structure which has residual blocks with strided convolution, batch normalization and ReLU activation but no skip connections between the encoding and decoding part. As one variation of our RNet we added a reparametrization layer in the bottleneck similar to a Variational Autoencoder (VAE). This forces the encoder to output a statistical distribution, whereby a continuous smooth latent feature representation is enforced. The encoding and decoding part consists out of four respective layers. For the training, the loss function between the input image $R \in \mathbb{R}^{l \times h \times w}$ and the reconstructed image $\widetilde{R} \in \mathbb{R}^{l \times h \times w}$ is denoted as $L_{Rec}(\widetilde{R}, R)$. For the AE network the Mean Squared Error (MSE) is used as a loss function to optimize the model's weights. As for the VAE, the reconstructed image $\widetilde{R}$ is represented through a distribution, and the Kullback-Leibler Divergence loss is used for the optimization.

2.2 Multi-task Networks

In multi-task learning, multiple tasks are optimized simultaneously. To reduce the risk of overfitting, we use hard parameter sharing, as our model needs to find an representation suitable for all task. To optimize for the classification and segmentation (MSNet) or classification and reconstruction (MRNet) task simultaneously, we added a classification branch (linear layer) after the bottleneck layer of the SNet and RNet, respectively (similar to [8]). In addition, an attention mechanism [12] is added to the third layer of the encoder.

The overall loss $L_{all}(\widetilde{C}, C, \widetilde{I}, I)$ is defined through the weighted sum of the loss for each task, where $\beta \in \mathbb{R}^+$ is the weighting parameter between the tasks:

$$L_{all}(\widetilde{C}, C, \widetilde{I}, I) = L_{Class}(\widetilde{C}, C) + \beta L_{Task}(\widetilde{I}, I). \tag{1}$$

The loss $L_{Task}(\widetilde{I}, I)$ is chosen as $L_{Seg}(\widetilde{S}, S)$, when segmentation, and $L_{Rec}(\widetilde{R}, R)$ when reconstruction is the surrogate task.

2.3 Incorporation of Non-imaging Data

Due to the predictive importance of several clinical parameters and to expand the available information for the model, tabular data was included to the input data. We explored two different strategies to incorporate the tabular information into the model. As a straightforward approach in CMNet, we added the tabular data after the encoder to the latent feature space. The tabular data was transformed to a numerical format before.

In our DMNet we use a more complex approach to include the non-imaging data. We use a Dynamic Affine Feature Map Transform (DAFT) [15]. This approach introduces an interaction between the clinical parameters and the imaging information. Hence, we replace the last encoding block with a corresponding DAFT block.

3   Materials and Experiments

3.1   Implementation Details

We selected relevant hyperparameters (learning rate, batch size, initial channel dimension, dimension of the latent space, data augmentations) by performing a grid search on SNet and RNet and fixed them for all experiments. We trained with intensity transformations (blurring), random spatial transformations, image flipping and synthetic MRI motion artifacts for data augmentation. The augmentation techniques were implemented using TorchIO [16]. For the final training of all models, we used a learning rate of 1e−3, a batch size of 16 and a initial channel dimension of 32. For the RNet, a latent space with a dimension of (256, 8, 8, 8) was selected. The training was run on a working station with 251 GB of RAM and AMD Ryzen Threadrupper 29600X 24.core processor and a NVIDIA Quadro RTX 8000 GPU.

3.2   Data

We used an in-house acquired MR dataset of 414 stroke patients, in which around every fifth patient suffered under long-term PSCI. The images (T_1, FLAIR and DTI Trace) were acquired within a few days after stroke diagnosis and clinical data were collected, including age, sex, education, stroke severity (NIHSS), information about health history and cognitive status (MoCA). The patients were followed-up after 12 months of stroke occurrence and categorized as *PSCI-negative* or *PSCI-positive* by a clinical expert based on the results of neurological examinations.

Infarct and WMH lesions were semi-automatically segmented and manually corrected by a clinical expert. The infarct lesions were segmented in the DTI Trace images and the WMH lesions in the FLAIR images. As preprocessing steps, the brain tissue is extracted from the T_1 images [17], mapped in an affine way to the Montreal Neurological Institute brain [18] using affine registration [19]. All other modalities where then registered to the T_1 image in atlas space and the image intensities are standardized. We split suitable patients into two groups with the same ratio of PSCI candidates, using 90 % for training and 10 % for testing. The training data was then further split into five subgroups for a 5-fold cross validation.

3.3   Evaluation Measures

Classification. As a reliable PSCI prediction is the main goal of our work, the evaluation of the classification performance plays an important role. To cope with any occurring imbalance, the balanced accuracy was selected as main evaluation metric for the classification. This measure is the arithmetic mean between the sensitivity and specificity of the classification model. To evaluate the overall quality of the model's prediction we evaluated the Area under the Curve (AUC).

Segmentation. For the evaluation of the segmentation performance, we compare the predicted segmentation with the reference segmentation. As overlap measure, we report the Dice score which indicates the overlap of two areas. As surface measures, the robust (95%) Hausdorff Distance (HD) and the average surface distance (ASD) are considered.

4   Results

We present three types of results: First, the baseline single-task model for classification and segmentation, second, the classification of PSCI with multi-task learning using imaging data only, and lastly the PSCI classification with multi-task learning using imaging and tabular data as input. For all models, we trained two configurations, depending on the imaging input (FLAIR or DTI Trace). Exemplary attention maps for all classification networks are shown in Fig. 3. These heat maps visualize the most important features that were identified by the network for the final prediction. The classification results for all experiments are visualized in Fig. 2.

For EncNet, the model trained on the FLAIR sequence achieved the highest balanced accuracy of 0.668 ± 0.106. For the DTI Trace modality, the balanced accuracy of the EncNet model was 0.569 ± 0.0814. This forms our baseline for further classification networks.

The segmentation results of SNet are summarized in Table 1 and compared to the other networks which solve segmentation as surrogate task. The infarct segmentations in DTI Trace achieved higher performances compared to the WMH segmentations in FLAIR images. This is due to the small size of the WHM lesions. It is harder to segment smaller structures and overlap measures, such as Dice and Jaccard, are very sensitive in this regard. We observe that the overlap measures for infarct segmentation are comparable for all four models. The multi-task models outperform the baseline SNet on the HD, indicating that the number of outliers is reduced due to the multi-task training. The best performing model is the CMNet. For WMH segmentation, the models MSNet and CMNet did not perform well, while the best results are obtained with DMNet.

We observe a different pattern for the multi-task models when trained on either FLAIR or DTI Trace images. The balanced accuracy does not improve for multi-task models when using FLAIR image compared to the EncNet performance (see Fig. 2 right, blue plots). Only the MRNet model using an AE was able to achieve a similar balanced accuracy of 0.655 ± 0.117 with an AUC increased to 0.867 ± 0.0563. On the other hand, the multi-task learning improved the PSCI classification performance when using the DTI Trace images as imaging data (see Fig. 2 left, blue plots). The MRNet model using an AE for reconstruction and DTI Trace brain images, was able to achieve the highest balanced accuracy of 0.736 ± 0.024 and an AUC of 0.769 ± 0.088. The MSNet model on DTI Trace using infarct segmentation was also able to further improve the classification performance compared to the EncNet, suggesting that the additional infarct segmentation benefits the pretext task. These results suggest that the

Table 1. Segmentation results of the single-task network SNet and the multi-task networks MSNet, MCNet and MDNet. Overall, the models were better able to segment the infarct in DTI Trace than the WMH areas in FLAIR.

Model	Lesion	Dice	Jaccard	Robust HD 95%	ASD
SNet	WMH	0.427 ± 0.018	0.287 ± 0.14	36.5 ± 24	9.2 ± 22.5
MSNet		0.118 ± 0.102	0.066 ± 0.061	54.2 ± 17.1	23.3 ± 15.1
CMNet		0.144 ± 0.183	0.090 ± 0.122	46.1 ± 17.8	23.7 ± 17.0
DMNet		**0.447 ± 0.175**	**0.303 ± 0.138**	**15.2 ± 18.5**	**4.7 ± 7.9**
SNet	infarct	0.662 ± 0.221	0.528 ± 0.209	19.5 ± 28.4	6.78 ± 22.6
MSNet		0.654 ± 0.250	0.528 ± 0.231	15.1 ± 31.2	8.12 ± 22.1
CMNet		**0.668 ± 0.210**	**0.533 ± 0.207**	**8.24 ± 21.3**	**3.79 ± 12.1**
DMNet		0.634 ± 0.260	0.509 ± 0.237	15.4 ± 31.9	8.26 ± 21.0

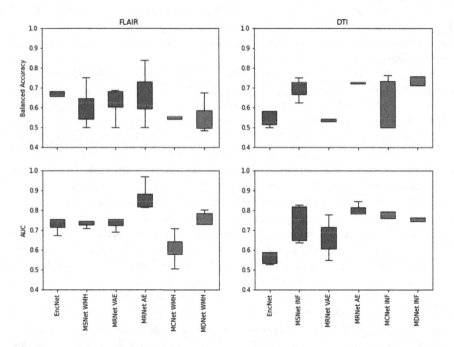

Fig. 2. Left: Network performances with FLAIR as MRI sequence for the imaging data. Right: Network performances of models trained on DTI Trace. The color determines, what type of data was used for input. (blue: only the MRI image was used as input, green: the MRI image and non-imaging clinical data was used as input). (Color figure online)

DTI Trace data and infarct lesion have a more predictive power than FLAIR and WMH lesions, but this has to be investigated in the future using more extensive experiments.

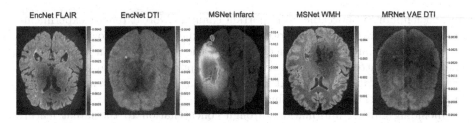

Fig. 3. Attention maps from different network architectures. The attention maps of the MSNet WMH and INF models focus on the brain lesions for their classification (green contour). While the EncNet focuses on the ventricles of the brain, the MRNet does not focus on a specific brain area. (Color figure online)

Analysing the attention maps in Fig. 3, the MSNet shows an increased attention to the segmented risk area. While the MRNet did not seem to focus on a specific brain area, the EncNet show a high focus on the ventricles of the brain. Especially the frontal horn of the lateral ventricle is receiving a high attention.

The results of multi-task learning (with segmentation as surrogate task) combined with tabular data is also shown in Fig. 2 (green plots). The naive approach of simply concatenating the vectorized tabular data to the latent space features did not improve PSCI classification results for either input data. The MDNet model using DAFT incorporated the tabular data more efficiently and the best model (MDNet on DTI data) achieved a mean balanced accuracy of 0.703 ± 0.161 and an AUC of 0.791 ± 0.086.

5   Discussion and Conclusion

In this work, we addressed the challenge of long-term PSCI prediction using brain MRIs and clinical non-imaging data. We proposed a multi-task approach for PSCI classification in combination with risk area segmentation or image reconstruction. The motivation for this approach is the advantage of multi-task learning, where learning two tasks simultaneously leverages the performance of the downstream task.

We found in our experiments that multi-task learning particularly improves PSCI prediction using DTI imaging data. A possible interpretation is that the infarct lesions, visible in DTI Trace images, are easier to segment and possibly more predictive for PSCI than the smaller lesions of WMH. Both segmentation and reconstruction are promising surrogate tasks to improve the feature extraction for PSCI classification. Using reconstruction as a subtask, the MRNet using an AE yielded to a higher classification performance than a VAE. This contradicts the assumption that a latent feature space, which is based on distributions, benefits the classification task. However, minor changes in the brain, which are responsible for PSCI development, might be underrepresented in such a distribution-based representation. Hence, this can cause the classification to miss such minor but nevertheless important changes. More extensive experiments are required to investigate the potential of AE and VAE as surrogate tasks.

We included an attention mechanism in the encoder of our models. The analyses of the attention maps strengthens the presumption that an awareness of the spatial location and/or extend of the brain lesions, as already suggested in [6], are beneficial for the classification task.

Including clinical information through concatenation to the latent feature space did not improve the performances of the models. This approach seems to be too naive to effectively incorporate tabular data into a CNN. In contrast, a DAFT layer in MDNet enables the network to receive image information in context to tabular data. This further improved the classification performance on the multi-task model segmenting the infarct area and represents the most promising approach of this work.

This work presents a first step towards reliable long-term PSCI predictions in stroke patients using DL. Our approach is able to make PSCI predictions with a good balanced accuracy of 0.70 on our test set and shows interesting research directions towards PSCI prediction. However, our results are only preliminary in the sense that more research is needed to confirm the conclusions and interpretations drawn from our experiments and explore other research avenues.

Specifically, we plan to further investigate the predictive power of different and/or multiple MR modalities. The visibility of each lesion differs in each modality. Enabling the network to process more than one modality at the same time could improve the expressiveness of the latent feature space. One approach could be to process FLAIR and DTI images at the same time and solve infarct and WMH segmentation as surrogate tasks simultaneously. Another approach could explore the reconstruction of T_1 images, as these have a high informative value and show different brain tissues and lesions than DTI and FLAIR.

Also, we will investigate different parameter sharing methods for multi-task learning. To this end, we adopted hard parameter sharing, where the core layers are shared between task. For very different tasks, as classification and lesion segmentation, a soft parameter sharing approach could be more suitable. Additionally, we want to further explore additional baseline and ablation studies. A pre-training of the encoder weights on a larger dataset could improve the performances of the single-task and multi-task learning models.

The relatively low dice scores indicate a high false positive and false negative rate of the segmentations. We plan to further investigate what influence a more stable segmentation has on the classification task.

Lastly, the exploration of different ways to incorporate non-imaging data is worth exploring. The non-imaging data (patient characteristics, health history, stroke severity, etc.) contain predictive parameters for PSCI prediction. Although DAFT already shows very promising results, other approaches are worth investigating. Also the positioning of the DAFT block and its influence on the data interaction can be explored in the future.

References

1. Betrouni, N., Yasmina, M., Bombois, S., Pétrault, M., Dondaine, T., Lachaud, C.: Texture features of magnetic resonance images: an early marker of post-stroke cognitive impairment. Transl. Stroke Res. **11**(4), 643–652 (2020). https://doi.org/10.1007/s12975-019-00746-3
2. Longstreth, W.T., Diehr, P.H., Yee, L.M., Newman, A.B., Beauchamp, N.J.: Brain imaging findings in elderly adults and years of life, healthy life, and able life over the ensuing 16 years: the Cardiovascular health study. J. Am. Geriatr. Soc. **62**(10), 1838–1843 (2014)
3. Zietemann, V., et al.: Early MoCA predicts long-term cognitive and functional outcome and mortality after stroke. Neurology **91**(20), e1838–e1850 (2018)
4. Georgakis, M.K., et al.: Cerebral small vessel disease burden and cognitive and functional outcomes after stroke: a multicenter prospective cohort study. Alzheimer's Dementia (2022)
5. Hénon, H., Pasquier, F., Leys, D.: Poststroke dementia. Cerebrovasc. Dis. **22**(1), 61–70 (2006)
6. Weaver, N.A., Kuijf, H.J., Aben, H.P., Abrigo, J., Bae, H.-J., Barbay, M., et al.: Strategic infarct locations for post-stroke cognitive impairment: a pooled analysis of individual patient data from 12 acute Ischaemic stroke cohorts. Lancet Neurol. **20**(6), 448–459 (2021)
7. Zhang, Y., Yang, Q.: A survey on multi-task learning. arXiv preprint arXiv:1707.08114 (2017)
8. Zimmer, V.A., et al.: Placenta segmentation in ultrasound imaging: addressing sources of uncertainty and limited field-of-view. arXiv preprint arXiv:2206.14746 (2022)
9. Crawshaw, M.: Multi-task learning with deep neural networks: a survey. arXiv preprint arXiv:2009.09796 (2020)
10. Zhou, Y., et al.: Multi-task learning for segmentation and classification of tumors in 3D automated breast ultrasound images. Med. Imag. Anal. **70**, 101918 (2021)
11. Lopes, R., et al.: Prediction of long-term cognitive function after minor stroke using functional connectivity. Neurology **96**(8), e1167–e1179 (2021)
12. Jetley, S., Lord, N.A., Lee, N., Torr, P.H.S.: Learn To Pay Attention. Proc, ICLR (2018)
13. Ronneberger, O., Fischer, P., Brox, T.: U-Net: convolutional networks for biomedical image segmentation. In: Navab, N., Hornegger, J., Wells, W.M., Frangi, A.F. (eds.) MICCAI 2015. LNCS, vol. 9351, pp. 234–241. Springer, Cham (2015). https://doi.org/10.1007/978-3-319-24574-4_28
14. Bank, D., Koenigstein, N., Giryes, R.: Autoencoders. arXiv preprint arXiv:2003.05991 (2020)
15. Pölsterl, S., Wolf, T.N., Wachinger, C.: Combining 3D image and tabular data via the dynamic affine feature map transform. In: de Bruijne, M., et al. (eds.) MICCAI 2021. LNCS, vol. 12905, pp. 688–698. Springer, Cham (2021). https://doi.org/10.1007/978-3-030-87240-3_66
16. Pérez-García, F., Sparks, R., Ourselin, S.: TorchIO: A Python library for efficient loading, preprocessing, augmentation and patch-based sampling of medical images in deep learning. Comput. Meth. Programs Biomed. **208**, 106236 (2021)
17. Ledig, C., et al.: Robust whole-brain segmentation: application to traumatic brain injury. Med. Image Anal. **21**(1), 40–58 (2015)

18. Evans, A.C., Collins, D.L., Mills, S.R., Brown, E.D., Kelly, R.L., Peters, T.M.: 3D statistical neuroanatomical models from 305 MRI volumes. In: Proceeding IEEE- Nuclear Science Symposium and Medical Imaging Conference, pp. 1813–1827 (1993)
19. Avants, B.B., Tustison, N., Song, G.: Advanced normalization tools (ANTS). Insight J. **2**(365), 1–35 (2009)

Quantifying the Predictive Uncertainty of Regression GNN Models Under Target Domain Shifts

Selim Yürekli⬤, Mehmet Arif Demirtaş, and Islem Rekik[✉]

BASIRA Lab, Faculty of Computer and Informatics Engineering,
Istanbul Technical University, Istanbul, Turkey
irekik@itu.edu.tr
http://basira-lab.com

Abstract. Predicting cognitive scores (e.g., intelligence quotient (IQ)) from functional brain connectomes enables the analysis of the underlying connectivity patterns that determine such abilities. In this context, recent works addressed IQ prediction from connectomes by designing graph neural network (GNN) architectures for regression. While effective, existing studies have two important drawbacks. *First*, the majority of these works train and evaluate regression GNNs on data from the same distribution. Thus, the performance of the models under domain shifts, where the *target* training and testing behavioral scores are drawn from different distributions, has not been considered. *Second*, the proposed architectures do not produce uncertainty estimates for their predictions, limiting their usage in critical real-world settings where data distribution may drastically change and render the predictions unreliable. To cope with this, a few studies proposed proposed Bayesian neural networks for estimating predictive uncertainty. However, these require heavy computation of the training process and have not been applied to regression GNNs. To address this problem, we unprecedentedly propose a *deep graph ensemble* of regression GNNs for estimating predictive uncertainty under domain shifts. Our main contributions are three-fold: (i) forming ensembles of regression GNNs for estimating their predictive uncertainties, (ii) simulating domain shift between training and test sets by applying clustering algorithms in the target domain, (iii) designing a novel metric for quantifying the uncertainty of GNN ensembles. We believe our study will inspire future research on the performance and uncertainty of GNNs under domain shifts, allowing their use in real-world scenarios. Our code is available at https://github.com/basiralab/predUncertaintywithDomainShift.

Keywords: Predictive uncertainty estimation · Domain shift · Regression GNNs · Brain connectivity

1 Introduction

Prediction of cognitive scores such as intelligence quotients (IQ) from functional brain connectomes has attracted the attention of the network neuroscience community as it

---

S. Yürekli and M. A. Demirtaş—Co-first authors.

I. Rekik et al. (Eds.): PRIME 2022, LNCS 13564, pp. 149–159, 2022.
https://doi.org/10.1007/978-3-031-16919-9_14

provides a method for discovering brain structures and connectivities that directly interact with cognitive abilities. Moreover, studies have shown a strong correlation between intelligence scores measured in childhood and academic success, and these scores have also been linked to health and mortality [1,2].

To this end, multiple works [3–7] applied learning-based methods for predicting behavioral and cognitive scores. For example, [3] proposed the first connectome-based predictive modeling method (CPM) by utilizing machine learning techniques. [4] applied this method to the problem of IQ prediction in both neurotypical (NT) and autism spectrum disorder (ASD) cohorts. Inspired by the recent works that showcase the predictive power of deep neural networks (DNN), [5] compared multiple DNN architectures for behavioral prediction. Most recently, [6] utilized geometric deep learning methods and designed a graph neural network (GNN) architecture for regression that leverages the underlying graph structure of the brain connectomes. Although these studies have promising prediction results, they have either focused on data drawn from a single cohort [3,5] or trained separate models for each cohort [4,6]. However, real-world applications of medical imaging encounter the problem of *domain shift*, where a model trained on a target data distribution (e.g., of the target score to predict) is tested on samples drawn from a different distribution [8].

To address the problem of domain shift in medical imaging, multiple domain adaptation techniques have been proposed. For example, [9] proposed a method for fine-tuning a trained model on a new domain with minimal annotated data. [10] compared multiple transfer learning tools for brain structure segmentation from magnetic resonance images (MRI). However, domain adaptation cannot be applied in all situations as data collection in each target domain is expensive and unfeasible for large-scale applications. An alternative approach to overcome this challenge is quantifying predictive uncertainty. For instance, [11] applies Bayesian inference to a classification problem for estimating predictive uncertainty, whereas [12] utilizes Bayesian neural networks for medical segmentation tasks. While Bayesian methods have proven effective for uncertainty quantification, they require high compute for training. To alleviate these problems, [13] proposed training deep ensembles. These ensembles have outperformed alternative approaches for accuracy and uncertainty estimation according to a large body of empirical research [14], and they were shown to be more robust against dataset shifts [15]. However, they have not been applied to graph neural networks for regression problems.

To address all these limitations, we propose the first method for quantifying the predictive uncertainty of regression GNN models under shifts of the target domain between the train and test sets. Our contributions include 1) estimating predictive uncertainties of regression GNNs by forming deep ensembles, 2) simulating domain shifts at training time by clustering the target domain outputs (i.e., target scores), and 3) designing a novel metric for measuring the uncertainty of the output of a deep ensemble.

2   Methods

In this section, we present the main steps of our deep graph ensemble method for predictive uncertainty estimation under target domain shift. Figure 1 provides an overview

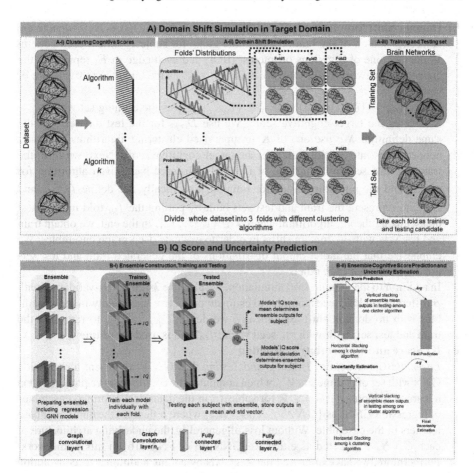

Fig. 1. *Illustration of the predictive uncertainty estimation with target domain shift using an ensemble of GNN architectures.* **A)** Preparing the cohort for the ensemble in order to evaluate the uncertainty estimation with target domain fracture **A-i)** using clustering algorithms in order to **A-ii)** build differently distributed **A-iii)** training and testing data in the output domain. **B)** To overcome the limitations of uncertainty in the target domain, we design a simple but effective ensemble method to predict uncertainty. **B-i)** First, we construct the ensemble with diverse base learners merely consisting of RegGNNs [6] and PNAs [16]. Moreover, each of the base learners is trained with built training sets. **B-ii)** Second, We evaluate the ensemble model with generated test sets. We calculate the target score and predictive uncertainty estimation of the ensemble by calculating the mean and standard deviation over all base learners in ensemble. Third, compute the mean of both cognitive score and uncertainty estimation among domain shift simulations.

of the proposed evaluation method: 1) clustering brain connectomes in the target output space (i.e. cognitive scores) using unsupervised clustering algorithms to simulate train and test sets with different distributions, 2) constructing and training deep graph ensembles, and 3) estimating predictive uncertainty with ensembles on test sets.

A) **Domain Shift Simulation in Target Domain.** Let $G_i(V_i, E_i) \in \mathbb{R}^{d \times d}$ denote the adjacency matrix of the brain connectome graph for subject i where each node in V_i denotes one of d regions of interest (ROI) and each edge in E_i represents the connection between two ROIs. We define $y_i \in \mathbb{R}$ as the target cognitive score of subject i.

Let $D_{train} = \{(G_i(V_i, E_i), y_i) \mid i \in \{1, \ldots, N\}\}$ as the training set where $y_i \in \mathbb{R}$ denotes the target cognitive score. We use D_{test} for the test dataset with the same definition. We use one of K unsupervised clustering algorithms to cluster connectomes into 3 folds based on the target cognitive score. Next, we form the train and test sets by using one of the folds clustered by a given algorithm for testing and the remaining folds for training. Specifically, we define $D_{train}^{k_f}$ and $D_{test}^{k_f}$ to represent the train and test sets built by putting the f_{th} fold into the test dataset using the kth algorithm, where $k \in \{1, \ldots, K\}$. In the end, we obtain train and test sets with K domain shifts in order to evaluate deep graph ensembles. We emphasize that the target output distributions of the generated train and test sets are different from each other.

In addition to the domain shift simulation, we also use 3-fold cross-validation with S different random seeds in order to estimate predictive uncertainty in our ensembles with no domain shift. Specifically, we define $D_{train}^{s_f}, D_{test}^{s_f}$ to represent the train and test sets built with s_{th} seed where f_{th} fold is used for testing.

B) **IQ Score and Uncertainty Prediction**

i) *Ensemble Construction, Training and Testing.* Let GNN_j represent a regression GNN with set of parameters W_j, which computes the cognitive score prediction via a learned mapping $f_j(G_i) \in \mathbb{R}$ for subject i in the dataset. We formed ensembles of regression GNNs as $\{GNN_1, \ldots, GNN_\alpha\}$ where α denotes the number of base learners in the ensemble. Without loss of generality, the underlying architecture of each GNN_j is selected as either RegGNN [6] or PNA [16] in this prime work. Furthermore, we have improved the RegGNN by adding additional n_c convolution layers and n_l linear layers in order to diversify the base learners in the ensemble as recommended by [14], noting that the diversification of the base learners in an ensemble increases the performance in terms of predictive uncertainty estimation. With this motivation, we achieve further diversification among the base learners in the ensemble by varying various parameters including dropout rates, convolutional layer counts n_c, linear layer counts n_l, and hidden sizes n_h.

We use either $D_{train}^{k_f}$ (with domain shift) or $D_{train}^{s_f}$ (without domain shift) to train an ensemble. We treat ensembles as uniformly-weighted mixture models and combine the predictions to predict the target cognitive score for subject i in $D_{test}^{s_f}$ as shown in Eq. 1:

$$M(G_i) = \frac{1}{\alpha} \sum_{j=1}^{\alpha} f_j(G_i) \tag{1}$$

ii) *Ensemble Cognitive Score Prediction and Uncertainty Estimation.* We estimate the predictive uncertainty for subject i in D_{test} by calculating the standard deviation of the predictions of the ensemble as shown in Eq. 2:

$$\sigma^2(G_i) = \frac{1}{\alpha} \sum_{j=1}^{\alpha} (f_j(G_i) - M(G_i))^2 \tag{2}$$

We reach the final predictions for uncertainty and target scores under target domain fracture by combining the predictions for subject i from different clustering algorithms using the following equation: $M(G_i) = \frac{1}{K} \sum_{k=1}^{K} M^k(G_i)$, where $M(G_i)$ denotes the final target score prediction, $M^k(G_i)$ is the predicted target score for subject i trained and tested with the kth clustering algorithm. $\sigma^2(G_i) = \frac{1}{K} \sum_{k=1}^{K} (\sigma^2)^k(G_i)$, where $(\sigma^2)^k(G_i)$ is the uncertainty estimation for subject i trained and tested with the kth clustering algorithm and $\sigma^2(G_i)$ denotes the final predictive uncertainty estimation. Similarly, same equations are applied in the case of seed shuffling for randomizing the cross-validation (i.e., perturbing the distributions of the training and testing sets). $M(G_i) = \frac{1}{S} \sum_{s=1}^{S} M^s(G_i)$ where $M(G_i)$ is the final target score prediction, $M^s(G_i)$ is the predicted target score for subject i trained and tested with the sth seed, $\sigma^2(G_i) = \frac{1}{S} \sum_{s=1}^{S} (\sigma^2)^s(G_i)$ where $(\sigma^2)^s(G_i)$ is the uncertainty estimation for subject i trained and tested with the sth seed and $\sigma^2(G_i)$ the final predictive uncertainty estimation.

We also propose a novel error metric to quantify the performance of ensembles according to the fitting error of the predicted target score and predictive uncertainty error. The intuition behind the presented metric is based on the motivation that if the prediction of the target score results in a high mean absolute error for any subject, then the model should have a high uncertainty and vice versa. Likewise, if the prediction of uncertainty results in high certainty, i.e. standard deviation, then the mean absolute error should be low. With this motivation, we introduce the following error metric e_U in Eq. 3:

$$e_U = \frac{\frac{1}{N} \sum_{i=1}^{N} \frac{\mu_i}{(\sigma_i^2+\epsilon)} + \frac{1}{N} \sum_{n=1}^{N} \frac{\sigma_i^2}{(\mu_i+\epsilon)}}{\frac{1}{N} \sum_{i=1}^{N} \frac{\mu_i}{(\sigma_i^2+\epsilon)} \times \frac{1}{N} \sum_{n=1}^{N} \frac{\sigma_i^2}{(\mu_i+\epsilon)}}, \tag{3}$$

where σ_i^2 is the squared standard deviation (i.e., predictive uncertainty estimate). μ_i is the mean absolute error for the predicted target cognitive score for subject i, and N is the size of the cohort.

3   Experimental Results and Discussion

Evaluation Dataset. For the experiments, we used a randomly selected subset of the Autism Brain Imaging Data Exchange (ABIDE) dataset [17] to account for imaging site bias. Preprocessed datasets are available online[1]. Each subject is represented by a functional brain connectome that is parcellated into 116 ROIs as defined in AAL [18]; they were obtained from resting-state functional magnetic resonance imaging (rs-fMRI) and corresponding full-scale intelligence quotients (FIQ) are given. Our subset contained 202 subjects in the autism spectrum disorder (ASD) cohort (with mean age = (15.4 ± 3.8) and mean FIQ = (106.102 ± 15.045)).

Parameter Setting. We trained our GNN models using the Adam [19] optimizer for 10 epochs with a learning rate of 0.001 and weight decay at 0.0005.

Evaluation and Comparison Methods. To evaluate the performance of deep ensembles with regression GNNs, we trained 8 ensemble models with varying architectures and parameters. The details of the proposed ensembles are explained in Tables 1a–1h.

To measure the predictive uncertainty of deep graph ensembles without domain shift, we trained and tested each ensemble using 3-fold cross-validation. To simulate the domain shift, we clustered the target output scores using a clustering algorithm and trained the ensemble on $N - 1$ clusters while using the Nth cluster as a test set, effectively simulating a fracture in the target output space.

For cross-validation, we repeated the experiments with 5 random seeds. For domain shift simulation, we repeated the experiments using 5 different clustering algorithms

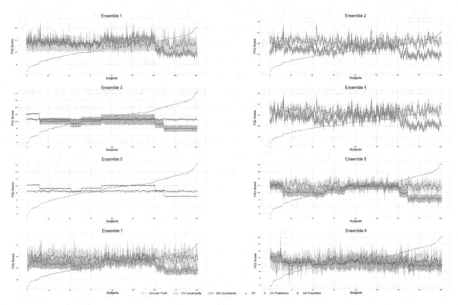

Fig. 2. *Uncertainty results for GNN regression ensembles.* In all plots, subjects are sorted increasingly by FIQ score on the x-axis and the scores are given on the y-axis. The light blue dotted curve represents the ground truth FIQ scores, the pink line represents the mean of the ensemble prediction under domain shift simulation and the green represents the mean under cross-validation. For both lines, the standard deviation of the predictions is given as the area chart of the corresponding color. (Color figure online)

---

[1] https://github.com/preprocessed-connectomes-project/abide.

Table 1. *Proposed regression GNN ensembles.* A total of 8 ensembles are proposed, with each ensemble including base learners obtained by varying one or more parameters of regression GNNs from previous works.

Ensemble 1				
Model	n_h	n_c	n_l	Dropout
RegGNN	64	0	0	0.3
PNA	64	0	0	0.3

(a)Varying architecture

Ensemble 2				
Model	n_h	n_c	n_l	Dropout
PNA	64	0	0	0.3
PNA	32	0	0	0.3
PNA	16	0	0	0.3
PNA	4	0	0	0.3

(b) Varying hidden size in PNA

Ensemble 3				
Model	n_h	n_c	n_l	Dropout
RegGNN	64	0	0	0.3
RegGNN	32	0	0	0.3
RegGNN	16	0	0	0.3
RegGNN	4	0	0	0.3

(c) Varying hidden size in RegGNN

Ensemble 4				
Model	n_h	n_c	n_l	Dropout
PNA	64	0	0	0.1
PNA	64	0	0	0.2
PNA	64	0	0	0.3
PNA	64	0	0	0.4

(d) Varying dropout in PNA

Ensemble 5				
Model	n_h	n_c	n_l	Dropout
RegGNN	64	0	0	0.1
RegGNN	64	0	0	0.2
RegGNN	64	0	0	0.3
RegGNN	64	0	0	0.4

(e) Varying dropout in RegGNN

Ensemble 6				
Model	n_h	n_c	n_l	Dropout
RegGNN	64	1	1	0.1
RegGNN	64	3	3	0.2
RegGNN	64	5	5	0.3
RegGNN	64	7	7	0.4

(f) Varying layer counts in RegGNN

Ensemble 7				
Model	n_h	n_c	n_l	Dropout
RegGNN	64	1	1	0.1
RegGNN	64	3	3	0.2
RegGNN	64	5	5	0.3
RegGNN	64	7	7	0.4
RegGNN	64	1	1	0.1
RegGNN	32	3	3	0.2
RegGNN	16	5	5	0.3
RegGNN	4	7	7	0.4

(g) Varying layer counts and dropout in RegGNN

Ensemble 8				
Model	n_h	n_c	n_l	Dropout
RegGNN	64	1	1	0.3
RegGNN	64	2	2	0.3
RegGNN	64	3	3	0.3
RegGNN	32	1	1	0.3
RegGNN	32	2	2	0.3
RegGNN	32	3	3	0.3
RegGNN	16	1	1	0.3
RegGNN	16	2	2	0.3
RegGNN	16	3	3	0.3
RegGNN	4	1	1	0.3
RegGNN	4	2	2	0.3
RegGNN	4	3	3	0.3

(h) Varying hidden sizes and layer counts in RegGNN

to eliminate biases stemming from the clustering algorithm of the target outputs. The clustering algorithms used are as follows.

- K-Means [20],
- Affinity Propagation [21],
- BIRCH [22],
- Agglomerative Clustering [23]
- Spectral Clustring [24].

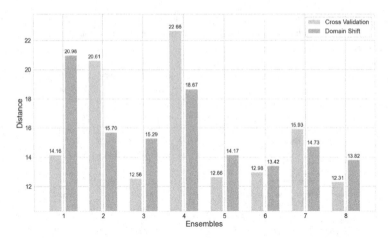

Fig. 3. *Comparison of GNN regression ensembles using the mean distance between the predicted target scores and the ground truth ones across subjects.* These values represent the distance between the ground-truth line displayed in blue in Fig. 2 and the red (under domain fracture) and green (cross-validation with no domain fracture) lines, respectively. (Color figure online)

In Fig. 2, evaluation results for the eight deep graph ensemble models are given with and without domain shift simulation. The uncertainty field obtained as a result of domain shift should be higher than the uncertainty field obtained as a result of the absence of domain shift. The model should not be confident of the target score predictions since the overall target score prediction and estimation of predictive uncertainty has been performed in the case of domain shift fracture. With this motivation, we conclude that ensemble 8 performs the most successful uncertainty estimation by probing the results in Fig. 2. On the other hand, we quantify the distance of the predicted target scores in Fig. 2 with and without domain shift where the distance is the mean of distance between the predicted target score line and ground truth line. The results are shown in Fig. 3 for the ensembles. While ensemble 8 and ensemble 3 perform better than other ensembles in the case of no domain shift, ensemble 6 and ensemble 8 achieve the best target score prediction under domain shift. It is important to note that all the successful ensembles in terms of the distance between the predicted target score and ground truth merely consist of RegGNNs. Therefore, we conclude from the results in Fig. 3 that ensembles including only RegGNN tend to perform more successfully than ensembles mixing RegGNN and PNA or having only PNA.

In Fig. 4, we compare the average performance of ensembles based on the mean absolute error (MAE). We note that the cross-validation errors are lower as the data is uniformly distributed across folds. We obtained higher error values under domain shift simulation as expected, proving that our simulation captures the shift between the train and test data distributions. We can conclude that Ensembles 3, 5, and 8 achieve the lowest errors with no domain shift. However, under the presence of domain shift simulation, the most successful model is Ensemble 8, which is the most diverse ensemble. Remarkably, this shows the robustness of diverse deep graph ensembles against domain

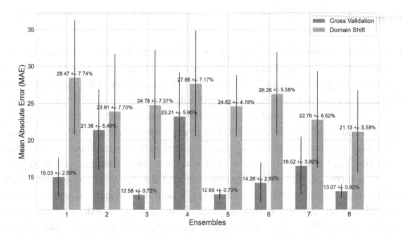

Fig. 4. *Comparison of ensembles using the mean absolute error (MAE).* Each ensemble is evaluated with and without domain shift simulation. Error bars represent the standard deviation of the predictions.

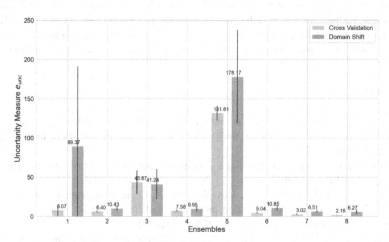

Fig. 5. *Comparison of ensembles using the proposed uncertainty error e_U.* Each ensemble is evaluated with and without domain shift simulation to estimate predictive uncertainty.

shift. Also, we observe that ensemble models formed with RegGNN perform better, which is in line with the previous work [6] stating that RegGNN outperforms PNA in regression despite its simple architecture.

In Fig. 5, we compare the performance of the GNN regression ensembles using the proposed predictive uncertainty measure e_U. We observe that Ensemble 8 has the lowest uncertainty error under both cross-validation and domain shift simulations, again showing its efficiency in minimizing uncertainty. We also concluded that when using larger deep graph ensembles with a diverse set of base learners helps optimize predictive uncertainty.

4   Conclusion

In this paper, we proposed a deep graph ensemble method with regression graph neural networks for quantifying the predictive uncertainty caused by target domain shifts. Moreover, we designed a method for domain shift simulation in the target output space and we proposed a novel predictive uncertainty measure to quantify the uncertainty of an ensemble. Our experimental results showed that diverse ensembles using regression GNNs reduce the predictive uncertainty error in both uniformly distributed data and under target domain shifts. [14] demonstrated that the generated ensembles with neural architectural search algorithms perform better than manually constructed deep ensembles in terms of uncertainty calibration and dataset shift robustness. With this motivation, in our future work, we aim to apply neural architectural search methods to the ensemble design in order to automatically construct optimal deep graph ensembles from a search space. We will also investigate the uncertainty *reproducibility* [25] across diverse datasets and models.

Acknowledgements. This work was funded by generous grants from the European H2020 Marie Sklodowska-Curie action (grant no. 101003403, http://basira-lab.com/normnets/) to I.R. and the Scientific and Technological Research Council of Turkey to I.R. under the TUBITAK 2232 Fellowship for Outstanding Researchers (no. 118C288, http://basira-lab.com/reprime/). However, all scientific contributions made in this project are owned and approved solely by the authors.

References

1. Colom, R., Escorial, S., Shih, P.C., Privado, J.: Fluid intelligence, memory span, and temperament difficulties predict academic performance of young adolescents. Pers. Individ. Differ. **42**, 1503–1514 (2007)
2. Gottfredson, L.S., Deary, I.J.: Intelligence predicts health and longevity, but why? Curr. Dir. Psychol. Sci. **13**, 1–4 (2004)
3. Shen, X., Finn, E.S., Scheinost, D., Rosenberg, M.D., Chun, M.M., Papademetris, X., Constable, R.T.: Using connectome-based predictive modeling to predict individual behavior from brain connectivity. Nat. Protoc. **12**, 506–518 (2017)
4. Dryburgh, E., McKenna, S., Rekik, I.: Predicting full-scale and verbal intelligence scores from functional connectomic data in individuals with autism spectrum disorder. Brain Imaging Behav. **14**, 1769–1778 (2020). https://doi.org/10.1007/s11682-019-00111-w
5. He, T., et al.: Deep neural networks and kernel regression achieve comparable accuracies for functional connectivity prediction of behavior and demographics. Neuroimage, **206**, 116276 (2020)
6. Hanik, M., Demirtaş, M.A., Gharsallaoui, M.A., Rekik, I.: Predicting cognitive scores with graph neural networks through sample selection learning. Brain Imaging Behav. **16**, 1123–1138 (2021). https://doi.org/10.1007/s11682-021-00585-7
7. Bessadok, A., Mahjoub, M.A., Rekik, I.: Brain graph synthesis by dual adversarial domain alignment and target graph prediction from a source graph. Med. Image Anal. **68**, 101902 (2021)
8. Wang, M., Deng, W.: Deep visual domain adaptation: a survey. Neurocomputing **312**, 135–153 (2018)

9. Zakazov, I., Shirokikh, B., Chernyavskiy, A., Belyaev, M.: Anatomy of domain shift impact on U-Net layers in MRI segmentation. In: de Bruijne, M., et al. (eds.) MICCAI 2021. LNCS, vol. 12903, pp. 211–220. Springer, Cham (2021). https://doi.org/10.1007/978-3-030-87199-4_20

10. Kushibar, K., et al.: Supervised domain adaptation for automatic sub-cortical brain structure segmentation with minimal user interaction. Sci. Rep. **9**, 1–15 (2019)

11. Hernández, S., López, J.L.: Uncertainty quantification for plant disease detection using Bayesian deep learning. Appl. Soft Comput. **96**, 106597 (2020)

12. Kwon, Y., Won, J.H., Kim, B.J., Paik, M.C.: Uncertainty quantification using Bayesian neural networks in classification: application to biomedical image segmentation. Comput. Stat. Data Anal. **142**, 106816 (2020)

13. Lakshminarayanan, B., Pritzel, A., Blundell, C.: Simple and scalable predictive uncertainty estimation using deep ensembles. In: Advances in Neural Information Processing Systems 30 (2017)

14. Zaidi, S., Zela, A., Elsken, T., Holmes, C.C., Hutter, F., Teh, Y.: Neural ensemble search for uncertainty estimation and dataset shift. Adv. Neural. Inf. Process. Syst. **34**, 7898–7911 (2021)

15. Ovadia, Y., et al.: Can you trust your model's uncertainty? evaluating predictive uncertainty under dataset shift. In: Advances in Neural Information Processing Systems 32 (2019)

16. Corso, G., Cavalleri, L., Beaini, D., Liò, P., Veličković, P.: Principal neighbourhood aggregation for graph nets. Adv. Neural. Inf. Process. Syst. **33**, 13260–13271 (2020)

17. Craddock, C., et al.: The neuro bureau preprocessing initiative: open sharing of preprocessed neuroimaging data and derivatives. Front. Neuroinform. **7**, 27 (2013)

18. Tzourio-Mazoyer, N., et al.: Automated anatomical labeling of activations in SPM using a macroscopic anatomical parcellation of the MNI MRI single-subject brain. Neuroimage **15**, 273–289 (2002)

19. Kingma, D.P., Ba, J.: Adam: a method for stochastic optimization. arXiv preprint arXiv:1412.6980 (2014)

20. MacQueen, J.: Classification and analysis of multivariate observations. In: 5th Berkeley Symposium on Mathematical Statistics and Probability, pp. 281–297 (1967)

21. Frey, B.J., Dueck, D.: Clustering by passing messages between data points. Science **315**, 972–976 (2007)

22. Zhang, T., Ramakrishnan, R., Livny, M.: Birch: a new data clustering algorithm and its applications. Data Min. Knowl. Disc. **1**, 141–182 (1997). https://doi.org/10.1023/A:1009783824328

23. Sibson, R.: Slink: an optimally efficient algorithm for the single-link cluster method. Comput. J. **16**, 30–34 (1973)

24. Shi, J., Malik, J.: Normalized cuts and image segmentation. IEEE Trans. Pattern Anal. Mach. Intell. **22**, 888–905 (2000)

25. Nebli, A., Gharsallaoui, M.A., Gürler, Z., Rekik, I., Initiative, A.D.N., et al.: Quantifying the reproducibility of graph neural networks using multigraph data representation. Neural Netw. **148**, 254–265 (2022)

Investigating the Predictive Reproducibility of Federated Graph Neural Networks Using Medical Datasets

Mehmet Yiğit Balık[1], Arwa Rekik[1,2], and Islem Rekik[1(✉)]

[1] BASIRA Lab, Faculty of Computer and Informatics Engineering,
Istanbul Technical University, Istanbul, Turkey
irekik@itu.edu.tr
[2] Faculty of Medicine of Sousse, Sousse, Tunisia
http://basira-lab.com

Abstract. Graph neural networks (GNNs) have achieved extraordinary enhancements in various areas including the fields medical imaging and network neuroscience where they displayed a high accuracy in diagnosing challenging neurological disorders such as autism. In the face of medical data scarcity and high-privacy, training such data-hungry models remains challenging. Federated learning brings an efficient solution to this issue by allowing to train models on multiple datasets, collected independently by different hospitals, in fully data-preserving manner. Although both state-of-the-art GNNs and federated learning techniques focus on boosting classification accuracy, they overlook a critical unsolved problem: *investigating the reproducibility of the most discriminative biomarkers (i.e., features) selected by the GNN models within a federated learning paradigm.* Quantifying the reproducibility of a predictive medical model against perturbations of training and testing data distributions presents one of the biggest hurdles to overcome in developing translational clinical applications. To the best of our knowledge, this presents the first work investigating the reproducibility of *federated GNN models* with application to classifying medical imaging and brain connectivity datasets. We evaluated our framework using various GNN models trained on medical imaging and connectomic datasets. More importantly, we showed that federated learning boosts both the accuracy and reproducibility of GNN models in such medical learning tasks. Our source code is available at https://github.com/basiralab/reproducibleFedGNN.

Keywords: Graph neural networks · Federated Learning · Reproducibility · Brain connectivity graphs · Predictive medicine

1 Introduction

Over the last years, artificial intelligence (AI) applied to medicine has witnessed exponential growth aiming to ease the diagnostic approach and propel, consequently, the

Supplementary Information The online version contains supplementary material available at
https://doi.org/10.1007/978-3-031-16919-9_15.

development of personalized treatment strategies. Specifically, advanced deep learning (DL) models such as convolutional neural networks (CNNs) have achieved a remarkable performance across of variety of medical imaging tasks including segmentation, classification, and registration [1,2]. However, such networks were primarily designed to handle images, thereby failing to generalize to non-euclidean data such as graphs and manifolds [3,4]. Recently, graph neural networks (GNNs) were introduced to solve this problem by designing novel graph-based convolutions [4,5]. A recent review paper [6] demonstrated the merits of using GNNs particularly when applied to brain connectomes (i.e., graphs) across different learning tasks including longitudinal brain graph prediction, brain graph super-resolution and classification for neurological disorder diagnosis. Althgouh promising, GNNs remain deep models which are data-hungry. Faced with the scarcity of medical imaging datasets and their high privacy and sensitivity, they can remain sub-optimal in their performance. In this perspective, federated learning [7] can bring a promising alternative to training GNNs models using decentralized data spread across multiple hospitals while boosting the accuracy of each local GNN model in a fully data-preserving manner. Although increasing the model accuracy through federation seems compelling, there remains a more important goal to achieve which is maximizing the *reproducibility* of a locally trained model. A model is defined as highly reproducible when its top discriminative features (e.g., biomarkers) remain unchanged against perturbations of training and testing data distributions as well as across other models [8–10]. Quantifying the reproducibility of a predictive medical model presents one of the biggest hurdles to overcome in developing translational clinical applications. In fact, this allows identifying the most *reproducible biomarkers* that can be used in treating patients with a particular disorder. To the best of our knowledge, reproducibility in federated learning remains an untackled problem.

[8] proposed the first framework investigating the reproducibility of GNN models. Specifically, the designed RG-Select framework used 5 different state-of-the-art GNN models to identify the most reproducible GNN model for a given connectomic dataset of interest. Although RG-Select solves both GNN reproducibility and non-euclidean data learning problems, it does not address the problem of model reproducibility when learning on decentralized datasets distributed across different hospitals. Undeniably, medical datasets carry information about patients and their medical conditions. Hence, the patient may be identified using such data. Patients have the right to control their personal information and keep it for themselves [11]. Such data must be held private between the patient and their health care workers. For such reasons, federated learning presents a great opportunity to learn without clinical data sharing and while boosting the model accuracy as well as its reproducibility.

We draw inspiration from the seminal work on decentralized learning where [7] proposed a federated averaging algorithm based on training many local models on their local datasets then aggregating the learned models at the server level. Next, the global server broadcasts their learned weights to each local modal for local updates. Several researchers were inspired by federated learning and adapted it to graphs [12,13]. Even though these proposed frameworks managed to boost the local accuracy of local models while handling decentralized data, they overlook the reproducibility of the most discriminative features (i.e., biomarkers). Will federated learning also boost the reproducibility of locally trained GNN models? Here we set out to address this prime question by quantifying the reproducibility of federated local models.

In order to ensure high accuracy, handle decentralized datasets and identify the most reproducible discriminative features, we federate GNN models and quantify their reproducibility by perturbing training and testing medical data distributions through random data splits. Our framework generalizes the seminal work of RG-Select [8] to federated models. Specifically, given a pool of GNN architectures to federate, we aim to identify the most reproducible GNN model across local hospitals and its corresponding biomarkers by quantifying the reproducibility of the global model. The key contributions of our framework are to: (1) Federate the learning of predictive GNN models with application to medical imaging and connectomic datasets. (2) Investigate and quantify the reproducibility of federated GNN models, and (3) identify the most *reproducible* biomarkers for neurological disorder diagnosis.

2   Proposed Method

In this section, we detail our federated reproducibility quantification framework as illustrated in Fig. 1. First, we divide the whole data into H different subsets. Each subset represents the local data of a particular hospital. Second, we train different GNN models using federated learning trained on each local dataset. Following the training, we extract the top K discriminative biomarkers (features) identified by each locally trained GNN model. Next, for each hospital, we produce a *hospital-specific GNN-to-GNN reproducibility matrix* where each element denotes the overlap ratio between the extracted top K biomarker sets by pairs of locally trained GNN models. We then construct the *global reproducibility matrix* by averaging all hospital-specific reproducibility matrices. Finally, we identify the most reproducible GNN model across hospitals in the federation process by identifying the central node with the highest overlap with other nodes in the global average reproducibility matrix. The selected model is then used to identify the most reproducible features.

Problem Statement. Given H hospitals with the local datasets $\mathcal{D}_h = (\mathcal{G}_h, \mathcal{Y}_h)$ that belongs to the hth hospital, where $h \in \{1, 2, \ldots, H\}$, let $\mathcal{D}_h$ denote a local dataset including subjects with their diagnostic states/labels (e.g., normal control and disordered). Let S denote the number of subjects in $\mathcal{D}_h$. $\mathcal{G}_h = \{\mathbf{G}_{h,1}, \mathbf{G}_{h,2}, \ldots, \mathbf{G}_{h,S}\}$ denotes the set of medical data graphs and their labels are denoted by $\mathcal{Y}_h = \{y_{h,1}, y_{h,2}, \ldots, y_{h,N}\}$. Each graph $\mathbf{G}_{h,n}$ is represented by an adjacency matrix $\mathbf{X}_{h,n} \in \mathbb{R}^{N \times N}$ and a label $y_{h,n} \in \{0, 1\}$ where N denotes the number of brain regions of interest (ROIs) for connectivity datasets or pixels for medical imaging datasets. Note that N also represents the number of nodes in the corresponding graph.

Given a pool of M GNNs $\{GNN_1, GNN_2, \ldots GNN_M\}$, we are interested in training a GNN model $GNN_{h,m} : \mathcal{G}_h \to \mathcal{Y}_h$ on the local dataset of hospital h. Our aim is to identify the most reproducible biomarkers or features that discriminate between the two classes. Hence, we extract the top K features $r_{h,m}^K \in \mathbb{R}^K$ learned by the mth local GNN model in the hth hospital, where $m \in \{1, 2, \ldots, M\}$. We calculate the intersection of the extracted local top K features $r_{h,m}^K \cap r_{h,l}^K$, where m and l are the indexes of GNN models in the GNN pool and h is the index of a hospital. In order to

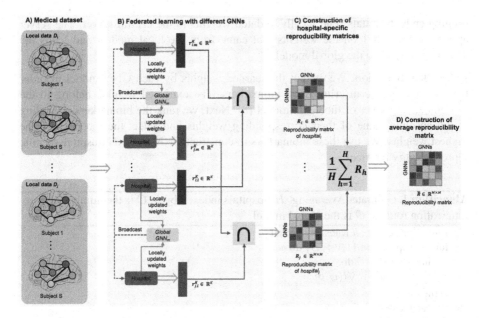

Fig. 1. *Overview of the proposed framework for quantifying the reproducibility of federated GNN models across decentralized datasets.* (**A**) **Medical datasets.** We split our dataset into H local datasets. (**B**) **Federated learning with different GNNs.** We use M GNN models to identify the most reproducible GNN model during the federation learning. For each local hospital model GNN_m where $m \in \{1, \ldots, M\}$, we extract its top K discriminative features and calculate their overlap ratio with discriminative feature sets selected by other GNN models. (**C**) **Construction of hospital-specific reproducibility matrix.** Using the intersections calculated in the previous step, we construct the hospital-specific reproducibility matrix where each element (i, j) denotes the overlap in the top K features identified by the locally trained GNN_i and GNN_j. (**D**) **Construction of average global reproducibility matrix across federated models.** Using the produced hospital-specific reproducibility matrices, we calculate the average global reproducibility matrix, thereby identifying the most reproducible features across models and hospitals.

calculate the reproducibility matrices, we extract the weights $\mathbf{w}_{h,m} \in \mathbb{R}^N$ learned by the hth hospital using the mth GNN architecture.

Definition 1. *Let GNN_i and GNN_j be two GNN models and let $\mathbf{w}_i \in \mathbb{R}^n$ and $\mathbf{w}_j \in \mathbb{R}^n$ be their weights, respectively. The top K biomarkers extracted using the weights $\mathbf{w}_i, \mathbf{w}_j$ are denoted by r_i^K and r_j^K, respectively. Reproducibility among models GNN_i and GNN_j is denoted by $\mathbf{R}_{i,j}^K$ which can be calculated as: $\mathbf{R}_{i,j}^K = \frac{|r_i^K \cap r_j^K|}{K}$.*

GNN Training Mode. Each local data is divided into 3 folds where 2 folds are used for training and the left-out fold is used for validation. We train each local GNN on its local dataset over E epochs and using B batches. Both global and local models communicate for C rounds. In each round, the global model sends a deep copy of the current GNN model to all local hospitals. Each hospital does training using its local data. When the training ends, hospitals send locally updated weights to the central server. The server applies Algorithm 1 on the weights that came from the local models and loads the averaged weights to the global model.

Biomarker Selection. We extract the learned weights by each GNN model in order to select the top K discriminative biomarkers. The extracted weights belong to the last embedding layer of the GNN model [8]. Next, we rank the biomarkers according to the absolute value of their corresponding weights and select the top K with the highest weights. We use these biomarkers to construct GNN-to-GNN hospital-specific reproducibility matrices.

Algorithm 1. FederatedAveraging. H hospitals indexed by h; C is the number of communication rounds; G is the global model

1: **LocalUpdate**(G) : // Runs on hospital h
2: **for** each epoch i in $\{1, \ldots, E\}$ **do**
3:     **for** batch b in B **do**
4:         $w \leftarrow w - \eta \nabla l(w; b)$
5: **return** w
6: **Server Executes:**
7: initialize global model G
8: **for** each round t in $\{1, \ldots, C\}$ **do**
9:     **for** each hospital h in $\{1, \ldots, H\}$ **do**
10:         $w_{t+1}^h \leftarrow$ LocalUpdate(deepCopy(G)) // Copy of global model sent to local update
11:     $w_{t+1} \leftarrow \sum_{h=1}^{H} \frac{w_{t+1}^h}{H}$

Algorithm 2. AvgRepMatrixConstruction. W weights of all GNNs; K is the threshold value

1: **RepMatrixConstruction**(W, K):
2: **for** w_i and w_j in $|W|$ **do** // absolute value of weights is used
3:     $r_i^K \leftarrow$ Top K features from w_i
4:     $r_j^K \leftarrow$ Top K features from w_j
5:     $\mathbf{R}_{ij}^K \leftarrow \frac{|r_i^K \cap r_j^K|}{K}$
6: **return** $\mathbf{R}^K$
7: **Execute:**
8: initialize $\bar{R} \in R^{M \times M}$ with zeros
9: **for** each hospital weights W_h where h in $\{1, \ldots, H\}$ **do**
10:     $\bar{R} \leftarrow \bar{R} +$ RepMatrixConstruction(W_h, K)
11: $\bar{R} \leftarrow \frac{\bar{R}}{H}$

GNN-to-GNN Reproducibility Matrix. Using the top K biomarkers, the overlap of each pair of GNN models is calculated thereby producing their GNN-to-GNN reproducibility score. This step is executed for each hospital individually to produce a hospital-specific reproducibility matrix. Repeating this operation for all H hospitals, the average of H hospital-specific matrices is then calculated, and the average global reproducibility matrix is constructed using Algorithm 2.

The Most Reproducible GNN and Biomarker Selection. In order to select the most reproducible GNN model, we use the average reproducibility matrix of the H hospital-specific reproducibility matrices. We consider this matrix as a graph where the GNN models are its nodes. We use the highest node strength to identify the most reproducible global federated model (Definition 2). In fact, such a hub GNN node implies a maximal overlap with other GNN models, thereby evidencing its reproducible power. Next, we find the most reproducible K biomarkers with the highest weights learned by the most reproducible GNN model.

Definition 2. *Given M GNN models to federate, let $\mathbf{R} \in \mathbb{R}^{M \times M}$ denote the constructed reproducibility matrix where each element encodes the intersection rate of the top K biomarkers identify by pairs of global GNN models. Let $\mathbf{r}_i$ be the ith row of $\mathbf{R}$ where $i \in \{1, 2, \ldots, M\}$. The $\mathbf{r}_i$ includes the top K biomarkers intersection ratios of GNN_i with all GNN models including itself. Let s_i denote the strength (i.e., score) of GNN_i defined as: $s_i = (\sum_{m=1}^{M} \mathbf{r}_{i,m}) - 1$ (minus one is for excluding the relation with itself).*

3   Results and Discussion

Evaluation of Biomedical Image Datasets. We evaluated our federated reproducibility framework on two large-scale biomedical image datasets which are retrieved from MedMNIST[1] public dataset collection [14]. The first biomedical image dataset (PneumoniaMNIST dataset) contains 5856 X-ray images, with a size of 28×28, and belonging to a normal control class or displaying pneumonia which is a respiratory infection that affects the lungs [15]. Out of the 5856 subjects, we randomly selected 1000 samples with balanced classes (normal and pneumonia). The second dataset (BreastMNIST dataset) contains 780 breast ultrasound images, with the size of 28×28, belonging to a normal control or diagnosed with malignant breast cancer. We randomly sampled 546 subjects where 399 subjects are labeled as normal and 147 as malignant. We used two different representations of the imaging datasets to feed into the models. In the first representation, we simply fed the original image to the target GNN whereas in the second representation we converted each image into weighted graph matrix. The weights of connectivity matrix were calculated using absolute differences in intensity between pixel pairs.

Evaluation of Connectomic Datasets. Additionally, we used the Autism Brain Imaging Data Exchange (ABIDE I) public dataset [16] to evaluate our federated reproducibility framework on morphological brain networks [17]. We used the left and right hemisphere brain connectivity datasets of autism spectrum disorder (ASD) and normal controls (NC). These datasets include 300 brain graphs with balanced classes. Both left

---

[1] https://medmnist.com/.

and right hemispheres are parcellated into 35 regions of interest (ROIs) using Desikan-Killiany Atlas [18] and FreeSurfer [19] software. The connectivity weight encodes the average morphological dissimilarity in cortical thickness between two cortical ROIs as introduced in [17,20].

Pool of GNNs. For our federated reproducibility framework, we used 2 state-of-the-art GNNs which are DiffPool [21] and GCN [22]. DiffPool includes a differentiable graph pooling module that is able to generate hierarchical representations of a given graph. Soft cluster assignments learned by DiffPool at each layer of GNN [21] to capture the graph nested modularity. The original aim of GCN is to perform node classification. However, we adapted the original GCN to handle whole-graph-based classification as in [8]. The code of [8][2] was used to develop our framework.

Training Settings and Hyperparameters. To train models in a federated manner, we divided each dataset into $H = 3$ local (independent) sets. We also divided each local data into 3-folds where two folds are used for training and the left one for testing. We selected all of the learning rates empirically. For DiffPool, the learning rate is set to 10^{-4} across all datasets. For GCN, the selected learning rates are 10^{-6}, 10^{-5}, 10^{-5} and 5×10^{-6} for the datasets PneumoniaMNIST, BreastMNIST, ASD/NC LH and ASD/NC RH, respectively. The threshold value K for the top features is set to 20 in our experiment. The epoch size E is fixed to 100 and batch size B is set to 1. The number of communication rounds C is set to 5.

Model Accuracy and Reproducibility Evaluation. We compared our federated reproducibility framework to the non-federated technique (without using Algorithm 1). The comparison was performed for both validation accuracies and average reproducibility matrices storing the intersection ratio of the top K discriminative biomarkers between global GNN models. Fig. 2 shows the comparison results of the classification accuracy and reproducibility matrices for two biomedical image datasets and two connectomic datasets. Notably, the classification accuracy was boosted across all datasets for each local model using federation. For the datasets, PneumoniaMNIST, ASD/NC LH and ASD/NC RH, an increase in the GNN reproducibility score is noted. However, a slight decrease was observed when we evaluated our federated reproducibility framework with the BreastMNIST dataset. The results of biomedical image datasets displayed in Fig. 2 were obtained when traininng GNN models on the original images directly. Supp. Fig. 1 displays the accuracy and reproducibility score comparison of the graph and image representations of the biomedical image datasets. Interestingly, according to Supp. Fig. 1, models performed better in terms of both accuracy and reproducibility when the original images were used without resorting to transforming them into graphs.

Most Reproducible Connectomic Biomarkers. Figures 3 and 4 shows the absolute value of the feature weights learned by the globally most reproducible GNN, which are the averages of the locally learned weights using ASD/NC LH and RH datasets, respectively. We considered the global GNN model rather than the hospital-specific local models to select the most reproducible biomarkers since the most reproducible model may change across hospitals. According to Fig. 4, the insula cortex and lingual

---

[2] https://github.com/basiralab/RG-Select.

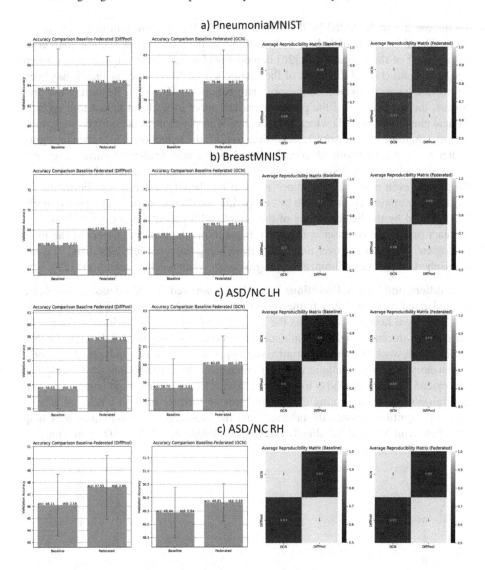

Fig. 2. *Accuracy and global reproducibility matrix comparison across datasets and GNN models.* Each row in the figure represents individual datasets. The first and second columns are the accuracy comparison results of DiffPool and GCN models, respectively. The third and fourth columns represent the baseline and federated reproducibility matrices, respectively.

gyrus are selected as the most reproducible biomarkers for both LH and RH datasets followed by the precuneus and the inferior parietal cortex. In patients presenting with autism, the insula cortex shows an important variation in T1 according to [23]. Such finding embodies the nature of this neurodevelopmental disorder mainly characterized by altered cognitive, emotional and sensory functions. These neurological aspects of the disease are orchestrated by the insular cortex [24] pinpointing further that autism is considered an insula pathology and highlighting the reliability of such biomarker as a fingerprint of the disease [25]. [26] demonstrated a significant relationship between ASD traits and cortical thickness of the lingual gyrus. As a matter of fact, it has been linked to the specific aspect of sensory disturbances in ASD [27]. Regarding the precuneus, the medial part of the posterior parietal lobe, it has been linked to a specific clinical phenotype of ASD which is associated with psychological comorbidities, such as post-traumatic stress disorder. According to [28], the reduction in the precuneus gray matter was correlated with adverse childhood experiences leading to intrusive reexperiencing in adults with ASD. Thus, the precuneus represents a potential biomarker of the disease even more valuable since it could be phenotype-dependant. Furthermore, the almost miror effect discernible by comparing both hemispheres (Fig 3 and 4) might be explained by the heterogeneity of the sample with patients' age ranging from 5 to 64 years (mean age of onset = 14 years). It pinpoints the evolving aspect of the morphological abnormalities over time going from being primarily left-lateralized to inter-hemispheric differences diminishing progressively when reaching adulthood [29].

Limitations and Future Directions. Even though we used different datasets to evaluate our federated reproducibility framework, it has several limitations. First, we assumed that each local hospital has almost the same number of samples –which might not be the case for decentralized medical datasets. Second, we only used 2 different GNNs. In our future work, we aim to optimize our hyperparameters using advanced methods, use an early stopping technique, consider imbalanced data distributions across hospitals and extend the pool of GNNs to obtain more results for an enhanced comparison and generalizability. Incorporating clinical features of patients such as a detailed assessment of cognition, sensory disturbances and the presence of comorbidities may help add phenotypic value to the already established biomarkers of the ASD in our study.

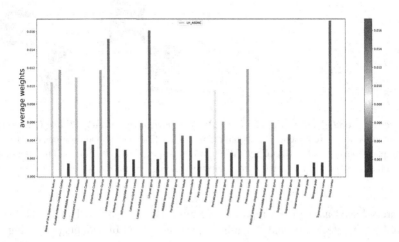

Fig. 3. *The learned weights of the cortical regions by the most reproducible GNN model for the dataset ASD/NC LH.*

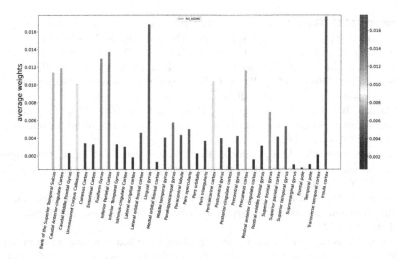

Fig. 4. *The learned GNN weights of the cortical regions by the most reproducible GNN model for the dataset ASD/NC RH.*

4 Conclusion

In this paper, we investigated and quantified the reproducibility of GNN models trained in a federated manner. We evaluated our federated reproducibility framework using several medical imaging and connectomic datasets. Our framework aims to calculate the most reproducible biomarkers or features while handling decentralized datasets and boosting the local model accuracies. In this prime work, we showed that federated learning not only increases the performance of locally trained GNN models but also boosts their reproducibility. In our future work, we will investigate federated GNN reproducibility when learning on non-IID clinical datasets and examine other state-of-the-art GNN models.

Acknowledgements. This work was funded by generous grants from the European H2020 Marie Sklodowska-Curie action (grant no. 101003403, http://basira-lab.com/normnets/) to I.R. and the Scientific and Technological Research Council of Turkey to I.R. under the TUBITAK 2232 Fellowship for Outstanding Researchers (no. 118C288, http://basira-lab.com/reprime/). However, all scientific contributions made in this project are owned and approved solely by the authors.

References

1. Lee, J.G., et al.: Deep learning in medical imaging: general overview. Korean J. Radiol. **18**, 570–584 (2017)
2. Shen, D., Wu, G., Suk, H.I.: Deep learning in medical image analysis. Annu. Rev. Biomed. Eng. **19**, 221 (2017)
3. Wolterink, J., Suk, J.: Geometric deep learning for precision medicine. Key Enabling Technol. Sci. Mach. Learn. **60**

4. Bronstein, M.M., Bruna, J., LeCun, Y., Szlam, A., Vandergheynst, P.: Geometric deep learning: going beyond euclidean data. IEEE Signal Process. Mag. **34**, 18–42 (2017)
5. Wu, Z., Pan, S., Chen, F., Long, G., Zhang, C., Philip, S.Y.: A comprehensive survey on graph neural networks. IEEE Trans. Neural Netw. Learn. Syst. **32**, 4–24 (2020)
6. Bessadok, A., Mahjoub, M.A., Rekik, I.: Graph neural networks in network neuroscience. arXiv preprint arXiv:2106.03535 (2021)
7. McMahan, B., Moore, E., Ramage, D., Hampson, S., y Arcas, B.A.: Communication-efficient learning of deep networks from decentralized data. In: Artificial intelligence and statistics, PMLR, pp. 1273–1282 (2017)
8. Nebli, A., Gharsallaoui, M.A., Gürler, Z., Rekik, I., Initiative, A.D.N., et al.: Quantifying the reproducibility of graph neural networks using multigraph data representation. Neural Netw. **148**, 254–265 (2022)
9. Georges, N., Mhiri, I., Rekik, I., Initiative, A.D.N., et al.: Identifying the best data-driven feature selection method for boosting reproducibility in classification tasks. Pattern Recogn. **101**, 107183 (2020)
10. Georges, N., Rekik, I.: Data-specific feature selection method identification for most reproducible connectomic feature discovery fingerprinting brain states. In: Wu, G., Rekik, I., Schirmer, M.D., Chung, A.W., Munsell, B. (eds.) CNI 2018. LNCS, vol. 11083, pp. 99–106. Springer, Cham (2018). https://doi.org/10.1007/978-3-030-00755-3_11
11. Forcier, M.B., Gallois, H., Mullan, S., Joly, Y.: Integrating artificial intelligence into health care through data access: can the GDPR act as a beacon for policymakers? J. Law Biosci. **6**, 317 (2019)
12. Chen, C., Hu, W., Xu, Z., Zheng, Z.: Fedgl: federated graph learning framework with global self-supervision. arXiv preprint arXiv:2105.03170 (2021)
13. He, C., et al.: Fedgraphnn: a federated learning benchmark system for graph neural networks. In: ICLR 2021 Workshop on Distributed and Private Machine Learning (DPML) (2021)
14. Yang, J., et al.: Medmnist v2: A large-scale lightweight benchmark for 2D and 3d biomedical image classification. arXiv preprint arXiv:2110.14795 (2021)
15. Gereige, R.S., Laufer, P.M.: Pneumonia. Pediatr. Rev. **34**, 438–456 (2013)
16. Di Martino, A., et al.: The autism brain imaging data exchange: towards a large-scale evaluation of the intrinsic brain architecture in autism. Mol. Psychiatry **19**, 659–667 (2014)
17. Soussia, M., Rekik, I.: Unsupervised manifold learning using high-order morphological brain networks derived from T1-w MRI for autism diagnosis. Front. Neuroinform. **12**, 70 (2018)
18. Fischl, B., et al.: Sequence-independent segmentation of magnetic resonance images. Neuroimage **23**, S69–S84 (2004)
19. Fischl, B.: Freesurfer. Neuroimage **62**, 774–781 (2012)
20. Mahjoub, I., Mahjoub, M.A., Rekik, I.: Brain multiplexes reveal morphological connectional biomarkers fingerprinting late brain dementia states. Sci. Rep. **8**, 1–14 (2018)
21. Ying, R., You, J., Morris, C., Ren, X., Hamilton, W.L., Leskovec, J.: Hierarchical graph representation learning with differentiable pooling. arXiv preprint arXiv:1806.08804 (2018)
22. Kipf, T.N., Welling, M.: Semi-supervised classification with graph convolutional networks. arXiv preprint arXiv:1609.02907 (2016)
23. Lou, B., et al.: Quantitative analysis of synthetic magnetic resonance imaging in Alzheimer's disease. Front. Aging Neurosci. **13**, 638731 (2021)
24. Gasquoine, P.G.: Contributions of the insula to cognition and emotion. Neuropsychol. Rev. **24**, 77–87 (2014). https://doi.org/10.1007/s11065-014-9246-9
25. Nomi, J.S., Molnar-Szakacs, I., Uddin, L.Q.: Insular function in autism: update and future directions in neuroimaging and interventions. Prog. Neuropsychopharmacol. Biol. Psychiatry **89**, 412–426 (2019)

26. Gebauer, L., Foster, N.E., Vuust, P., Hyde, K.L.: Is there a bit of autism in all of us? autism spectrum traits are related to cortical thickness differences in both autism and typical development. Res. Autism Spectr. Disord. **13**, 8–14 (2015)
27. Habata, K., et al.: Relationship between sensory characteristics and cortical thickness/volume in autism spectrum disorders. Transl. Psychiatry **11**, 1–7 (2021)
28. Kitamura, S., et al.: Association of adverse childhood experiences and precuneus volume with intrusive reexperiencing in autism spectrum disorder. Autism Res. **14**, 1886–1895 (2021)
29. Khundrakpam, B.S., Lewis, J.D., Kostopoulos, P., Carbonell, F., Evans, A.C.: Cortical thickness abnormalities in autism spectrum disorders through late childhood, adolescence, and adulthood: a large-scale MRI study. Cereb. Cortex **27**, 1721–1731 (2017)

Learning Subject-Specific Functional Parcellations from Cortical Surface Measures

Roza G. Bayrak[1](✉), Ilwoo Lyu[2], and Catie Chang[1,3,4]

[1] Computer Science, Vanderbilt University, Nashville, TN 37235, USA
`rozgns@gmail.com`
[2] Computer Science and Engineering, UNIST, Ulsan 44919, Korea
[3] Biomedical Engineering, Vanderbilt University, Nashville, TN 37235, USA
[4] Vanderbilt University Institute of Imaging Science, Nashville, TN 37235, USA

Abstract. Cortical parcellations that are tailored to individual subjects have been shown to improve functional connectivity prediction of behavior and provide useful information about brain function and dysfunction. A hierarchical Bayesian (HB) model derived from resting-state fMRI (rs-fMRI) is a state-of-the art tool for delineating individualized, spatially localized functional parcels. However, rs-fMRI acquisition is not routine in clinical practice and may not always be available. To overcome this issue, we hypothesize that functional parcellation may be inferred from more commonly acquired T1- and T2-weighted structural MRI scans, through cortical labeling with deep learning. Here, we investigate this hypothesis by employing spherical convolutional neural networks to infer individualized functional parcellation from structural MRI. We show that the proposed model can achieve comparable parcellation accuracy against rs-fMRI derived ground truth labels, with a mean Dice score of 0.74. We also showed that our individual-level parcellations improve areal functional homogeneity over widely used group parcellations. We envision the use of this framework for predicting the expected spatially contiguous areal labels when rs-fMRI is not available.

Keywords: Structural features · Cortical surface · Individual-specific · Functional boundaries

1 Introduction

Complex human cognition is enabled through communication between functionally synchronized distributed networks that are comprised of computational units across the brain. To study human behavior and brain function, there has been a significant interest in mapping these localized functional regions using non-invasive brain imaging techniques such as magnetic resonance imaging (MRI). These delineations of distinct functional units across the brain, also called parcellations, are widely used to facilitate investigations into cognition and disease [1,2].

© The Author(s), under exclusive license to Springer Nature Switzerland AG 2022
I. Rekik et al. (Eds.): PRIME 2022, LNCS 13564, pp. 172–180, 2022.
https://doi.org/10.1007/978-3-031-16919-9_16

Earlier efforts focused on defining brain areas through histological examination of post-mortem brains [3]. With the advent of MRI, architectonic and topographical features could be examined noninvasively (e.g., Harvard-Oxford, Juelich atlases). In addition to structural and anatomic features, functional MRI has also been used to find temporally coherent regions across the brain [4,5]. Computational atlases, both structural and functional, are typically summarized at the population level [5,6] and are designed to correspond across subjects, thus capturing stable units that are shared in common across individuals.

However, there is considerable variability across people that the group-level mappings fail to capture. Indeed, it has been shown that the neuroscientific validity of statistical inferences may improve greatly when using individualized parcellations [7–10]. Subject-specific spatial features (i.e. spatial boundaries or parcel size) are shown to associate with behavior [7] and functional state [9]. Individualized mapping of functional architecture is also a fundamental requirement of clinical procedures such as surgical planning and brain stimulation therapies [11]. A range of automated techniques have been developed for deriving individual parcellations [8,12,13], including a multi-session hierarchical Bayesian (HB) model derived from resting-state fMRI (rs-fMRI) proposed by [10]. This latter approach is currently the state-of-the-art tool for delineating individualized, spatially localized functional parcellations and has shown to improve behavioral predictions from functional connectivity, demonstrating its utility in determining individualized functional parcels.

However, application of this approach broadly relies on the availability and quality of rs-fMRI data. Of note, rs-fMRI acquisitions are not routine in clinical practice, and when available they may be brief in duration. The reproducibility and test-retest reliability of connectivity estimates have been shown to be compromised by the length of the rs-fMRI scan [14] rendering short rs-fMRI acquisitions (<10 min [15]) of limited utility. In a separate body of literature, structural MRI has been found to provide architectonic markers that exhibit some degree of correspondence with functionally distinct areas in individual subjects [17,18], and are more widely performed in clinical brain scans compared to resting-state fMRI. Therefore, to generate individualized parcellations in the absence of rs-fMRI data (or of sufficiently long rs-fMRI scans), we hypothesize that functional parcellations derived from state-of-the-art rs-fMRI methods may be inferred from more commonly acquired structural MRI scans, through cortical labeling with deep learning.

In this paper, we propose a novel way to infer individualized functional parcellations using only cortical surface measures reconstructed from commonly acquired T1-and T2-weighted MRI scans, by employing spherical convolutional neural networks. We train our models using cortical surface measures and evaluate the resulting functional parcels using rs-fMRI data. As ground truth labels, we use individualized functional parcellations from [10], which were derived from rs-fMRI using a multi-session Hierarchical Bayesian modeling approach. We evaluate the generalizability of our parcellations to out-of-sample subjects in terms of segmentation accuracy using Dice correlation coefficient. We also compare our proposed approach with a group-level parcellation [5] and with the previously defined rsfMRI-based individual-level parcellations [10] in terms of areal homogeneity (temporal similarity of vertices within a given parcel). To the best of our knowledge, this is the first work to capture a mapping between cortical surface features and functionally (temporally) coherent regions.

The remainder of the paper is organized as follows. Section 2 briefly explains the dataset, preprocessing, model training and evaluation. In Sect. 3, the predicted labels are compared against population-based and ground truth individualized parcellations (derived from rs-fMRI) both qualitatively and through functional homogeneity. In Sect. 4, we discuss the implications and limitations of this work.

2   Methods

2.1   Dataset

The Human Connectome Project (HCP) is a large-scale data collection effort. The S1200 release consists of structural MRI (sMRI), resting-state fMRI (rs-fMRI) and behavioral measures [16]. T1-weighted images (T1w) were acquired using a 3D-magnetization-prepared rapid acquisition with gradient echo (MPRAGE) sequence and T2-weighted (T2w) images were acquired using a 3D T2-sampling perfection with application-optimized contrasts by using flip angle evolution (SPACE) sequence, both with spatial resolution of 0.7 mm isotropic [22]. Surface data was already preprocessed according to [17] using both T1w and T2w images. Briefly, surface extraction was performed using the standard FreeSurfer protocol [19] and shape features (convexity, thickness, etc.) were calculated. Surface data was then mapped to a standard 32k reference mesh. Resting-state functional MRI (rs-fMRI) images were obtained by multiband gradient echo-planar imaging with the following parameters: temporal resolution (TR) of 0.72 s, duration of 1200 frames per run (14.4 min), and spatial resolution of 2 mm isotropic [22]. Rs-fMRI was preprocessed according to [20,23] and each volume was mapped to a standard 32k reference mesh. Since the units of fMRI signals are arbitrary, we temporally normalized all signals to zero mean and unit variance. In addition, following [10], we reduced potential sources of artifact by regressing out the global signal and head motion parameters, along with their temporal derivatives. In this project, we randomly selected 150 subjects for training. Another set of randomly selected 300 subjects from the same HCP release was used for testing and subsequent analyses (Fig. 1).

2.2   Cortical Surface Features

For the cortical surface features, we used sulc (average convexity) [19], curv (mean curvature), cortical thickness, and bias corrected cortical myelin maps. Here we employ data augmentation to generate extra surface features through geometric transformations. Following [25], we compute decomposable deformation trajectories (ranging from rigid body alignment to more local non-rigid deformation) encoded by spherical harmonics coefficients [21] and generate the intermediate deformation of each cortical feature as augmented data.

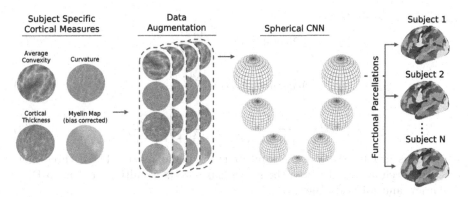

Fig. 1. The pipeline for learning functional parcellations from structural data is shown. Four surface measures (average convexity, curvature, cortical thickness, and bias corrected myelin map) are used to create an augmented dataset. Augmentation is achieved through geometric transformations. The resulting augmented set is provided to the spherical convolutional neural network (CNN) that is already adapted for cortical segmentation as input. The output is individual-specific functional parcellations.

2.3   Model Training

The spherical CNN architecture by [24, 25] is used for the segmentation task. In our framework, four cortical shape measures with their augmentation are provided as input, and 200 labels (corresponding to individualized parcels from the left hemisphere, described next) are predicted. The MS-HBM [10] parcellation, consisting of 400 regions of interest (200 on the left hemisphere), was used as ground truth labels. Within the set of 150 training subjects, 5-fold cross validation was used for model training, using a 60/20/20 split respectively for training, validation and testing by rotating partitions. We used cross-entropy loss and the ADAM optimizer, and networks were allowed to train up to 30 epochs. All networks were trained with learning rate 0.01 with decay of factor 0.1 and patience 2. The best models were saved based on the validation loss. A batch size of 2 was used at icosahedral subdivision level 6. The experiments were performed on an NVIDIA RTX 3090 GPU. Programs were implemented with Python using the Pytorch deep learning library.

2.4   Generating and Evaluating Predicted Parcellations on the Test Set

We subsequently turned to the set of 300 subjects that were held out from training. For each subject in this test set, 5 sets of segmentations (individualized parcellations) are predicted, corresponding to the 5 models (one from each fold) of the aforementioned 5-fold CV (that had been performed on the training set of 150 subjects). These segmentations are combined using majority vote to form one final segmentation. Segmentation accuracy is calculated using Dice coefficient, accuracy and Intersection-Over-Union (IoU, Jaccard Index):

$$Dice(A, B) = \frac{2\,A \cdot B|}{|A| + |B|} \tag{1}$$

$$Accuracy(A, B) = \frac{|A \cdot B|}{|A|} \tag{2}$$

$$IoU(A, B) = \frac{|A \cdot B|}{|\max(A, B)|} = \frac{|A \cdot B|}{|A| + |B| - |A \cdot B|} \tag{3}$$

where A is ground truth parcel and B is predicted parcel. These three metrics were each averaged across the set of 200 parcels, resulting in a mean Dice, Accuracy, and IoU value per scan.

2.5   Assessment of Homogeneity

To further evaluate the utility of the predicted parcellations in investigations of brain function, we assess the homogeneity (similarity) of time courses within a given parcel, based on the assumption that parcellations that follow an individual's functional boundaries ought to contain voxels with highly similar time courses. Therefore, higher homogeneity indicates better parcellation quality. For each subject, we computed homogeneity for all four runs separately (two fMRI sessions on two consecutive days). Vertex time-courses are extracted using a set of labels (i.e. Schaefer, Kong, or predicted parcellations). For each parcel, within-parcel homogeneity is calculated by averaging the pairwise Pearson's correlations between rs-fMRI time courses of all vertices within that parcel. An overall homogeneity value is then constructed by averaging across the within-parcel homogeneities of all 200 parcels, adjusted for parcel size [10]:

$$Homogeneity = \frac{\sum_{l=1}^{L} \rho_l |l|}{\sum_{l=1}^{L} |l|} \tag{4}$$

where ρ_l is the homogeneity of parcel l and $|l|$ is the number of vertices (or voxels) for parcel l.

3   Results

Evaluation of the proposed framework indicates that functional parcellations can be approximated solely from anatomic (cortical shape) features. Individualized parcellations derived from cortical surface features on a held-out test cohort showed moderate agreement against multi-session hierarchical Bayesian-based ground truth labels derived from rs-fMRI data, with a mean Dice score of 0.740.

Figure 2a shows two example subject predictions, along with their ground truth labels, for subjects in the held-out test set. Figure 2b demonstrates the

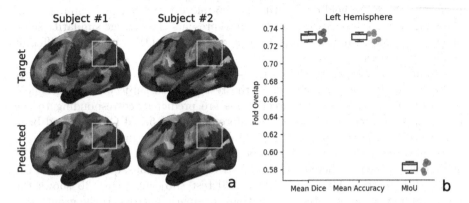

Fig. 2. (a) Two example subjects were randomly selected for visual inspection. Predicted and ground truth labels are projected onto their respective inflated surfaces. The yellow box highlights that indeed the model was able to capture individual differences. (b) During training, 5-fold cross-validation is performed. Three separate scores, capturing the similarity of the predicted labels against ground truth, are reported separately on the test split for each fold. Both the mean Dice and mean accuracy are 0.730 ± 0.004 and mean intersection of union (IoU) is 0.583 ± 0.005 across 5 folds. (Color figure online)

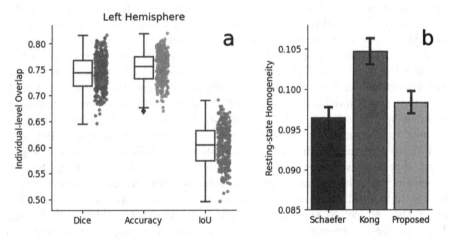

Fig. 3. For each subject in the held-out test set: (a) similarity with ground truth parcellations was calculated using the same 3 metrics as in Fig. 2. Scores recorded consisted of mean Dice $= 0.740 \pm 0.032$, accuracy $= 0.753 \pm 0.028$ and intersection of union (IoU) $= 0.604 \pm 0.037$; (b) 5 sets of parcellations are predicted, corresponding to the 5 models of the 5-fold CV (one from each fold). These parcellations were then applied to all four rs-fMRI runs. Resting-state homogeneity is calculated for Schaefer group-level, Kong individual-level (ground truth) and the predicted individual-level parcellation from the proposed model. Proposed method outperformed the group-level atlas, showing higher parcel homogeneity.

performance on the held-out partitions of 5-fold CV (within the training set of 150 subjects). Each data point in Fig. 2b represents the average similarity score across all parcels (and all subjects in a given test fold), using three different similarity metrics.

Results on a separate set of held-out test data are shown in Fig. 3. As described above, for each subject in the test set (300 subjects) that was held out from training, 5 sets of parcellations are predicted, corresponding to the 5 models (one from each fold) of the aforementioned 5-fold CV that had been performed on the training set of 150 subjects. These segmentations are combined using majority vote to form one final segmentation. Figure 3a shows the similarity between predicted and ground-truth parcellations, quantified with the same three metrics, for each of these 300 test subjects. Figure 3b shows the temporal homogeneity of the parcellations, comparing across (i) the group-level parcellation (Schaefer, which uses the same parcels for all subjects), (ii) the individualized parcellations from rs-fMRI data (Kong; here used as ground truth), and (iii) the parcellation resulting from the proposed method. The proposed method outperformed the group-level parcellation, indicating that it is able to learn information about individualized functional boundaries.

4   Discussion and Conclusion

We demonstrate a novel way of inferring individual-specific functional parcellations from cortical features derived from structural (T1w, T2w) MRI. Functional parcellations are most commonly derived using rs-fMRI data, as coherent activity across rs-fMRI time courses has been shown to correspond with subject-specific functional networks and behavioral measures more closely than those defined from traditional anatomic subdivisions [28]. By contrast, the present work indicates that structural brain images contain information about these functional boundaries, suggesting that functional parcellations could be inferred without the need to measure brain activity time courses with a resting-state fMRI scan.

Indeed, compared with the population-based [5] atlas parcellation, the proposed approach estimated more homogeneous regions during resting state, in agreement with the claims of [10]. Of note, the aim of this approach was to achieve individual precision (i.e., to outperform the population-based atlas) rather than to exceed the quality of the individualized rs-fMRI parcellations that were used as ground truth for training. Therefore, any improvement over a group-level parcellation (that is extracted from fMRI data) using solely structural features exceeds the current expectations of the neuroimaging community.

Importantly, the ability to delineate functional parcellations solely from structural MRI has important implications both in clinical applications and research. In preoperative planning and brain stimulation therapies, the ability to precisely localize functional boundaries in an individual will enable individualized treatment and can potentially improve patient outcome. In addition, an increasing number of studies suggest that individual differences in the size or shape of functional parcels can be related to cognition and behavior [7,9], and may therefore present informative non-invasive biomarkers. Together with the aforementioned studies, our ability to extract functionally relevant units from anatomic images underscores a prominent link between structure and function.

Recent work by [9,27] has suggested that the brain parcellations reconfigure dynamically and across different cognitive states. Accordingly, identifying parcellations within their dynamic states would improve reproducibility and quality over "static" parcellations. Similar to the argument of [10], our study does not challenge this notion. It is possible that computationally stable units across the brain could potentially reconfigure to form dynamic networks that change moment-to-moment, and the degree to which cortical shape features can predict parcellations corresponding to different brain states is an area of future investigation. Our study, and that of Kong et al., may be delineating parcellations that are most stable - on average - in an individual.

In future work, the dataset can be extended to fully utilize all 1029 subjects and explore a coarser or finer labeling scheme from the same individual labeling protocol [2]. As this study used only resting-state data from healthy young adult subjects, another potential avenue of investigation could be to examine the generalizability and impact of this approach on task fMRI data and patient populations.

References

1. Arslan, S., et al.: Human brain mapping: a systematic comparison of parcellation methods for the human cerebral cortex. Neuroimage **170**, 5–30 (2018)
2. Eickhoff, S.B., Yeo, B.T., Genon, S.: Imaging-based parcellations of the human brain. Nat. Rev. Neurosci. **19**(11), 672–686 (2018)
3. Vergleichende Lokalisationslehre der Grosshirnrinde in ihren Prinzipien dargestellt auf Grund des Zellenbaues. Barth (1909)
4. Shen, X., et al.: Groupwise whole-brain parcellation from resting-state fMRI data for network node identification. Neuroimage **82**, 403–415 (2013)
5. Schaefer, A., et al.: Local-global parcellation of the human cerebral cortex from intrinsic functional connectivity MRI. Cereb. Cortex **28**(9), 3095–3114 (2018)
6. Yeo, B.T., et al.: The organization of the human cerebral cortex estimated by intrinsic functional connectivity. J. Neurophysiol. (2011)
7. Bijsterbosch, J.D., et al.: The relationship between spatial configuration and functional connectivity of brain regions. Elife **7**, e32992 (2018)
8. Wang, D., et al.: Parcellating cortical functional networks in individuals. Nat. Neurosci. **18**(12), 1853–1860 (2015)
9. Salehi, M., et al.: There is no single functional atlas even for a single individual: functional parcel definitions change with task. NeuroImage **208**, 116366 (2020)
10. Kong, R., et al.: Individual-specific areal-level parcellations improve functional connectivity prediction of behavior. Cereb. Cortex **31**(10), 4477–4500 (2021)
11. Lang, S., Duncan, N., Northoff, G.: Resting-state functional magnetic resonance imaging: review of neurosurgical applications. Neurosurgery **74**(5), 453–465 (2014)
12. Gordon, E.M., et al.: Generation and evaluation of a cortical area parcellation from resting-state correlations. Cereb. Cortex **26**(1), 288–303 (2016)
13. Chong, M., et al.: Individual parcellation of resting fMRI with a group functional connectivity prior. Neuroimage **156**, 87–100 (2017)

14. Birn, R.M., et al.: The effect of scan length on the reliability of resting-state fMRI connectivity estimates. Neuroimage **83**, 550–558 (2013)
15. Gonzalez-Castillo, J., et al.: The spatial structure of resting state connectivity stability on the scale of minutes. Front. Neurosci. **8**, 138 (2014)
16. van Essen, D.C., et al.: The WU-Minn human connectome project: an overview. Neuroimage **80**, 62–79 (2013)
17. Glasser, M.F., van Essen, D.C.: Mapping human cortical areas in vivo based on myelin content as revealed by T1-and T2-weighted MRI. J. Neurosci. **31**(32), 11597–11616 (2011)
18. Di Biase, M.A., et al.: Cell type-specific manifestations of cortical thickness heterogeneity in schizophrenia. Mol. Psychiatry **27**(4), 2052–2060 (2022)
19. Fischl, B.: FreeSurfer. Neuroimage **62**(2), 774–781 (2012)
20. Griffanti, L., et al.: ICA-based artefact removal and accelerated fMRI acquisition for improved resting state network imaging. Neuroimage **95**, 232–247 (2014)
21. Lyu, I., et al.: Hierarchical spherical deformation for cortical surface registration. Med. Image Anal. **57**, 72–88 (2019)
22. van Essen, D.C., et al.: The human connectome project: a data acquisition perspective. Neuroimage **62**(4), 2222–2231 (2012)
23. Robinson, E.C., et al.: MSM: a new flexible framework for multimodal surface matching. Neuroimage **100**, 414–426 (2014)
24. Jiang, C., et al.: Spherical CNNs on unstructured grids. arXiv preprint arXiv:1901.02039 (2019)
25. Parvathaneni, P., et al.: Cortical surface parcellation using spherical convolutional neural networks. In: Shen, D., et al. (eds.) MICCAI 2019. LNCS, vol. 11766, pp. 501–509. Springer, Cham (2019). https://doi.org/10.1007/978-3-030-32248-9_56
26. Boykov, Y., Kolmogorov, V.: An experimental comparison of min-cut/max-flow algorithms for energy minimization in vision. IEEE Trans. Pattern Anal. Mach. Intell. **26**(9), 1124–1137 (2004)
27. Boukhdhir, A., et al.: Unraveling reproducible dynamic states of individual brain functional parcellation. Netw. Neurosci. **5**(1), 28–55 (2021)
28. Dadi, K., et al.: Fine-grain atlases of functional modes for fMRI analysis. NeuroImage **221**, 117126 (2020)

A Triplet Contrast Learning of Global and Local Representations for Unannotated Medical Images

Zhiwen Wei, Sungjoon Park, and Jaeil Kim[✉]

Kyungpook National University, 80 Daehak-ro, Buk-gu, Daegu, Republic of Korea
`jaeilkim@knu.ac.kr`

Abstract. Recently, self-supervised learning(SSL) has shown its great potential in representation learning and been applied to various computer vision tasks. With the success of SSL, which showed performance improvement in natural images, SSL research is actively being conducted in medical image analysis. In this paper, we present a triplet network for the medical image representation learning to learn robust patterns of medical images against global and local changes by comparing latent feature distance between positive and negative pairs with anchors. This approach does not require large batches or the asymmetry of the network. It has been experimentally shown that the proposed method can outperform ImageNet pretrained models and the state-of-the-art SSL methods.

Keywords: Self-supervised Learning · Triplet Network · Triplet Margin Loss · Medical Image Classification · Chest X-Ray

1 Introduction

Self-supervised learning (SSL) aims to improve the feature extraction capability of a model by designing proxy tasks that explore the representations of the data itself and to transfer the learned representations to fine-tune them on a new labeled task. Therefore, the design of proxy tasks has become an important topic in SSL. In this context, various self-supervised learning methods have been introduced, and most of them have adopted the contrast learning architecture. That is, the representation is learned by making the distance of one similar sample smaller and the distance of different samples larger. However, contrastive learning methods like SimCLR[4], MoCo[5] need to find ways to construct as many negative samples as possible to learn different features, hence the increased memory burden. Recent methods such as BYOL[7] and PixPro[15] modified the network structure by adding projection heads to inject asymmetry and to update the weights using gradient stopping or momentum update structure. This type of contrastive learning approaches throws away negative samples and relies solely on training tactics to avoid model collapse. Despite their success with natural

I. Rekik et al. (Eds.): PRIME 2022, LNCS 13564, pp. 181–190, 2022.
https://doi.org/10.1007/978-3-031-16919-9_17

images, the contrastive learning approaches are not widely utilized in medical image analysis due to the differences between medical images and natural images. For example, abnormal lesions are not stereotyped in images, they may appear in small sizes, and these regional variations are not easy to model using the contrastive learning using ordinary instance-level self-supervised structures.

In this paper, we present a self-supervised learning method based on a triplet comparison network [9] to learn anomaly features in medical images more effectively by putting in global changes representing body structure and local changes focusing on texture. The global view takes the overall body structure as positive and the local view looks at the detailed texture of the image as negative. Then using triplet loss brings the global structure closer and closer to the original image, while local details are further and further away from the original image. The whole and the local are learned simultaneously to promote a multi-level feature representation. Our model does not require large batches like [4] or large queues to store negative samples like [5] or asymmetry to prevent model collapse like [7] compared to other methods, and only requires small amounts of data to meet or even exceed the state-of-the-art model.

2   Related Work

Self-supervised Learning in Computer Vision. In recent years, self-supervised learning in natural still images regard gained promising results. For example, in the context-based jigsaw puzzle model[11], the pictures are divided into 9 patches that were out of order. Patches were then restored to the correct order as a proxy task. In contrastive-based MoCoV2, a queue was designed to store negative samples. Different data from the same image are augmented as positive samples. Data in the queue are negative samples. The contrastive loss function[13] is used to make the positive samples more similar and the negative samples less similar. PixPro[15] builds pixel-level counterparts to the excuse task through different views of a single image. If the distance between pixels in different views is greater than a threshold value of 1 and less than a threshold value of 0. PixPro[15] not only looks at local information, but also does not require a large queue size, but loses sight of global features.

Self-supervised Learning in Medical Image. Self-supervised learning has also been frequently applied to medical data in recent years to mitigate the problems such as small medical datasets and difficult annotation. Some works are designed with special pretext tasks[2,19] and some are based on contrasting works with positive and negative pairs[1,3,14]. The work closest to us is C2L[18]. C2L proposes to construct homogeneous and heterogeneous data pairs by mixup[17] data augmentation and mixing feature batches. And instead of contrastive loss simplifies the calculation with cross-entropy loss.

Limitations of Self-supervised Learning. Medical image data sets usually relate to the structure of the human body and the abnormal white (increased density) or abnormal black (decreased density) due to disease. And, now most of self-supervised learning models only focus on the location information of the thorax, airway, lung, heart, etc. Center the data as a whole and ignore local textures.

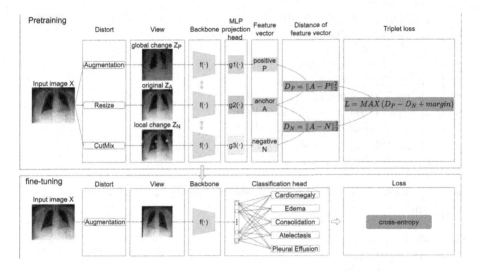

Fig. 1. An illustration of the proposed method which is based on a triplet network. Each of the three well-made views is passed into the backbone network with shared weights (shown as blue rectangles) and then they are cast to the projection head (green pink and yellow rectangles indicate no shared weights) to obtain the three feature vectors. The loss is calculated using the triplet loss. The fine-tuning stage picks up the backbone network to add to the classification head for training. (Color figure online)

3 Proposed Method

Inspired by recent contrastive learning algorithms, proposed method learns data information through the synergy of the global and the local. Figure 1 and Algorithm 1 provides the overall workflow. As exhibited in Fig. 1, this framework includes the following five main components.

First, the pretrained model is composed of a global view and a local view by image enhancement and cutmix[16] respectively. Secondly, the global, local, and original views are fed into a backbone network with shared weights across views. The resulting feature vectors are then placed into the projection head separately to obtain the positive, anchor, and negative, which are finally computed with triplet loss[12]. The fine-tuning process migrates only the backbone network and adds untrained classification head to train the classification task.

Algorithm 1: pseudocode for our approach (one epoch)

Input: batch size $N \times C \times W \times H$, number of crop Crop, Crop size I

1   **for** X *in minibatch* **do**
2      $Z_P = \text{augment}(X)$ // Create global change view
3      $Z_A = \text{resize}(X)$ // Create local change view with cutmix
4   **for** *index = 1 to Crop* **do**
5          $shuffle\_index = shuffle\_batch(N)$;
6          $Z_N = X.\text{clone}()$;
7   // Get coordinates of crops
8          $cx = randint(W)$;
9          $cy = randint(H)$;
10         $x_1 = Clip(cx - I \;//\; 2, 0, W)$;
11         $x_2 = Clip(cx + I \;//\; 2, 0, W)$;
12         $y_1 = Clip(cy - I \;//\; 2, 0, H)$;
13         $y_2 = Clip(cy + I \;//\; 2, 0, H)$;
14   // Cut and paste crops
15         $Z_N[:\,,:\,, \text{x1:x2, y1:y2}] = X[\text{shuffle\_index},:\,, \text{x1:x2, y1:y2}]$;
16   **end**
17   // Put three different views into network
18      $\mathcal{P} = g_1(\text{f}(Z_P))$;
19      $\mathcal{A} = g_2(\text{f}(Z_A))$;
20      $\mathcal{N} = g_3(\text{f}(Z_N))$;
21   // TripletLoss
22   **define** $\mathcal{L}(\mathcal{A}, \mathcal{P}, \mathcal{N})$ **as** $\mathcal{L}(\mathcal{A}, \mathcal{P}, \mathcal{N}) = \max(\text{d}(\mathcal{A}, \mathcal{P}) - \text{d}(\mathcal{A}, \mathcal{N}) + \text{marge}, 0)$;
23   loss += $\mathcal{L}(\mathcal{A}, \mathcal{P}, \mathcal{N})$;
24   Backward(loss);
25 **end**

3.1 Local Change

For the building of local variations, we have chosen cutmix enhancements[16]. Simply put, another image is selected from the batch and a part of the image is cropped and superimposed on top of the original image X as the local change Z_N. Lung images rely mainly on lung texture, and cropped patches may carry features that are the opposite of the original image. For example, the original image is a healthy lung, yet the cropped patch may be located exactly where it carries information about the disease. Such an alteration is not part of the information that the original image would have carried, so the local change can be considered negative.

3.2 Global Change

As is done in most contrastive learning methods, the proposed method constitutes a global change Z_P by sampling an augmentation view from the single image X. The image augmentation pipeline is made up of colorJitter, elastic, and patch rotation[6]. We also experimented with other combinations of data augmentations and compared them with our approach (see Table 3). The first transformation colorJitter is always applied. And elastic can simulate the deformation of some chest x-rays due to lung disease. Patch rotation is the process of dividing the original image into a number of patches and then randomly selecting whether or not to rotate and at what angle. Because the change in local change is made up of patches, we chose to Patch Rotation that looks similar to Cutmix. This was done to mimic and add difficulty to the proxy task, interfere with global change and give the illusion of local change.

Besides images with global and local changes, the original image X is fed it into the network after resizing as an anchor.

3.3 Network

The network is divided into backbone $f(\cdot)$ (e.g., ResNet [8]) and MLP projection head $g(\cdot)$. The MLP projection head consists of adding the ReLU activation function between the three linear layers. Previous work [4, 7] has shown that the use of such projections can improve performance. At the beginning of place the created local change view Z_N, the global change view Z_P and the original image Z_A in a triplet network where the three backbones use the same network and share weights. In this step, feature vectors extracted from backbone networks are obtained. The feature vectors are subsequently sent into the projection head to acquire negative samples N, positive samples P, and anchor A. Proposed method uses a projection head with non-shared weights to map the feature vectors to the space of contrasts. The aim of using a projection head is to pull in anchor A and positive P distances and push away anchor A and negative N distances.

3.4 Triplet Loss

Triplet loss[12] was first proposed as an algorithm in the field of face recognition. It is mainly known for sibling face differentiation. It is obvious that triplet loss can distinguish non-identical and very similar samples. Since the advantage of triplet loss is in detail differentiation, it can easily be extended to lung image processing. As shown in Fig. 2 the definition of the triplet loss function in the proposed method is based on three different views A, N, and P. We expect the distance between the three views to satisfy Eq. 1 A and P to be much smaller than the distance between A and N even when marge is added.

$$\|A - P\|_2^2 + margin < \|A - N\|_2^2 \tag{1}$$

Equation1 can be further expressed as Eq. 2.

$$\|A - P\|_2^2 - \|A - N\|_2^2 + margin < 0 \tag{2}$$

When Eq. 2 is greater than 0, the loss is greater than zero and the parameters are updated. When Eq. 2 is less than 0, the loss is zero and the parameters are not updated because the objective has been achieved. The final triplet loss can be expressed as Eq. 3.

$$\sum_{i=0}^{N} \left[\|A_i - P_i\|_2^2 - \|A_i - N_i\|_2^2 + margin \right]_+ \tag{3}$$

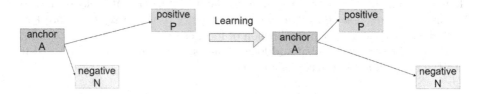

Fig. 2. The principle of triplet loss. The training brings the anchor and the positive closer together and pushes the negative farther apart.

3.5   Fine-Tuning

Through pretraining, this model has learned general features such as body structure and texture information in images. Although the extracted features are consistent but the type of downstream and excuse tasks are not, we keep the backbone network replacing the projection head used for comparison with the classification head used for classification and retrain for the downstream task.

4   Experiments

Datasets. CheXpert[10] is a large public dataset comprising 224,316 frontal and lateral chest X-rays of 65,240 patients. The dataset contains information on the labeling of 14 common chest radiographic observations, all of which were manually labeled by three certified radiologists. We randomly selected 500 frontal chest X-rays from each of the 14 observations of frontal chest X-rays in the pretraining phase, for a total of 7000 X-rays. In the fine-tuning phase, all frontal chest X-rays were selected and the test index included the mean AUC for five chest diseases (Atelectasis, Cardiomegaly, Consolidation, Edema, Pleural Effusion).

Implementation Details. In the pretraining phase, we first resized the chest image to a size of 224 × 224 as the original image. When constructing a local change view, 10 images are randomly selected in the batch to crop 10 patches of size 16 × 16 and pasted onto the original image. Apply elastic, colorJitter, and crop rotation to the original image when building a global change view. The crop rotation patch size is also 16 × 16 as is the local change, which can

Table 1. Comparison of transfer learning performance of our self-supervised approach with previous methods across 5 classes. All models use a ResNet-50 backbone. The best results for the category are shown in bold.

Method	Average	Cardiomegaly	Edema	Consolidation	Atelectasis	Pleural effusion
MoCoV2	87.14	81.81	91.22	86.58	**83.87**	92.22
C2L	87.81	82.61	93.30	87.85	83.20	92.09
ImageNet	87.87	81.37	**94.02**	89.71	82.09	92.14
PixPro	88.53	84.00	93.54	88.01	83.38	**93.72**
Jigsaw	88.81	86.16	93.44	89.12	82.61	92.71
Ours	**89.42**	**86.89**	93.48	**90.29**	83.41	93.05

Table 2. Data augmentation should only be applied to the performance of global changes and the performance of global changes and local changes all added to the data augmentation.

view	ColorJitter	GaussianBlur
global	88.71	88.05
global + local	88.37	87.88

add difficulty to the proxy task. We use ResNet-50[8] as the backbone network. All three branches use the same backbone network and share weights. Following BYOL [7], we are adding 3-layer MLP as a projection head and a feature vector of size 2048 is obtained. The margin of the triplet loss is set to 1. We use SGD as the optimizer where the initial learning rate is le-5 and a weight decay is le-4. We train each model for 300 epochs and the batch size is 64. The fine-tuning phase takes away the pretrained backbone network and replaces the projection head with a fully connected classification head. And the image size was resized to 320×320 with a batch size of 64 and trained 30 epochs.

Comparison with Previous Results. We examined the improvement in AUC when the backbone was ResNet-50. Table 1 compares our results with previous methods. Our proposed method achieved the best results at two observations(Cardiomegaly, Consolidation) and a mean AUC of 89.94%. Although the other three observations did not reach the optimal AUC, they did almost reach the top two. The competitiveness of our proposed approach can be seen.

Data Augmentations Ablations. Table 2 reports the results of local change using the same data augmentation as global change on top of cut and paste. Because the same data augmentation reduces the difficulty of the proxy task, the effect is lower than without.

In Table 3, we investigate the effects of various data enhancements. We found that colorJitter, elastic, and crop rotation were the top three individual data enhancements. We have since combined them to obtain the final result.

Table 3. The effect of individual data augmentations and the effect of progressively increasing data augmentations.

GaussNoise	GaussianBlur	GridDistortion	Elastic	Crop rotation	ColorJitter	Average
✓						87.93
	✓					88.05
		✓				88.24
			✓			88.30
				✓		88.33
					✓	88.71
			✓		✓	88.82
			✓	✓	✓	**89.42**

Network Explorations. Mapping features to the same space using projection head has become popular since projection head was first introduced in SimCLR [4]. BYOL[7] adds to this by doing prediction to prevent network collapse. Table 4 reports the results on whether projection head, predication head, and update methods are utilized. The results show that prediction head does not help for the proposed method and that the best AUC is achieved in the case of training the projection head alone.

Table 4. The result of whether to include projection head, prediction head and whether to share the weights.

baseline	Projection head	Prediction head	Average AUC
a	share weights	share weights	88.57
b	no share weights	no share weights	88.70
c	share weights	✗	89.15
d	no share weights	✗	**89.42**
e	✗	✗	89.24

5   Conclusion

In this paper, we introduce a pre-trained self-supervised learning method using the triplet loss. Comparisons of global and local variations are used to learn information from multiple ranges of medical images. We also demonstrate the performance improvement of the proposed method in X-Ray image classification over the previous pre-training and state-of-the-art self-supervised methods.

Acknowledgments. This work was supported by the Technology Innovation Program (20011875, Development of AI based diagnostic technology for medical imaging devices) funded By the Ministry of Trade, Industry & Energy(MOTIE, Korea).

References

1. Azizi, S., et al.: Big self-supervised models advance medical image classification. In: Proceedings of the IEEE/CVF International Conference on Computer Vision (ICCV), pp. 3478–3488 (2021)

2. Bai, W., et al.: Self-supervised learning for cardiac MR image segmentation by anatomical position prediction. In: Shen, D., et al. (eds.) MICCAI 2019. LNCS, vol. 11765, pp. 541–549. Springer, Cham (2019). https://doi.org/10.1007/978-3-030-32245-8_60

3. Chaitanya, K., Erdil, E., Karani, N., Konukoglu, E.: Contrastive learning of global and local features for medical image segmentation with limited annotations. In: Larochelle, H., Ranzato, M., Hadsell, R., Balcan, M., Lin, H. (eds.) Advances in Neural Information Processing Systems. vol, 33, pp. 12546–12558. Curran Associates, Inc. (2020). https://proceedings.neurips.cc/paper/2020/file/949686ecef4ee20a62d16b4a2d7ccca3-Paper.pdf

4. Chen, T., Kornblith, S., Norouzi, M., Hinton, G.: A simple framework for contrastive learning of visual representations. In: III, H.D., Singh, A. (eds.) Proceedings of the 37th International Conference on Machine Learning. Proceedings of Machine Learning Research, vol. 119, pp. 1597–1607. PMLR (13–18 Jul 2020). https://proceedings.mlr.press/v119/chen20j.html

5. Chen, X., Fan, H., Girshick, R.B., He, K.: Improved baselines with momentum contrastive learning. CoRR abs/2003.04297 (2020). https://arxiv.org/abs/2003.04297

6. Du, X., et al.: Vision checklist: towards testable error analysis of image models to help system designers interrogate model capabilities. CoRR abs/2201.11674 (2022). https://arxiv.org/abs/2201.11674

7. Grill, J.B., et al.: Bootstrap your own latent - a new approach to self-supervised learning. In: Larochelle, H., Ranzato, M., Hadsell, R., Balcan, M., Lin, H. (eds.) Advances in Neural Information Processing Systems, vol. 33, pp. 21271–21284. Curran Associates, Inc. (2020). https://proceedings.neurips.cc/paper/2020/file/f3ada80d5c4ee70142b17b8192b2958e-Paper.pdf

8. He, K., Zhang, X., Ren, S., Sun, J.: Deep residual learning for image recognition. In: Proceedings of the IEEE Conference on Computer Vision and Pattern Recognition (CVPR) (2016)

9. Hoffer, E., Ailon, N.: Deep metric learning using triplet network. In: Feragen, A., Pelillo, M., Loog, M. (eds.) Similarity-Based Pattern Recognition, pp. 84–92. Springer International Publishing, Cham (2015). https://doi.org/10.1007/978-3-319-24261-3_7

10. Irvin, J., et al.: CheXpert: a large chest radiograph dataset with uncertainty labels and expert comparison. CoRR abs/1901.07031 (2019). http://arxiv.org/abs/1901.07031

11. Noroozi, M., Favaro, P.: Unsupervised learning of visual representations by solving jigsaw puzzles. In: Leibe, B., Matas, J., Sebe, N., Welling, M. (eds.) ECCV 2016. LNCS, vol. 9910, pp. 69–84. Springer, Cham (2016). https://doi.org/10.1007/978-3-319-46466-4_5

12. Schroff, F., Kalenichenko, D., Philbin, J.: FaceNet: A unified embedding for face recognition and clustering. In: Proceedings of the IEEE Conference on Computer Vision and Pattern Recognition (CVPR) (2015)

13. Sohn, K.: Improved deep metric learning with multi-class n-pair loss objective. In: Lee, D., Sugiyama, M., Luxburg, U., Guyon, I., Garnett, R. (eds.) Advances in Neural Information Processing Systems, vol. 29. Curran Associates, Inc. (2016). https://proceedings.neurips.cc/paper/2016/file/6b180037abbebea991d8b1232f8a8ca9-Paper.pdf
14. Sowrirajan, H., Yang, J., Ng, A.Y., Rajpurkar, P.: MoCo pretraining improves representation and transferability of chest x-ray models. In: Heinrich, M., Dou, Q., de Bruijne, M., Lellmann, J., Schläfer, A., Ernst, F. (eds.) Proceedings of the Fourth Conference on Medical Imaging with Deep Learning. Proceedings of Machine Learning Research, vol. 143, pp. 728–744. PMLR (07–09 Jul 2021). https://proceedings.mlr.press/v143/sowrirajan21a.html
15. Xie, Z., Lin, Y., Zhang, Z., Cao, Y., Lin, S., Hu, H.: Propagate yourself: Exploring pixel-level consistency for unsupervised visual representation learning. In: Proceedings of the IEEE/CVF Conference on Computer Vision and Pattern Recognition (CVPR), pp. 16684–16693 (2021)
16. Yun, S., Han, D., Oh, S.J., Chun, S., Choe, J., Yoo, Y.: CutMix: regularization strategy to train strong classifiers with localizable features. In: Proceedings of the IEEE/CVF International Conference on Computer Vision (ICCV) (2019)
17. Zhang, H., Cissé, M., Dauphin, Y.N., Lopez-Paz, D.: mixup: beyond empirical risk minimization. CoRR abs/1710.09412 (2017). http://arxiv.org/abs/1710.09412
18. Zhou, H.-Y., Yu, S., Bian, C., Hu, Y., Ma, K., Zheng, Y.: Comparing to learn: surpassing imagenet pretraining on radiographs by comparing image representations. In: Martel, A.L., et al. (eds.) MICCAI 2020. LNCS, vol. 12261, pp. 398–407. Springer, Cham (2020). https://doi.org/10.1007/978-3-030-59710-8_39
19. Zhuang, X., Li, Y., Hu, Y., Ma, K., Yang, Y., Zheng, Y.: Self-supervised feature learning for 3D medical images by playing a Rubik's cube. In: Shen, D., et al. (eds.) Medical Image Computing and Computer Assisted Intervention - MICCAI 2019, pp. 420–428. Springer International Publishing, Cham (2019). https://doi.org/10.1007/978-3-030-32251-9_46

Predicting Brain Multigraph Population from a Single Graph Template for Boosting One-Shot Classification

Furkan Pala and Islem Rekik$^{(\boxtimes)}$

BASIRA Lab, Faculty of Computer and Informatics Engineering,
Istanbul Technical University, Istanbul, Turkey
irekik@itu.edu.tr
http://basira-lab.com

Abstract. A central challenge in training one-shot learning models is the limited representativeness of the available shots of the data space. Particularly in the field of network neuroscience where the brain is represented as a graph, such models may lead to low performance when classifying brain states (e.g., typical vs. autistic). To cope with this, most of the existing works involve a data augmentation step to increase the size of the training set, its diversity and representativeness. Though effective, such augmentation methods are limited to generating samples with the same size as the input shots (e.g., generating brain connectivity matrices from a single shot matrix). To the best of our knowledge, the problem of generating brain multigraphs capturing multiple types of connectivity between pairs of nodes (i.e., anatomical regions) from a single brain graph remains unsolved. In this paper, we unprecedentedly propose a hybrid graph neural network (GNN) architecture, namely Multigraph Generator Network or briefly MultigraphGNet, comprising two subnetworks: (1) *a many-to-one GNN* which integrates an input population of brain multigraphs into a single template graph, namely a connectional brain temple (CBT), and (2) *a reverse one-to-many* U-Net network which takes the learned CBT in each training step and outputs the reconstructed input multigraph population. Both networks are trained in an end-to-end way using a cyclic loss. Experimental results demonstrate that our MultigraphGNet boosts the performance of an independent classifier when trained on the augmented brain multigraphs in comparison with training on a single CBT from each class. We hope that our framework can shed some light on the future research of multigraph augmentation from a single graph. Our MultigraphGNet source code is available at https://github.com/basiralab/MultigraphGNet.

Keywords: Multigraph augmentation from a single graph · One-shot learning · Brain connectivity · Connectional brain template

1 Introduction

Brain graphs present powerful tools in modeling the relationship between different anatomical regions of interest (ROIs) as well as fingerprinting neural states

I. Rekik et al. (Eds.): PRIME 2022, LNCS 13564, pp. 191–202, 2022.
https://doi.org/10.1007/978-3-031-16919-9_18

(e.g., typical and atypical) [1]. Recently, graph neural network (GNN) models have achieved remarkable results across different brain graph learning tasks [2] such as time-dependent prediction [3,4], super-resolution [5,6] and classification [7,8]. Despite their ability to extract meaningful and powerful representations from labelled brain graph data, they might fail to handle training data with a limited number of samples. Particularly, such data-hungry architectures might struggle to converge and produce a good performance within a few-shot learning (FSL) paradigm [9–11] –let alone one-shot learning [12].

Such problem is usually remedied by data augmentation where labeled samples are generated from the available shots to better generalize to unseen distributions of testing samples. Several FSL works [13] proposed novel methods to solve medical image-based learning tasks. For instance, [14] presented a learning-based method that is trained on a few samples while leveraging data augmentation and unlabeled image data to enhance model generalizability. [15] used the meta-train data from common diseases for rare disease diagnosis and tackled the low-data regime problem while leveraging meta-learning. [16] presented a novel task-driven and semi-supervised data augmentation scheme to improve medical image segmentation performance in a limited data setting. However, to the best of our knowledge and as revealed by this recent GNN in network neuroscience review paper [2], one-shot GNN learning remains unexplored in the field of network neuroscience –with the exception of [12] where one-shot GNN architectures are trained for brain connectivity regression and classification tasks. Specifically, representative connectional brain templates (CBTs) [17] were used to train GNN architectures in one-shot fashion. Such graph templates present a compact representation of a particular brain state.

However, this landmark work did not resort to any data augmentation strategies or generative models to better estimate the unseen distributions of the classes to discriminate. Besides, existing graph augmentation methods are limited to generating graphs with the same size as the input shots (e.g., generating brain connectivity matrices from a single shot matrix). To the best of our knowledge, the problem of generating brain multigraphs capturing multiple types of connectivity between pairs of nodes (i.e., anatomical regions) from a single brain graph remains unsolved. Note that a brain multigraph is encoded in a tensor, where each frontal view captures a particular type of connectivity between pairs of brain ROIs (e.g., morphological or functional). In this paper, we set out to boost a one-shot brain graph classifier *by learning how to generate multi-connectivity brain multigraphs from a single template graph*. Specifically, we propose a hybrid graph neural network (GNN) architecture, namely Multigraph Generator Network or briefly MultigraphGNet, comprising two subnetworks: (1) *a many-to-one GNN* which integrates an input population of brain multigraphs into a single CBT graph using deep graph normalizer (DGN) [18], and (2) *a reverse one-to-many convolutional neural network (CNN)* which takes the learned CBT in each training step and outputs the reconstructed input multigraph population. Our prime contributions are listed below:

1. We are the first to learn how to generate brain multigraphs from a single graph template (namely CBT).
2. We propose a hybrid cyclic GNN architecture for multigraph graph augmentation from a single CBT.
3. We show that the augmented brain multigraphs can boost the performance of an independent classifier across various evaluation metrics.

2 Methodology

In this section, we explain our proposed MultigraphGNet in detail. We represent tensors by calligraphic font capital letters, e.g., $\mathcal{X}$, matrices by boldface capital letters, e.g., $\mathbf{X}$, vectors by boldface lowercase letters, e.g., $\mathbf{x}$ and scalars by letters, e.g., x. Table 1 summarizes the mathematical notations we used throughout the paper.

Table 1. Mathematical notations followed in the paper

Mathematical notation	Definition
S	Training set
n_r	Number of region of interests (ROIs) in the brain
n_v	Number of connectomic views in the brain multigraph (tensor)
$\mathcal{X}_s$	Brain graph tensor $\in \mathbb{R}^{n_r \times n_r \times n_v}$ of subject s
$\mathbf{X}_s^v$	Brain graph matrix $\in \mathbb{R}^{n_r \times n_r}$ of the view v and subject s
$\mathbf{C}_s$	Subject-driven connectional brain template (CBT) $\in \mathbb{R}^{n_r \times n_r}$ of the subject s
$\hat{\mathcal{X}}_s$	Reconstructed brain graph tensor $\in \mathbb{R}^{n_r \times n_r \times n_v}$ for the subject s

Problem Statement. A brain connectome can be encoded in a single view (i.e., matrix) or multiple views (i.e., matrices forming a tensor) so that each view sits on a different manifold and captures a specific relationship, e.g., morphological or functional, between anatomical brain regions of interest. Since multiview connectomic data is scarce, we set out to learn how to predict brain connectivity tensors (i.e., multigraphs) from a single graph template (i.e., brain connectivity matrix). Thus, we propose a one-to-many brain graph augmentation approach. Specifically, given a set of multi-view brain graphs where each view models a specific relationship between pairs of brain ROIs, our goal is to first collapse these graphs to a single view graph-based representation, i.e., connectional brain template (CBT), then, reconstruct the original brain graphs using the generated CBT, so that we can augment new multi-view brain graphs by adding small noise to the global CBT which can be considered as an average connectome over all subjects and views.

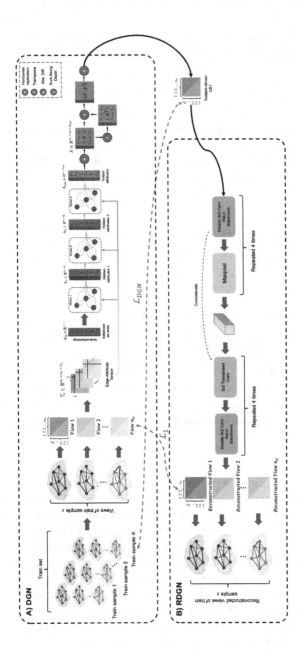

Fig. 1. *The proposed MultigraphGNet architecture to predict a population of brain multigraphs from a single graph template shot.* **A)** **CBT generation from a population of brain multigraphs.** To represent the multiple views of a brain graph in a single view, Deep Graph Normalizer (DGN) [18] network learns the node embeddings using three edge conditioned graph convolutional layers followed by differentiable tensor operations to generate a subject specific CBT. DGN Loss computes the mean Frobenius distance between the CBT and each view in the training subjects. **B)** **Reverse brain multigraph reconstruction from the learned CBT.** To reconstruct the original views of the training subject, we propose a novel Reverse-DGN (RDGN) network that uses a U-Net architecture to first encode the CBT into a lower-dimensional representation using the same convolution and maxpool layers in DGN, then up-sample to multiple views via transposed convolution layers. We optimize the reconstructed tensor population by minimizing the L1 distance between the original and reconstructed views for each training subject. DGN and RDGN are trained in a cyclic and end-to-end manner to ensure that (i) the learned CBT captures the connectivity patterns shared across brain views and subjects and (ii) the tensor views of each training subject can be reconstructed using the learned CBT solely.

Definition 1. Let $\mathbf{C}_s$ denote a subject-driven connectional brain template, which is a centered representation of subject s with respect to the training population tensor (i.e., multigraph) distribution. Specifically, $\mathbf{C}_s$ is encoded in a single-view brain connectivity matrix which is a normalized graph-based representation of the multi-view brain graph (i.e., tensor) of subject s.

2.1   CBT Learning

The first block (Fig. 1-A) of our MultigraphGNet utilizes the Deep Graph Normalizer (DGN) [18] network to produce a subject-driven CBT $\mathbf{C}_s$ for each training subject s. We represent a brain graph view i as $G_i(V_i, E_i)$ where V_i is the set of n_r nodes each corresponds to a brain ROI and E is a set of edges each encoding a particular type of relationship between two ROIs (e.g., structural). Thus, we can define a multi-view brain graph for subject s as a tensor $\mathcal{X}_s \in \mathbb{R}^{n_r \times n_r \times n_v}$, where n_r and n_v denote the number of ROIs and views, respectively. Since self-connections do not carry important information, we set the diagonal entries in the tensor to zero. The DGN network takes a node embedding matrix $\mathbf{V^0} \in \mathbb{R}^{n_r \times d_0}$, where d_0 is the initial node embedding size and a multi-view edge embedding tensor $\mathcal{X}$. Since we do not have any node/ROI features initially, we set the $\mathbf{V^0}$ to 1. DGN utilizes 3 edge-conditioned graph convolution layers [19] with a ReLU at the end of each layer to learn the node embeddings. Each layer $l \in \{1, 2, 3\}$ includes a dense filter neural network $F^l : \mathbb{R}^{n_v} \mapsto \mathbb{R}^{d_l \times d_{l-1}}$ that implements the message passing between ROIs i and j given the edge embeddings $\mathbf{e}_{ij} \in \mathbb{R}^{n_v \times 1}$ as follows

$$\mathbf{v}_i^l = \boldsymbol{\Theta}^l . \mathbf{v}_i^{l-1} + \frac{1}{|\mathcal{N}(i)|} \left(\sum_{j \in \mathcal{N}(i)} F^l(\mathbf{e}_{ij}; \mathbf{W}^l) \mathbf{v}_j^{l-1} + \mathbf{b}^l \right)$$

$$F^l(\mathbf{e}_{ij}; \mathbf{W}^l) = \boldsymbol{\Theta}_{ij},$$

where $\mathbf{v}_i^l$ is the node embedding corresponding to the ith ROI in layer l. The dense filter neural network F^l with weights $\mathbf{W}^l$ and bias $\mathbf{b}^l$ produces new edge weights in each layer for the edges between node i and its neighbour $j \in \mathcal{N}(i)$. The resulting node embeddings tensor $V^3 \in \mathbb{R}^{n_r \times d_3}$ is first repeated horizontally to get a tensor, then, we compute the element-wise absolute difference between its transpose. Here we use the absolute difference since the original brain connectivity tensors were generated using this operation. One can use any other operation that is differentiable for the back propagation process. The final output is obtained by summing along the z-axis which gives us the subject-driven CBT $\mathbf{C}_s \in \mathbb{R}^{n_r \times n_r}$ for subject s.

We use the Subject Normalization Loss (SNL) as proposed in the DGN. SNL for training subject s is defined as the mean Frobenius distance between the learned CBT and each training subject view as follows:

$$SNL_s = \frac{1}{n_v \times |S|} \sum_{v=1}^{n_v} \sum_{i \in S} ||\mathbf{C}_s - \mathbf{X}_i^v||_F \times \lambda_v,$$

where S is the training set and λ_v is the loss weight computed for each view v as follows:

$$\lambda_v = \frac{\frac{1}{\mu_v}}{\max\left\{\frac{1}{\mu_j}\right\}_{j=1}^{n_v}},$$

where μ_v is computed by taking the mean of edge attributes for view v. Next, we define and optimize the DGN Loss using the following objective function [18]:

$$\mathcal{L}_{\text{DGN}} = \frac{1}{|S|} \sum_{s \in S} SNL_s$$

2.2   Reverse Mapping

The second block (Fig. 1-B) of our MultigraphGNet aims to reverse the DGN process, thus we call it reverse DGN (RDGN) network by taking the learned CBT $\mathbf{C}_s$ and mapping it back into the original brain multigraph tensor $\mathcal{X}_s$ for subject s. We use the U-Net [20] architecture to design the RDGN, which consists of an encoder and a decoder. Specifically, in each iteration of the optimization process, the encoder takes the learned CBT and applies the same convolution operation with a kernel size of 3, stride and padding of 1 two times, each followed by a ReLU non-linearity and a batch normalization layer. To down-sample the resulting feature map, we use a max pooling layer with a kernel size and stride of 2. The number of output channels is doubled at the end of the down-sampling. We repeat this process 4 times to get the feature map with 1024 channels. In the decoder part, we first up-sample using a 2×2 transposed convolutional layer with a stride of 2 that halves the number of output channels which is followed by a concatenation with the feature map from the counterpart in the encoder. As for the decoder, we apply the same convolution operation twice. This process is repeat 4 times, as well. The final layer consists of a 1×1 convolution layer that outputs the reconstructed tensor $\hat{\mathcal{X}}_s \in \mathbb{R}^{n_r \times n_r \times n_v}$. To preserve the similarity to the original tensor, we additionally minimize the $L1$ distance, i.e., mean absolute error (MAE), between the original ($\mathcal{X}$) and reconstructed ($\hat{\mathcal{X}}$) tensor views as follows:

$$\mathcal{L}_{L1} = ||\mathcal{X} - \hat{\mathcal{X}}||_1$$

We train the DGN and RDGN in an end-to-end and fully cyclic manner to ensure that the generated CBT can well collapse the multiple views into a single connectivity matrix, which in turn is used to reconstruct back the original brain multigraph using the U-Net augmentation process. Thus, we define our RDGN loss as follows:

$$\mathcal{L}_{cyclic} = \mathcal{L}_{DGN} + \lambda \mathcal{L}_{L1}$$

2.3   Multigraph Data Augmentation from a Single Graph

The trained RDGN is able to generate multiple views from a given single-view CBT, which makes it possible to predict a multigraph from a single representative template graph. Hence, by slightly modifying the an particular input CBT, RDGN can produce unique brain multigraphs where it acts as a *one-to-many augmentation network*. To augment new brain multigraphs from a single CBT, we first obtain a subject-driven CBT for each training subject as follows:

$$S_{CBT} = \left\{ \mathbf{C}_s | \forall s \in S \right\}$$

$$\mathbf{C}_s = DGN(\mathcal{X}_s)$$

Next, we construct a global CBT $\mathbf{C}$ by taking the element-wise median of all the subject-driven CBTs in S_{CBT}. $\mathbf{C}$ can be considered as an average brain network over all the training brain multigraph set. To create diversity in our augmented multigraphs, we add a small noisy matrix $\mathbf{W}_i \sim \mathcal{N}(\mu_{\mathbf{C}}, \sigma_{\mathbf{C}}^2)$ to the global CBT for each augmented new sample i as follows:

$$\tilde{\mathbf{C}}_i = \mathbf{C} + c\mathbf{W}_i,$$

where $\mu_{\mathbf{C}}$ denotes the CBT mean and $\sigma_{\mathbf{C}}$ its standard deviation. c is a scaling coefficient to control the added noise. Note that we re-sample the added noise in each augmentation step. We augment new samples as follows:

$$S_{aug} = \left\{ \hat{\mathcal{X}}_i | i \in \{1, 2, \ldots, k\} \right\}$$

$$\hat{\mathcal{X}}_i = RDGN(\tilde{\mathbf{C}}_i),$$

where k is the number of samples that we want to augment.

3   Experimental Results and Discussion

Evaluation Dataset. We evaluated our framework on the Autism Brain Imaging Data Exchange (ABIDE-I) public dataset[1] using a random subset including 150 normal control (NC) and 150 subjects with autism spectrum disorder (ASD), each wit 6 views of morphological brain connectomes (extracted from the maximum principal curvature, the mean cortical thickness, the mean sulcal depth, the average curvature, the minimum principle area and the cortical surface area) of the left cortical hemispheres (LH). The cortical surface is split into 35 ROIs via Desikan-Killiany atlas [21] after the reconstruction from T1-weighted MRI using the FreeSurfer pipeline [22]. Next, the brain network is obtained by taking the absolute difference between the cortical measurements in each pair of ROIs. We used 5-fold cross-validation with 5 different seeds to evaluate the generalizability of our MultigraphGNet. We implemented our framework in PyTorch and PyTorch-Geometric [23] libraries.

---

[1] http://preprocessed-connectomes-project.org/abide/.

Table 2. Testing classification results of independent SVM classifiers trained using (i) a single CBT from each class and (ii) samples augmented using the trained RDGN network. We report the average accuracy, precision, recall and F1 score obtained when training on 10, 25 and 50 augmented samples. Each row displays the mean of the results over the 5 cross-validation folds with different random seeds for the train-test split.

	One-shot CBT				Augmented multigraphs			
	Acc	Prec	Rec	F1	Acc	Prec	Rec	F1
Seed #1	0.929	0.944	0.916	0.928	0.989	0.953	0.993	0.989
Seed #2	0.960	0.993	0.928	0.959	0.956	0.939	1.000	0.964
Seed #3	0.948	0.993	0.903	0.944	0.971	0.985	0.955	0.968
Seed #4	0.961	0.981	0.941	0.960	0.965	0.991	0.935	0.958
Seed #5	0.954	0.992	0.915	0.952	0.968	0.961	0.979	0.969
Avg	0.950	**0.981**	0.921	0.949	**0.970**	0.966	**0.972**	**0.970**

Hyperparameters. In DGN, we used 3 edge-conditioned graph convolution layers followed by ReLU non-linearity and each layer has an output node embedding size of 36, 24 and 5, respectively. In RDGN, we used a U-Net architecture. For the optimizer, we chose AdamW [24] with a learning rate of 0.001, beta1 and beta2 of 0.9 and 0.999, and a weight decay of 0.01. We set $\lambda = 1$ in the total loss function and $c = 0.2$ for the added noise in the CBT augmentation using RDGN.

Evaluation and Comparison Methods. To evaluate the effectiveness of our brain multigraph augmentation strategy from a single CBT, we trained two support vector machine (SVM) classifiers in each cross-validation fold. Note that we provided the same seeds in both DGN/RDGN and SVM training so that neither our augmentation framework nor the classifier have seen the test set before.

One-shot CBT. We generated two global CBTs $\mathbf{C}_{ASD}$ and $\mathbf{C}_{NC}$ using the trained DGN for ASD and NC training sets, respectively. We vectorized the upper-triangular part of both CBTs to get two feature vectors $\mathbf{c}_{ASD}, \mathbf{c}_{NC} \in \mathbb{R}^{\frac{n_r \times n_r - 1}{2}}$. In the testing step, we created a subject-driven CBT using the trained DGN for each brain multigraph in the test set since the SVM was not trained on multiple views.

Augmented samples. We augmented $k = 10, 25, 50$ multigraphs as explained in the Sect. 2.3 and vectorized the upper-triangular parts of each view to get the feature vector $\mathbf{x}_i \in \mathbb{R}^{\frac{n_v \times n_r \times n_r - 1}{2}}$ for each augmented sample $i \in \{1, 2, \ldots, k\}$. Next, we trained a new SVM classifier on the augmented set and tested it on the left-out test set. In this case, there is no need for generating subject-driven CBTs in the testing phase since the SVM was already trained on multi-view tensors. We report the comparison between the classification accuracy, precision, recall and F1 scores for the both methods in the Table 2 for both methods. It can be clearly seen that our framework is able to reconstruct the initial brain graph views and

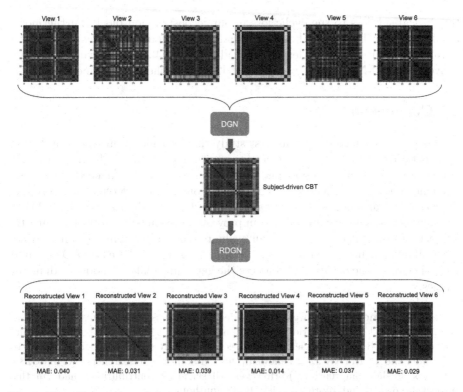

Fig. 2. Visual inspection of the reconstructed brain multigraph from a single CBT. On top, we display the brain tensor including 6 connectivity views for a randomly selected ASD testing sample. In the middle, we present the subject-driven CBT obtained using the trained DGN network. In the bottom, we compare the reconstructed views by the trained RDGN network given the learned CBT as input. We also measure the MAE between the corresponding ground-truth and predicted views.

produces relevant features for the ASD/NC classification task. While one-shot CBT is considerably enough to distinguish between ASD and NC subjects, our framework further boosts the independent classifier performance by augmenting multiple multi-view brain connectomes using only one single-view CBT.

Visual Inspection. In Fig. 2, we show the original and reconstructed brain multigraph tensor including 6 views as well as the learned CBT for a randomly selected ASD testing subject. In addition, we report the mean absolute error (MAE) between reconstructed and original views. Obviously, RDGN network is able to expand and decode the CBT into multiple views with a low error.

Limitations and Future Directions. Although the L1 Loss between the the ground truth and reconstructed views produced very promising reconstructions and is resistant to data outliers, it only considers the element-wise similarity in connectivity weights without examining the topological properties (e.g., hubness) of the augmented multigraphs. Hence in our future work, we will add a topological sub-loss to the cyclic loss in our reconstruction block. Furthermore, the RDGN can be further boosted by adding a discriminator network to the U-Net under an adversarial learning paradigm as in [4]. We also will replace the convolutional U-Net with a graph U-Net [25] for further improvement.

4   Conclusion

In this paper, we introduced the first study that provides a one-to-many U-Net augmentation framework for generating multi-view brain graphs from a single connectional template to boost one-shot learning classifiers. Given the high-cost of connectomic data collection and processing, our framework offers an affordable approach to learning how in a frugal setting with limited data. We showed that the augmented samples are able to improve the classification results of autistic subjects. In our future work, we will evaluate our MultigraphGNet on subjects with different neurological disorders such as Alzheimer's Disease (AD) or mild cognitive impairment (MCI) and assess the generalizability of model to different classes.

Acknowledgements. This work was funded by generous grants from the European H2020 Marie Sklodowska-Curie action (grant no. 101003403, http://basira-lab.com/normnets/) to I.R. and the Scientific and Technological Research Council of Turkey to I.R. under the TUBITAK 2232 Fellowship for Outstanding Researchers (no. 118C288, http://basira-lab.com/reprime/). However, all scientific contributions made in this project are owned and approved solely by the authors.

References

1. van den Heuvel, M.P., Sporns, O.: A cross-disorder connectome landscape of brain dysconnectivity. Nat. Rev. Neurosci. **20**, 435–446 (2019)
2. Bessadok, A., Mahjoub, M.A., Rekik, I.: Brain graph synthesis by dual adversarial domain alignment and target graph prediction from a source graph. Med. Image Anal. **68**, 101902 (2021)
3. Tekin, A., Nebli, A., Rekik, I.: Recurrent brain graph mapper for predicting time-dependent brain graph evaluation trajectory. In: Albarqouni, S., et al. (eds.) DART/FAIR -2021. LNCS, vol. 12968, pp. 180–190. Springer, Cham (2021). https://doi.org/10.1007/978-3-030-87722-4_17
4. Gürler, Z., Nebli, A., Rekik, I.: Foreseeing brain graph evolution over time using deep adversarial network normalizer. In: Rekik, I., Adeli, E., Park, S.H., Valdés Hernández, M.C. (eds.) PRIME 2020. LNCS, vol. 12329, pp. 111–122. Springer, Cham (2020). https://doi.org/10.1007/978-3-030-59354-4_11
5. Isallari, M., Rekik, I.: Brain graph super-resolution using adversarial graph neural network with application to functional brain connectivity. Med. Image Anal. **71**, 102084 (2021)
6. Mhiri, I., Nebli, A., Mahjoub, M.A., Rekik, I.: Non-isomorphic inter-modality graph alignment and synthesis for holistic brain mapping. In: Feragen, A., Sommer, S., Schnabel, J., Nielsen, M. (eds.) IPMI 2021. LNCS, vol. 12729, pp. 203–215. Springer, Cham (2021). https://doi.org/10.1007/978-3-030-78191-0_16

7. Oh, K.H., et al.: Diagnosis of schizophrenia with functional connectome data: a graph-based convolutional neural network approach. BMC Neurosci. **23**, 1–11 (2022)
8. Nebli, A., Gharsallaoui, M.A., Gürler, Z., Rekik, I., Initiative, A.D.N., et al.: Quantifying the reproducibility of graph neural networks using multigraph data representation. Neural Netw. **148**, 254–265 (2022)
9. Kadam, S., Vaidya, V.: Review and analysis of zero, one and few shot learning approaches. In: Abraham, A., Cherukuri, A.K., Melin, P., Gandhi, N. (eds.) ISDA 2018 2018. AISC, vol. 940, pp. 100–112. Springer, Cham (2020). https://doi.org/10.1007/978-3-030-16657-1_10
10. Sun, Q., Liu, Y., Chua, T.S., Schiele, B.: Meta-transfer learning for few-shot learning. In: Proceedings of the IEEE/CVF Conference on Computer Vision and Pattern Recognition, vol. 403–412 (2019)
11. Li, X., Sun, Z., Xue, J.H., Ma, Z.: A concise review of recent few-shot meta-learning methods. arXiv preprint arXiv:2005.10953 (2020)
12. Guvercin, U., Gharsallaoui, M.A., Rekik, I.: One representative-shot learning using a population-driven template with application to brain connectivity classification and evolution prediction. In: Rekik, I., Adeli, E., Park, S.H., Schnabel, J. (eds.) PRIME 2021. LNCS, vol. 12928, pp. 25–36. Springer, Cham (2021). https://doi.org/10.1007/978-3-030-87602-9_3
13. Kotia, J., Kotwal, A., Bharti, R., Mangrulkar, R.: Few shot learning for medical imaging. In: Das, S.K., Das, S.P., Dey, N., Hassanien, A.-E. (eds.) Machine Learning Algorithms for Industrial Applications. SCI, vol. 907, pp. 107–132. Springer, Cham (2021). https://doi.org/10.1007/978-3-030-50641-4_7
14. Zhao, A., Balakrishnan, G., Durand, F., Guttag, J.V., Dalca, A.V.: Data augmentation using learned transformations for one-shot medical image segmentation. In: Proceedings of the IEEE/CVF Conference on Computer Vision and Pattern Recognition, pp. 8543–8553 (2019)
15. Li, X., Yu, L., Jin, Y., Fu, C.-W., Xing, L., Heng, P.-A.: Difficulty-aware meta-learning for rare disease diagnosis. In: Martel, A.L., et al. (eds.) MICCAI 2020. LNCS, vol. 12261, pp. 357–366. Springer, Cham (2020). https://doi.org/10.1007/978-3-030-59710-8_35
16. Chaitanya, K., et al.: Semi-supervised task-driven data augmentation for medical image segmentation. Med. Image Anal. **68**, 101934 (2021)
17. Chaari, N., Akdag, H.C., Rekik, I.: Comparative survey of multigraph integration methods for holistic brain connectivity mapping. arXiv preprint arXiv:2204.05110 (2022)
18. Gurbuz, M.B., Rekik, I.: Deep graph normalizer: a geometric deep learning approach for estimating connectional brain templates. In: Martel, A.L., et al. (eds.) MICCAI 2020. LNCS, vol. 12267, pp. 155–165. Springer, Cham (2020). https://doi.org/10.1007/978-3-030-59728-3_16
19. Simonovsky, M., Komodakis, N.: Dynamic edge-conditioned filters in convolutional neural networks on graphs. In: Proceedings of the IEEE Conference on Computer Vision and Pattern Recognition, vol. 3693–3702 (2017)
20. Ronneberger, O., Fischer, P., Brox, T.: U-Net: convolutional networks for biomedical image segmentation. In: Navab, N., Hornegger, J., Wells, W.M., Frangi, A.F. (eds.) MICCAI 2015. LNCS, vol. 9351, pp. 234–241. Springer, Cham (2015). https://doi.org/10.1007/978-3-319-24574-4_28
21. Fischl, B., et al.: Automatically parcellating the human cerebral cortex. Cereb. Cortex **14**, 11–22 (2004)

22. Fischl, B.: Freesurfer. Neuroimage **62**, 774–781 (2012)
23. Fey, M., Lenssen, J.E.: Fast graph representation learning with pytorch geometric. arXiv preprint arXiv:1903.02428 (2019)
24. Loshchilov, I., Hutter, F.: Fixing weight decay regularization in adam (2018)
25. Gao, H., Ji, S.: Graph u-nets (2019)

Meta-RegGNN: Predicting Verbal and Full-Scale Intelligence Scores Using Graph Neural Networks and Meta-learning

Imen Jegham[1,2,3] and Islem Rekik[2,3](✉)

[1] LATIS - Laboratory of Advanced Technology and Intelligent Systems, Université de Sousse, Ecole Nationale d'Ingénieurs de Sousse, 4023 Sousse, Tunisie
[2] Horizon School of Digital Technologies, 4023 Sousse, Tunisie
[3] BASIRA Lab, Faculty of Computer and Informatics Engineering, Istanbul Technical University, Istanbul, Turkey
irekik@itu.edu.tr
http://basira-lab.com/

Abstract. Decrypting intelligence from the human brain construct is vital in the detection of particular neurological disorders. Recently, functional brain connectomes have been used successfully to predict behavioral scores. However, state-of-the-art methods, on one hand, neglect the topological properties of the connectomes and, on the other hand, fail to solve the high inter-subject brain heterogeneity. To address these limitations, we propose a novel regression graph neural network through meta-learning namely Meta-RegGNN for predicting behavioral scores from brain connectomes. The parameters of our proposed regression GNN are explicitly trained so that a small number of gradient steps combined with a small training data amount produces a good generalization to unseen brain connectomes. Our results on verbal and full-scale intelligence quotient (IQ) prediction outperform existing methods in both neurotypical and autism spectrum disorder cohorts. Furthermore, we show that our proposed approach ensures generalizability, particularly for autistic subjects. Our Meta-RegGNN source code is available at https://github.com/basiralab/Meta-RegGNN.

Keywords: Meta-learning · Graph neural networks · Behavioral score prediction · Brain connectivity regression · Functional brain connectomes

1 Introduction

Autism, or Autism Spectrum Disorder (ASD), is a neurodevelopmental disorder that affects how a person feels, thinks, interacts with others, and encounters their environment. Research has shown that subjects with ASD have higher rates of health issues throughout childhood, adolescence, and adulthood and this can

© The Author(s), under exclusive license to Springer Nature Switzerland AG 2022
I. Rekik et al. (Eds.): PRIME 2022, LNCS 13564, pp. 203–211, 2022.
https://doi.org/10.1007/978-3-031-16919-9_19

lead to a high risk of early mortality. ASD diagnosis remains a challenging task due to the wide range in the severity of its symptoms and the lack of a patho-physiological marker [1,2]. Recently, machine learning techniques have become a primary route for computer-aided diagnosis, and have been broadly used to analyze autism disorders [3–5]. Intelligence, in particular, is a key aspect of ASD. State-of-the-art methods successfully used functional brain connectomes to pre-dict cognitive measures such as Intelligence Quotient (IQ) scores in both disor-dered and healthy cohorts [6–8]. Indeed, functional brain connectomes describe the brain network structure and are derived from resting-state magnetic reso-nance imaging (MRI). They are modeled as graphs whose nodes depict anatom-ical regions of interest (ROIs) and edges represent the correlations in activity between ROI pairs [9].

To improve generalizability across contexts and populations, Shen et al. [10] developed a data-driven protocol for Connectome-based Predictive Modeling (CPM) of brain-behavior relationships by training linear regression model using cross-validation. To ameliorate the obtained results, Dryburgh et al. [6] studied how neural correlates of intelligence scores are altered by atypical neurodevel-opmental disorders by performing their analysis in both Neuro Typical (NT) subjects and subjects with ASD. For that, they adopted CPM and evaluated neg-ative and positive correlations of brain regions separately. However, these meth-ods flatten the brain connectome matrix though vectorization which neglects the graph structure of the connectomes. Thus, the local and global topological properties of the connectomes that are rich of information are not exploited.

To overcome this issue, Graph Neural Networks (GNNs) have been proposed. They can handle complex graph data and have proven their exclusive ability in learning in non-Euclidean spaces including graphs with complex topologies and a wide range of graphs [11]. GNN is firstly proposed in 2005 [12] to be then elaborated on in detail [13]. GNNs are a class of deep learning techniques with graph convolutional layers that outperform existing methods in a large range of computer vision applications [14]. Recently, they have received large attention thanks to their exclusive ability in effectively modeling the correlation between samples. They provide an efficient solution to integrate diverse information. How-ever, a lack of works that explored GNN for the prediction of cognitive scores has been noticed. Hanik et al. [7] was the first to propose a GNN architecture, called RegGNN, specialized in regressing brain connectomes to a cognitive score to predict. To better improve the performance of GNN, they also proposed a learning-based sample selection method that selects training samples with the highest predictive power. However, existing GNN-based models present a major drawback which is the lack of flexibility which means that the model fails to be used for independent testing [15].

As a key challenge for the cognitive score prediction is high heterogeneity across individual brains, standard learning approaches fail when applied in dif-ferent conditions than used for training. To decrease this covariate shift that drastically affects the usefulness of machine learning models and improve the generalizability of proposed methods, meta-learning approaches have been proposed and achieved a tremendous success in recent years [16]. The basic idea of meta-learning or learn to learn is to gradually enhance the performance of a model by learning multiple different tasks. It is similar to transfer learning [17]. In transfer learning, model parameters are learned after being trained with lots of data and then fine-tuned to obtain good parameters, while in meta-learning, good model parameters that are sensitive to small changes and give large improvement on loss function for a particular task are learned. Meta-learning aims to rapidly learn a new task from a small amount of new data, and the model is trained by the meta-learner to be able to learn on several existing tasks [18]. There are different meta-learning approaches including one-shot learning with memory augmented neural networks [19], optimization as a model for few-shot learning [20] and Model Agnostic Meta-Learning (MAML) [21]. The latter may be directly applied to any learning model that is trained with a gradient descent procedure. With minimal modification, it can simply manage several architectures and multiple problem settings, including policy gradient reinforcement learning, classification and regression. However, despite their important role to ensure generalizability and solve data fracture problem, this method has not been previously employed in predicting cognitive scores.

In this paper, we introduce *the first regression GNN network through meta-learning*, namely Meta-RegGNN that regresses functional brain connectomes to predict cognitive scores. Our Meta-RegGNN network on one hand properly includes the graph structure of functional brain connectomes and effectively models the correlation between them, and on the other hand, thanks to meta-learning, makes the regression GNN model more flexible while decreasing the impact of the high brain variability and domain fracture issues.

The main contributions of our method can be summarized as follows:

1. We introduce a novel meta-learning regression graph neural network that shows an exclusive ability in modeling the correlation between data and incorporates global and local topological properties of the functional brain connectomes to predict behavioral scores.
2. We present the first work on meta-learning for regression graph neural networks rooted in inductive learning and which boosts the prediction performance by decreasing the effect of sample heterogeneity. This network shows a good trade-off between flexibility and performance and can be used in other application fields suffering from high intra-class variability issues.
3. We illustrate a pipeline, consisting of Meta-RegGNN, which outperforms state-of-the-art models in predicting Verbal Intelligence Quotient (VIQ) and Full-scale Intelligence Quotient (FIQ) from functional brain connectomes in neurotypical and autism spectrum disorder cohorts.

2   Methodology

In this section, we detail the architecture and the algorithm of our proposed. **Figure** 1 shows the layout of the overall process of Meta-RegGNN. In our proposed approach, meta-training is implemented as episodic tasks on support and query sets. A few-shot learning framework is used for the query set. The goal of this few-shot regression is to predict the behavioral scores from only a few samples after training on many samples with similar statistical properties. During the meta-testing, predicted behavioral scores are obtained using unseen samples that are provided with the optimized weights obtained from the meta-learning stage.

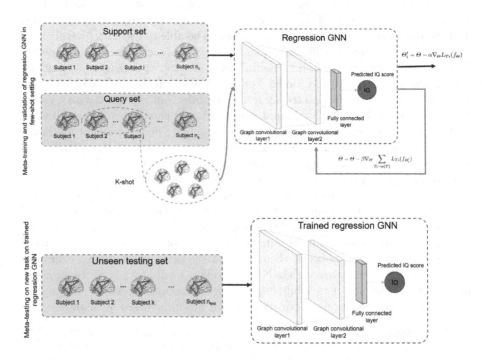

Fig. 1. Illustration of the proposed meta-training and validation of regression GNN in a few-shot setting.

- **Problem statement.** We consider a regression GNN model, denoted f, that maps brain graphs g to behavioral scores s. During meta-learning, the regression GNN model is trained to be able to adapt to a large number of tasks. We present a generic notion of a learning task below. Each task $T = \{L(g_1, s_1, ..., g_H, s_H), q(g_1), q(g_{t+1}|g_t, s_t), H\}$ consists of a loss function L, a distribution over initial observations $q(g_1)$, a transition distribution $q(g_{t+1}|g_t, s_t)$ and an episode length H (in our case, we can define $H = 1$ and drop the time-step t on x_t, as the model is used for supervised learning and accepts one input and gives one output). For regression, the loss function is defined as follows:

$$L_{Ti} = \sum_{g^{(j)}, s^{(j)} \sim T_i} \|f(g^{(j)}) - s^{(j)}\|_2^2, \tag{1}$$

where $g^{(j)}, s^{(j)}$ represent respectively the input and output sampled from task T_i. In our model agnostic meta-learning scenario, we define a distribution over tasks $p(T)$ that we want our regression GNN model to adapt to. In the K-shot learning setting, the regression GNN is trained to learn a new task T_i from $p(T)$ from only K samples drawn from q_i and the feedback L_{Ti} produced by T_i. At the end of meta-training, new tasks are sampled from $p(T)$, and meta-performance is measured by the model's performance after learning from K samples.

- **Meta-RegGNN algorithm.** The aim of our Meta-RegGNN is to prepare our regression GNN model for fast adaptation. Thus, the GNN might learn internal features of functinal brain connectomes that are relevant to all tasks in $p(T)$. For that, we first find the RegGNN model parameters that are responsive to modifications in the given task, so that small modifications in the parameters produce large improvements on the loss function of any task from $p(T)$. Let us consider our regression GNN model represented by a parametrized function f_Θ with parameters Θ. The latter is updated to Θ' when adapting to a new task T_i. The updated Θ is defined as:

$$\Theta'_i = \Theta - \gamma \nabla_\Theta L_{Ti}(f_\Theta), \tag{2}$$

where γ represents the step size hyperparameter. The meta-optimization is achieved over the regression GNN model parameters Θ, while the objective is calculated using the updated regression GNN model parameters Θ'. Indeed, our Meta-RegGNN aims to optimize the model parameters so that one or a small number of gradient steps on a new task generate effective behavior.

The meta-optimization through tasks is conceived in order to update the regression GNN model parameters Θ as follows:

$$\Theta = \Theta - \eta \nabla_\Theta \sum_{T_i \sim p(T)} L_{Ti}(f_{\Theta'_i}) \tag{3}$$

where η presents the meta-step size. The meta-training algorithm is outlined in Algorithm 1.

- **Regression GNN.** To properly take into account the graph structure of the brain connectomes and effectively model the correlation between data samples, we used a regression GNN network that consists of two graph convolution layers and a fully connected layer (**Fig. 1**). Given a correlation matrix of a connectome C is symmetric, that can have zero or positive eigenvalues, we may simply regularize it to be symmetric positive definite according to:

$$I' = C + \mu I, \tag{4}$$

where I represents the identity matrix and $\mu > 0$ [22]. In fact, since positive correlations have been demonstrated to be more important in analyzing brain networks [23], all negative eigenvalues are set to zero to train our regression GNN [7]. Thus, regression GNN receives the regularized positive adjacency matrix I' of a connectome and predicts the corresponding behavioral scores

---

Algorithm 1. Meta-training regression GNN algorithm.

Require: p(T)= Distribution over tasks
Require: γ, η: Step size hyperparameters
1: Initialize Θ randomly
2: **while** not done **do**
3:     Sample tasks batch $T_i \sim p(T)$
4:     **for all** Ti **do**
5:         Randomly choose k samples $D = \{g^{(i)}, s^{(i)}\}$ from Ti
6:         Evaluate $\nabla_\Theta L_{Ti}(f_\Theta)$ with respect to k using D and L_{Ti} in Eq. 1
7:         Compute adapted parameters Θ'_i according to Eq. 2
8:     Update Θ according to Eq. 3 using L_{Ti} in Eq. 1
9: **end**

---

using graph convolutions. This reduces the size of the brain connectomes and learns an embedding for the brain connectomes. After the first graph convolution operation, we add a dropout layer for regularization. Finally, the obtained embedding goes through a fully connected layer which produces a scalar output (IQ scores).

3   Experimental Results and Discussion

Evaluation Dataset. To highlight the utility of our proposed Meta-RegGNN, we evaluated our method on subjects drawn from the Autism Brain Imaging Data Exchange (ABIDE) preprocessed dataset [24]. The preprocessed datasets are available online[1]. They contain two cohorts: ASD and NT. The ASD cohort comprises 202 patients (with mean age = (15.4 $\pm$ 3.8)), while the NT cohort includes 226 subjects (with mean age = (15 $\pm$ 3.6)). VIQ and FIQ scores in the ASD cohort have means 106.102 $\pm$ 15.045 and 103.005 $\pm$ 16.874 whereas VIQ and FIQ scores in the NT cohort have means 111.573 $\pm$ 12.056 and 112.787 $\pm$ 12.018, respectively. The connectomes of the brain were derived from resting-state fMRI using the parcellation from [25] into 116 ROIs.

Parameter Settings. To evaluate the generazabilty and the effectiveness of our Meta-RegGNN, we used 3-fold cross-validation on ASD and NT cohorts for VIQ and FIQ prediction. Based on empirical observations, we trained our proposed method for 300 epochs with a weight decay at 0.0005 and a learning rate of 0.001. The dropout rate was set to 0.2. For the meta-training, we used one gradient update with K=5 shots with a step size $\gamma = 10^{-7}$ and employed Adam optimizer as meta-optimizer [26]. For all methods, we state the Mean Absolute Error (MAE) and the Root Mean Squared Error (RMSE).

Evaluation and Comparison Method. To benchmark our method, we chose the first and unique deep learning method proposed in the literature that uses

---

[1] http://preprocessed-connectomes-project.org/abide/.

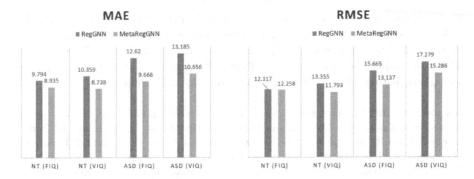

Fig. 2. Cognitive scores prediction results using different evaluation metrics on the NT and ASD cohorts.

GNN to predict cognitive scores [7] without the proposed sample selection step. The results for the ASD and NT cohorts for FIQ and VIQ are shown in **Fig.** 2. These results present the average of more than 40 random repetitions of our 3-fold cross-validation.

Compared to the NT cohort, the ASD cohort achieved the worst results across all methods. The difficulty of predicting behavioral scores in the ASD cohort may be explained by the high inter-subject heterogeneity [27]. A general improvement by our Meta-RegGNN is noticed in all learning tasks. Our method dealt with the correlation of functional brain connectomes and combined the prior knowledge with automatically learned similarity. Therefore, a high improvement in the ASD cohort is recorded that can be explained by the generalizability improvement. Even with the repeated randomized runs, our Meta-RegGNN displayed the lowest prediction error across both cohorts and metrics, which indicates the stability of our model under data distribution shifts. The best results in terms of MAE and RMSE are noted in the NT cohort which may be explained by the similarity between neurotypical brains.

Compared with previous studies on predicting behavioral scores, our model achieved a good trade-off between flexibility and performance requiring fewer samples for training. Moreover, it can deal with test samples that are different from those of the training samples (brains diagnosed with Alzheimer's Disease for example). Despite its multiple advantages, this prime work needs to be further validated on other datasets and different brain connectivity classes.

4   Conclusion

In this paper, we proposed the first GNN for regression through meta-learning namely Meta-RegGNN, for behavioral score prediction from brain connectomes. Our network nicely provides an efficient solution which handles the topological properties of functional brain connectomes. Furthermore, it ensures model flexibility and enables inductive learning, thereby enhancing the model generalizability to unseen data. Our key contributions consist in designing a graph neural network for regression that predicts behavioral scores and training our GNN via model agnostic meta-learning. Our proposed method outperforms state-of-the-art methods in terms of prediction results. In our future work, we will investigate the explainability aspect of our Meta-RegGNN in order to identify connectivity biomarkers distinguishing between typical and atypical brain states.

Acknowledgements. This work was funded by generous grants from the European H2020 Marie Sklodowska-Curie action (grant no. 101003403, http://basira-lab.com/normnets/) to I.R. and the Scientific and Technological Research Council of Turkey to I.R. under the TUBITAK 2232 Fellowship for Outstanding Researchers (no. 118C288, http://basira-lab.com/reprime/). However, all scientific contributions made in this project are owned and approved solely by the authors.

References

1. Smith-Young, J., Chafe, R., Audas, R., Gustafson, D.L.: " I know how to advocate": parents' experiences in advocating for children and youth diagnosed with autism spectrum disorder. Health Serv. Insights **15**, 11786329221078803 (2022)
2. Hodges, H., Fealko, C., Soares, N.: Autism spectrum disorder: definition, epidemiology, causes, and clinical evaluation. Transl. Pediatr. **9**, S55 (2020)
3. Rahman, M.M., Usman, O.L., Muniyandi, R.C., Sahran, S., Mohamed, S., Razak, R.A.: A review of machine learning methods of feature selection and classification for autism spectrum disorder. Brain Sci. **10**, 949 (2020)
4. Xu, M., Calhoun, V., Jiang, R., Yan, W., Sui, J.: Brain imaging-based machine learning in autism spectrum disorder: methods and applications. J. Neurosci. Methods **361**, 109271 (2021)
5. Hyde, K.K., et al.: Applications of supervised machine learning in autism spectrum disorder research: a review. Rev. J. Autism Dev. Disord. **6**, 128–146 (2019). https://doi.org/10.1007/s40489-019-00158-x
6. Dryburgh, E., McKenna, S., Rekik, I.: Predicting full-scale and verbal intelligence scores from functional connectomic data in individuals with autism spectrum disorder. Brain Imaging Behav. **14**, 1769–1778 (2020). https://doi.org/10.1007/s11682-019-00111-w
7. Hanik, M., Demirtaş, M.A., Gharsallaoui, M.A., Rekik, I.: Predicting cognitive scores with graph neural networks through sample selection learning. Brain Imaging Behav. **16**, 1123–1138 (2021). https://doi.org/10.1007/s11682-021-00585-7
8. Yamin, M.A., Tessadori, J., Akbar, M.U., Dayan, M., Murino, V., Sona, D.: Geodesic clustering of positive definite matrices for classification of mental disorder using brain functional connectivity. In: 2020 International Joint Conference on Neural Networks (IJCNN), pp. 1–5. IEEE (2020)
9. Liu, M., Zhang, Z., Dunson, D.B.: Graph auto-encoding brain networks with applications to analyzing large-scale brain imaging datasets. Neuroimage **245**, 118750 (2021)
10. Shen, X., et al.: Using connectome-based predictive modeling to predict individual behavior from brain connectivity. Nat. Protoc. **12**, 506–518 (2017)
11. He, T., et al.: Deep neural networks and kernel regression achieve comparable accuracies for functional connectivity prediction of behavior and demographics. Neuroimage **206**, 116276 (2020)

12. Gori, M., Monfardini, G., Scarselli, F.: A new model for learning in graph domains. In: Proceedings. In: 2005 IEEE International Joint Conference on Neural Networks, vol. 2, pp. 729–734 (2005)

13. Scarselli, F., Gori, M., Tsoi, A.C., Hagenbuchner, M., Monfardini, G.: The graph neural network model. IEEE Trans. Neural Networks **20**, 61–80 (2008)

14. Bessadok, A., Mahjoub, M.A., Rekik, I.: Graph neural networks in network neuroscience. arXiv preprint arXiv:2106.03535 (2021)

15. Song, X., Mao, M., Qian, X.: Auto-metric graph neural network based on a meta-learning strategy for the diagnosis of Alzheimer's disease. IEEE J. Biomed. Health Inform. **25**, 3141–3152 (2021)

16. Wang, J.X.: Meta-learning in natural and artificial intelligence. Curr. Opin. Behav. Sci. **38**, 90–95 (2021)

17. Torrey, L., Shavlik, J.: Transfer learning. In: Handbook of Research on Machine Learning Applications and Trends: Algorithms, Methods, and Techniques, pp. 242–264. IGI global (2010)

18. Bai, Y., et al.: How important is the train-validation split in meta-learning? In: International Conference on Machine Learning, PMLR, pp. 543–553 (2021)

19. Santoro, A., Bartunov, S., Botvinick, M., Wierstra, D., Lillicrap, T.: Meta-learning with memory-augmented neural networks. In: International Conference on Machine Learning, PMLR, pp. 1842–1850 (2016)

20. Ravi, S., Larochelle, H.: Optimization as a model for few-shot learning. In: ICLR. (2017)

21. Finn, C., Abbeel, P., Levine, S.: Model-agnostic meta-learning for fast adaptation of deep networks. In: International Conference on Machine Learning, PMLR, pp. 1126–1135 (2017)

22. Wong, E., Anderson, J.S., Zielinski, B.A., Fletcher, P.T.: Riemannian regression and classification models of brain networks applied to autism. In: Wu, G., Rekik, I., Schirmer, M.D., Chung, A.W., Munsell, B. (eds.) CNI 2018. LNCS, vol. 11083, pp. 78–87. Springer, Cham (2018). https://doi.org/10.1007/978-3-030-00755-3_9

23. Fornito, A., Zalesky, A., Bullmore, E.: Fundamentals of Brain Network Analysis. Academic Press, Cambridge (2016)

24. Craddock, C., et al.: The neuro bureau preprocessing initiative: open sharing of preprocessed neuroimaging data and derivatives. Front. Neuroinform. **7**, 27 (2013)

25. Tzourio-Mazoyer, N., et al.: Automated anatomical labeling of activations in SPM using a macroscopic anatomical parcellation of the MNI MRI single-subject brain. Neuroimage **15**, 273–289 (2002)

26. Kingma, D.P., Ba, J.: Adam: a method for stochastic optimization. arXiv preprint arXiv:1412.6980 (2014)

27. Tordjman, S., et al.: Reframing autism as a behavioral syndrome and not a specific mental disorder: implications of genetic and phenotypic heterogeneity. Neurosci. Biobehav. Rev. **80**, 210 (2017)

Author Index

Printed in the United States
by Baker & Taylor Publisher Services